The Sacramental Mystery

The Sacramental Mystery

Paul Haffner

First published in 1999

Reprinted 2006

Gracewing
2 Southern Ave, Leominster
Herefordshire HR6 0QF

Nihil Obstat:
Mgr. Cyril Murtagh, Censor Deputatus

Imprimatur:
+Crispian Hollis, Bishop of Portsmouth
3 September 1998

ISBN 0 85244 476 1

Typesetting by Reesprint
Radley, Oxfordshire, OX14 3AJ

Contents

Foreword

This book is a short introduction to sacramental theology which I hope will be helpful to the clergy, religious and laity who wish to deepen their awareness of these God-given gifts of our Christian life. It is a forthright exposition of the sacramental mystery and it embraces biblical, patristic, theological and spiritual themes interwoven with recent Magisterial pronouncements on the subject. It traces some of the chief aspects of the historical development of the Church's understanding of the mystery of the sacraments. The book does not attempt to be particularly novel in its approach, but rather aims to present an organic synthesis of these saving signs of Christ's presence in His Church. It is my hope that these pages will help Christians deepen their understanding of the sacraments, assist them in loving and appreciating those great moments of grace when Christ touches our lives through them, and thus promote a more frequent and devotional sacramental attendance among the faithful.

I warmly commend this work on the subject of sacramental theology, published at the auspicious time of the threshold of the Third Millenium. It should help Christians rediscover the sacramental dimension of their lives, and promote that reconciliation which is so much a part of the Holy Year, the Great Jubilee Year 2000.

His Grace Archbishop Csaba Ternyák
Secretary of the Congregation for the Clergy
Vatican City
24th June 1998

Preface

This book has been prepared to fulfil a need for an introductory text on sacramental theology. The treatment is from the standpoint of Catholic dogmatic theology. Liturgical, pastoral and canonical aspects are therefore only treated secondarily as are areas concerning spirituality. The work is written with College students of theology in mind; it is also intended for the non-scholarly reader who wishes to deepen his or her theological knowledge of this central aspect of Christian life.

The sacraments may seem to have changed a great deal in the past fifty years, especially in regard to the way they are carried out. However, this work seeks to highlight the continuity of the ongoing Tradition of the Church in order to stress the underlying continuity and essence of these sacred signs. In doing so, while respecting the value of scholarship, this text does not accept that theological truth derives from a consensus among thinkers, but rather from adherence to the revealed deposit of faith, which must of course be expressed with clarity for every epoch of the Church.

Several different schemes could have been chosen as a way of ordering the chapters. I have decided to follow the sequence followed by the Catechism of the Catholic Church. Thus the book starts with the three sacraments of initiation, Baptism, Confirmation and the Holy Eucharist. Then the book moves to consider the sacraments of healing, namely Penance and Anointing of the Sick. Finally, the sacraments which serve Christian communion are treated, Sacred Orders and Holy Matrimony.

The sacramental mystery is indeed the "mystery of mysteries" for here the human and the divine, the material and the spiritual realms are intimately intertwined. The mystery is the work of the Most Holy Trinity and in this context the book is offered as a Jubilee Year meditation. The sacraments are the chief means in the Church via which mankind is reconciled to the Father, through His Son, by the power of the Holy Spirit.

I should like to thank the people who helped to bring this book to fruition. First of all, my gratitude goes to Rt. Rev. Crispian Hollis, Bishop of Portsmouth. Also I am very grateful to Archbishop Csaba Ternyák, Secretary of the Vatican Congregation for the Clergy who kindly wrote the Foreword. Next, several priest colleagues helped me on one point or another, and here my thanks are given to Fr. Matteo Byeon, Fr. Gabriel Delgado, Fr. Fintan Gavin and Fr. Christopher Kunze, L.C. At the publishers, Mr. Tom Longford and Jo Ashworth deserve my gratitude for being the "midwives" through whom this offspring came to birth. This book is dedicated to Frank and Philomena Whitesell.

Rome, 31st May 1998
Trinity Sunday

Abbreviations

AAS   *Acta Apostolicae Sedis. Commentarium officiale.*
Rome: Vatican Polyglot Press, 1909– .

CCC   *Catechism of the Catholic Church*
Dublin: Veritas, 1994.

CCEO *Code of Canons of the Eastern Churches*
Vatican City: 1990.

CCL   *Corpus Christianorum series latina*
Tournai: Brepols, 1954–.

CIC   *Code of Canon Law*
Vatican City: 1983.

DS   H. Denzinger and H. Schönmetzer. *Enchiridion
Symbolorum, Definitionum et Declarationum de rebus fidei et
morum.*
Barcelona/Freiburg im Breisgau/Rome: Herder, 1976.

ED   Pontifical Council for Christian Unity, *Ecumenical
Directory*
Vatican City: Vatican Polyglot Press, 1993

EV   *Enchiridion Vaticanum.* Documenti ufficiali della
Chiesa.
Bologna: Edizioni Dehoniane.

IG   *Insegnamenti di Giovanni Paolo II.*
Vatican City: Vatican Polyglot Press, 1978– .

IP   *Insegnamenti di Paolo VI*
       Vatican City: Vatican Polyglot Press, 1963–1978.

ND   J Neuner and J. Dupuis, *The Christian Faith in the Doctrinal Documents of the Catholic Church*. Sixth edition.
       New York: Alba House, 1996.

OR   *L'Osservatore Romano*, daily Italian edition.

ORE   *L'Osservatore Romano*, weekly English edition.

PG   J.P. Migne. *Patrologiae cursus completus, series graeca*. 161 vols. Paris: 1857–1866.

PL   J.P. Migne. *Patrologiae cursus completus, series latina*. 221 vols. Paris: 1844–1864.

SW   P.F. Palmer. *Sacraments and Worship. Liturgy and Doctrinal Development of Baptism, Confirmation and the Eucharist*.
       Westminster, MD: The Newman Press, 1955.

SF   P.F. Palmer. *Sacraments and Forgiveness. History and Doctrinal Development of Penance, Extreme Unction and Indulgences*.
       Westminster, MD: The Newman Press, 1961.

The Scriptural quotations and abbreviations in this work are from the New Jerusalem Bible.

The Vulgate numbering of the psalms is employed.

1

Sacraments in General

*Forth from the Father He comes with His sevenfold
mystical dowry,
Pouring on human souls infinite riches of God.*

"Salve festa dies", from the York Processional

The sacramental mystery lies at the very heart of Christian life in the Church. For it is through the Church and in sacraments, that God the Father through His Son, by the working of the Holy Spirit communicates His divine life to His people. Although God is not bound by these efficacious sacred signs instituted by His Son, in general they are the privileged channels where He touches the lives of His faithful. This chapter introduces some general themes which are common to all of the sacraments, in order to render easier an understanding of each one when it is treated separately; it also indicates what underlies the sacramental understanding of Christian experience.

1.1 Christ, the Sacrament of the Father

In a sense, the sacramental dynamic starts with the inner life of the Most Holy Trinity. It is the initiative of God. However, before there can be a sacramental system, there has to be a material creation, which in its turn makes possible the mystery of the Incarnation. God has prepared His sacramental economy at the heart of His plan of salvation. Christ has

1

come to reveal and make present among people the life and love of the Holy Trinity. Christ is the Sacrament of the Father, the One who is sent by the Father, and who makes Him visible, in the power of the Holy Spirit. In this sense, the sacramental mystery is rooted in the mystery of the Most Holy Trinity. However, it is a gratuitous gift, for God was never bound from external or internal necessity to create, and never bound to reveal Himself, and never bound to share His Life and Love.

Before the theme of the Incarnation can be addressed, it is necessary to consider the dogma of Creation, the first article of the creed, as the logical and ontological basis for all theology. This first step is also important because of the fundamental difference between the Judaeo-Christian vision of creation and other approaches. The Christian vision is marked by order, coherence, rationality, goodness, linearity with respect to time, a rejection of superstition, where man and woman are stewards of creation. Ancient and modern pagan approaches often involve a chaotic or chance vision of reality, some idea that matter is evil, and a cyclical notion of history. The Christian vision of creation brings in its wake philosophical realism which is also a necessary foundation of the sacramental economy. Sacramental theology is bound up with a realist approach to the fabric of space and time.

The creation of man and woman provides a further foundation for sacramental understanding. For the human person is both material and spiritual, external and internal, visible and invisible. These elements must be present therefore in the sacraments and liturgy to correspond with human nature. Since a sacrament is an outward sign of inward grace, it harmonizes with the composite characteristics of human nature as both material and spiritual. Material elements are used in sacraments, for example water, wine, bread, oil. The sacramental system is consonant with the nature of the human person as body and soul, material and spiritual, external and internal.

The outward signs of the sacraments are themselves made possible by the creation, and were prefigured in various ways in the Old Testament. The Old Testament covenant involved some important signs like the rainbow (Gn 9:11–17), circumcision (Gn 17:6–13), the Passover (Ex 12), the covenant ratification with bull's blood (Ex 24:1–11), the tent (Ex 29:43–45) and the Temple (I K 6). Sacred signs were perfected in the New Testament to express Christ's power and His Kingdom, for instance the changing of water into wine at the Wedding Feast at Cana (Jn 2:1–12) and the Feeding of the Five Thousand (Jn 6:1–15) which prefigure the Holy Eucharist.

In the Christian picture, the Incarnation brings about a new meaning to Creation and History and brings together the Transcendence and Immanence of God. Christ is outside of time and yet in Him time and eternity meet. Christ, God and man, is a Mystery and a Revelation. The sacraments therefore must be based on two fundamental pivots: the nature of man and woman and also the mystery of the Incarnation. Hence sacraments are a fusion in harmony of the external and internal, the material and spiritual, the human and the Divine, grace and nature. However, the sacramental economy must also take account of the reality of sin and evil, in the concrete forms of the Fall, original sin and actual sin, sickness, suffering and death. Christ came to heal and redeem fallen man. The Creation and Incarnation must, as a result of the Fall, be seen in the light of redemption through the paschal mystery. The sacraments are regarded especially by the Eastern Fathers of the Church as the application of healing by Christ, the Divine Physician.

1.2 The Church, the Sacrament of Christ

Christ desired to found a Church and its sacraments. Sacraments have always been viewed in relation to the Church, although understanding of this link has undergone and continues to undergo a theological development. Discussions about non-Christian ministers of Baptism in the early Church and the efficacy of sacraments administered to non-Catholics bear witness to this type of question. A very fruitful line of approach regards the Church herself as a

sacrament, but in an analogous way to the application of the
term to the seven sacraments. Locating the sacramental
economy within the context of the Church as the sacrament
of Christ sheds light on the recurrent theme of the relation
between the individual and community emphases in the celebration of the sacraments. The sacraments are essentially
ecclesial and in this perspective any tension between the
individual and the community can be resolved. Seeing the
sacraments in an ecclesial context also indicates that they are
manifestations of Christ's power, theophanies which reveal
and make present God's love. They are a privileged point of
encounter with God in today's world.

The unity between Christ and His Church set up by the
redemptive Incarnation forms the basis for the efficacy of the
sacramental system. This Trinitarian sacramental economy
is already present in outline in the Pauline letters: "He has
let us know the mystery of His purpose the hidden plan He
so kindly made in Christ from the beginning...." (Ep 1:9).
The gradual unfolding of a mystery of revelation is the basis
for understanding the Church's continuing role in this economy: "Without any doubt, the mystery of our religion is very
deep indeed: He was made visible in the flesh...." (I Tm
3:16).

Indeed, the word "mystery" rendered by *mystérion* in
Greek and by the Latin *sacramentum*, is at the etymological
root of the English word "sacrament." This leads to the idea
that the basis of the Church seen as sacrament is both the
Incarnation and the Redemption or Paschal Mystery. In the
Incarnation, Christ reveals the mystery of the Holy Trinity.
The Redemption opens the way for union with God which
had been lost by sin. Christ is both God and man. As God He
has the power to institute the sacraments: as Man He carries
out this institution for us. The Passion, Death and Resurrection of Christ opens up the way to a relationship with God, in
the Church, which is the sacrament of Christ. Developments
in ecclesiology over the past century led to the Church being
regarded as the primordial sacrament. The theology of the
whole Church as a sacrament was developed last century by

J.H. Oswald and M.J. Scheeben. During this century, O. Semmelroth further unfolded this idea[1]. The Second Vatican Council made this approach its own by stating: "The Church, in Christ, is in the nature of sacrament — a sign and instrument, that is, of communion with God and of unity among men."[2] The concept of the Church as sacrament gives meaning to those various other descriptions such as new people of God, mystical Body of Christ, Bride of Christ.

The model of the Church which best squares with the flavour of this book is the bridal image in which Christ is the Bridegroom and the Church His mystical Bride. This picture was prepared and prefigured in the Old Testament in the bridal image of the Song of Songs, which St. Hippolytus, Origen, St. Athanasius, St. Gregory of Nyssa, St. Bernard of Clairvaux, St. John of the Cross and other Fathers and Doctors of the Church have interpreted as symbolic of union between Christ and the Church. The bridal imagery has many implications, but it applies especially to Christ and the Church (cf. Ep 5:32). One of the sacraments, Matrimony, thus becomes an image for the nature of the Church as a primordial sacrament. The permanent character imparted by some of the sacraments reflects the indissoluble bond between Christ and His Church. Christ cares for His Bride though the sacraments, in the power of the Holy Spirit. He washes her clean through Baptism, anoints and strengthens her with the oil of chrism in Confirmation and feeds her with His own Body and Blood in the Eucharist. Christ heals the sins of her members through Penance, soothes their sickness in Anointing. He ministers to His mystical Bride in the sacrament of Orders and reflects His love for her in Holy Matrimony.

1.3   The concept of sacrament

Certain sacred signs in the Old Covenant foreshadowed the sacramental economy brought about by Christ. In the New Testament, salvation and eternal life are transmitted through matter and the word, as is seen in St. Paul's bridal imagery for the Church: "He made her clean by washing her

with water with a form of words" (Ep 5:26). This divine life
communicated by the sacraments of the new law is the fulfilment of the Old Testament promises: "How much more
effectively the Blood of Christ, who offered Himself as a perfect sacrifice to God through the eternal Spirit, can purify our
inner self from dead actions so that we can do our service to
the living God"(Heb 9:14).

St. Paul's reference to the bridal imagery of Christ and His
Church involved the expression "mystery", a term which is
open to various interpretations (See Ep 5:32). The Greek
word *mysterion* (or *musterion*) which denotes mystery here,
derives from the expression *muo* meaning "to shut the
mouth". The expression *mysterion* in biblical terms refers to a
hidden thing, a secret or a mystery, and in rabbinic writings
denoted the mystic or hidden sense of an Old Testament saying or of an image seen in a vision. In its turn, the Latin word
sacramentum renders the equivalent of *mysterion* in the Vulgate. The English word *sacrament* is a translation of the Latin
word, which for the early Christians had the sense of something sacred, secret, involving initiation to some type of service. Among the Romans the expression was used specifically
for the oath which soldiers took on entering the service of the
emperor. Tertullian (steeped in the Roman legal tradition)
was one of the first to apply the word in the context of Christian rites, especially those of initiation.

Before the Church arrived at a unified vision of the sacraments it took nearly eleven centuries. During this time, it
became necessary to distinguish the sacraments from other
sacred realities in the life of the Church. The Greeks, following the Alexandrian school in the works of Clement of Alexandria and Origen, used the word *mysterion* or its plural
mysteria. They thought in Platonic categories, according to
which the world of the senses is a world of images and symbols, above which lies the true world of divine ideas. Origen
used the expression *mysterion* to refer to baptism and the
Eucharist, and by the beginning of the fourth century this
usage seems to be common. At the end of the fourth century,
St. John Chrysostom used the formulation "the mysteries"

to refer to the Holy Eucharist. Unfortunately among certain pagan rites such as those of Mithras, the cult was also described in terms of *mysteria*. As the pagan religions faded away, the word *mysteria* was used increasingly also in the West so that two words evolved into use for the idea of sacrament in the Latin West, *sacramentum* and *mysterium*.[3] Gradually, in the West, one of the two words became more favoured for the rites and this was *sacramentum*, while *mysterium* was used to denote the realities of the faith and salvation in themselves, like the mystery of the Holy Trinity.

Thereafter, in the West, controversies took place which refined the usages of the expression *sacramentum*. St. Augustine made the important distinction between the sign (*signum*) and content (*res*). This distinction was used in the struggle against the Donatists. The Donatists arose from a development of the dispute between the See of Rome and that of Carthage over the re-baptism of apostates and heretics. St. Cyprian and the Church in Carthage maintained that an apostate needed to be re-baptized. Pope Stephen I objected to this, because it was a departure from the Tradition of the Church. In the year 256, Pope Stephen wrote to Cyprian stating that, in accordance with Tradition, heretics should be reconciled by the sacrament of penance, and not by re-baptism.[4] Then later in the fourth and fifth centuries, the Donatists emerged in North Africa, denying the truth that Baptism is once and for all. The Donatists, while believing that re-baptism was necessary, twisted the doctrine of Baptism to their own end maintaining that as they really had the sacrament of Baptism (and this could not be denied after Stephen I had spoken), then they were the Church of Christ. In this context, St. Augustine gave the word *sacramentum* the refinements which have remained with it ever since. St. Augustine had to distinguish between the sacramental sign (*signum*) and the grace content (*res*). In this formulation, the Donatists received the sacrament validly, but not the grace, as they put an obstacle in the way by opposing the true Church of Christ.

St. Augustine stressed the visible sign aspect of the sacrament, and its relation to the spiritual reality which it signifies. Further steps in sacramental theology led to the medieval picture. Isidore of Seville (d. 636) distinguished more sharply than Augustine between sign and reality; although he used the word sacrament in many senses, he was the first to offer the idea of sacrament to a unified picture of baptism, confirmation and the Eucharist.[5] St. Isidore was therefore a bridge in sacramental theology linking St. Augustine with medieval thought. Hugh of St. Victor conceived the sacraments as containing grace rather like a vessel contains liquid: "A sacrament is a corporal or material element manifested externally, which represents by resemblance, signifies by institution and contains by sanctification a certain spiritual or invisible grace."[6] Around the year 1150, Peter Lombard arrived at his famous definition in the Fourth Book of the Sentences: "A sacrament is properly said to be such a sign of the grace of God and form of invisible grace as to be at the same time the image and cause of it."[7] These ideas paved the way for St. Thomas who defined a sacrament in the proper sense of the word to be a sign of a sacred reality inasmuch as it sanctifies man.[8] The Council of Trent took up Augustinian and Thomistic ideas by regarding a sacrament as a "visible form of invisible grace."[9] Traditionally sacraments have been understood as outward signs of inward grace instituted by Jesus Christ. More recently they have been defined as "efficacious signs of grace, instituted by Christ and entrusted to the Church," which are God's masterpieces in the new and everlasting covenant.[10]

1.4   Divine institution of the sacraments

The Church and its most important treasures were directly founded by Christ the Saviour. Among these treasures are the inspired Word of God, the Papacy and the sacraments. In most of the cases where there are details in the New Testament concerning Christ's institution of each individual sacrament, there is a reference which deals with an institution before the first Easter and one after the first Easter. The reason is that the pre-Paschal institution lays the foundation for the sacrament, while the post-Paschal institution brings the sacrament about in its fulness. Only after the accomplishment of the Paschal Mystery can the sacraments become fully effective as they draw their efficacy from Christ's Sacrifice and His Resurrection. Since the sacraments are signs which bring about the effects of Christ's redemption in the lives of individuals and in the Church as a whole, then since Christ is the only Saviour of mankind, therefore it is only He who could have the power to set up these sacred signs. It is a defined dogma of the faith that each sacrament has been divinely instituted by Jesus Christ.[11] Some concrete details of this divine institution will be explored for each sacrament.

The teaching that all the sacraments are part of the deposit of Revelation contrasts sharply with the Modernist error that sacraments just "evolved" into the life of the Church as a means of arousing faith; this error was condemned at the turn of this century.[12] Nor is the theory of K. Rahner adequate, when he proposed that Christ instituted some of the sacraments only implicitly, "included" in the foundation of the Church as a primordial sacrament.[13] Christ instituted the sacraments, by assigning the grace and also the external rite which signified it. However, it is evident that many aspects of the external rite were left to the Church to determine more fully, and discussion about the matter and form of some of the sacraments (such as confirmation and ordination) continued for many centuries. The doctrine that Christ founded a sacramental economy and also a specific series of sacred rites leads on to the fact that the number of sacraments instituted is seven.

1.5   Number of the sacraments

That there are seven sacraments is part of the deposit of faith; however it took some time for the Church to become fully aware of this truth. In the early centuries, there was never any denial that any of the seven was truly a sacrament, but rather other signs were also held to be "sacraments".

This was partly due to the fact that in the patristic era, as has been seen, the expressions sacrament and mystery were still used in the broad sense. Thus, holy water, exorcisms and the recital of the Our Father were called sacraments. Later these were defined as *sacramentals*. At the same time, many Fathers wrote tracts on the individual sacraments. For example, Tertullian wrote about Baptism, Confirmation, the Eucharist, Holy Orders and Marriage. St. Augustine listed all the sacraments more than once, apart from the Anointing of the Sick. Nevertheless, during the same period, in the year 416, Pope Innocent I wrote a letter to Decentius, Bishop of Gubbio, on the subject of Anointing.[14]

In the early Middle Ages, the seven sacred signs were increasingly thrown into greater relief as the only sacraments. Theologians like Otto of Bamberg, Master Roland Bandinelli (later Pope Alexander III) and Hugh of St. Victor were among the first theologians to affirm that there were only seven sacraments. Through the influence of Peter Lombard on scholastic theology, the recognition that there were seven sacraments passed into the theological collections of the thirteenth century. In the Middle Ages, some theologians thought that there were more than seven sacraments. For example, the consecration of a king or queen was regarded by some of the medievals as the eighth sacrament, as can be seen from versions of this rite in the Roman Pontifical dating from before the Second Vatican Council.[15] However, from the middle of the thirteenth century onwards, the existence of the seven sacraments was considered to be a truth of faith. The Church professed this truth at the Council of Lyons in the year 1274: "The same Holy Roman Church also holds and teaches that there are seven sacraments of the Church."[16] Again at the Council of Florence in 1439 the Church professed her faith in the "seven sacraments of the New Law, namely Baptism, Confirmation, the Eucharist, Penance, Extreme Unction, Order and Matrimony."[17] The Council of Trent solemnly defined that the number of sacraments was no "more or fewer than seven".[18] The Tridentine definition was directed at the idea of Luther who held only

Baptism and the Eucharist as sacraments; earlier he had vac-
illated considering Penance as a sacrament, at other times he
thought there were five sacraments. The Augsburg Confession drawn up by Melanchton, one of Luther's disciples,
admitted only three sacraments, Baptism, the Lord's Supper
and Penance. Melanchton left the way open for the other
five sacred signs to be considered as "secondary sacraments".
However, Zwingli, Calvin and most of the later Reformed
tradition accepted only Baptism and the Lord's Supper as
sacraments, but in a highly symbolic sense. Some Protestants such as Leibniz[19] defended the existence of seven sacraments. Traditionally, the Anglicans considered that there
were only two sacraments instituted by the Lord, namely
Baptism and the Lord's Supper.[20] Nevertheless, some representatives of the so-called High Church tried to renew interest in the "secondary" five sacraments.

The Orthodox Churches all believe that there are seven
sacraments, and have upheld this truth since the thirteenth
century. The acceptance of this truth in common with the
Church of Rome indicates that, in essence, it must have been
a truth of the primitive Church. The Orthodox would not
have been likely to accept this truth only because it had been
defined by Rome. The instance of Orthodox faith in the
seven sacraments is an indication that they belong to the
deposit of revelation handed down from the Apostles. The
Orthodox have held on to this belief in the sevenfold sacramental system despite attempts by the Protestants in centuries past to convince them of the Reformed position.

Among the sacraments there is a hierarchy. The Council of
Trent made it clear that not all the sacraments are equal.[21]
The Eucharist occupies a place of primacy among the sacraments, and "all the other sacraments are ordered to it as to
their end."[22] The sacramentality of the Church goes beyond
the celebration of the seven sacraments, and in fact shapes
all her actions and touches the deepest level of her being.[23]

1.6   Sacramental causality

God mediates His truth and life in many ways but always through some personal agent. The Scriptures were written by men under the guidance of the Holy Spirit. The Church is Christ's way, but always through other human beings is this way mediated. In all cases God assures His people of the efficacy of these means and guarantees them. In the case of the Scriptures, this occurs via the guarantee of inerrancy; in the Church the Spirit bestows the charism of infallibility. With the sacraments, God guarantees them by an intrinsic objective efficacy, *ex opere operato*, which is also a special work of the Holy Spirit.

The *ex opere operato* efficacy of the sacraments should not be confused with magic. By definition, magic "is a belief and practice according to which men are convinced that they may directly affect natural powers and each other among themselves either for good or evil by their own efforts in manipulating the superior powers."[24] On the other hand, the whole initiative for the sacramental economy and its causality starts from God the Holy Trinity as remarked above.

The Scriptures do not use the expression *ex opere operato* but indicate the truth which it signifies. The New Testament describes situations where, through the carrying out of an external sign, an interior grace is communicated to the subject. Examples are Jesus' conversation with Nicodemus concerning baptism (Jn 3:5), baptism in the Acts of the Apostles (Ac 2:38), the Eucharist (I Co 10:16ff). During the patristic era, faith in the intrinsic efficacy of the sacraments was manifested by the practice of the baptism of infants. The Fathers held that whenever the sacramental sign is correctly carried out, the sacrament takes place validly. Thus, just as the sun is reflected in its integrity from a dirty puddle, the sacramental character of Baptism is not soiled by the sin of the minister. The Fathers stressed that in each sacrament, it is Christ who acts through His unworthy minister. St. Augustine stated that "Peter may baptize, but still it is

Christ who baptizes; Judas may baptize, but it is still Christ who baptizes."[25]

The distinction between the *opus operans* and *opus operatum* started its theological life in Christology, as a means of distinguishing between the good and bad aspects of the Crucifixion of Christ. The terminology was also applied to the issue of man's merit. The formulae *ex opere operato* and *ex opere operantis* were first used by William of Auxerre in the early part of the thirteenth century and were rapidly adopted in the course of that century.

The concept of sacramental causality was sharpened in the context of various controversies. During the thirteenth century, the followers of Peter Waldo desired to reform the disorderly lifestyle of some of the clergy at that time. In their exaggerated zeal, they made the validity of the sacraments depend on the worthiness of the minister. The profession of faith which Pope Innocent III prescribed to the Waldensians indicates the belief of the Church that the validity of the sacraments is independent of the goodness of the minister.[26] Wyclif and Hus maintained a similar error, namely that a sinful minister could not perform valid sacraments. The General Council of Constance and later Pope Martin V effectively reaffirmed the traditional teaching that "a bad priest who uses the correct matter and form and has the intention of doing what the Church does, truly performs the Eucharist, truly absolves, truly baptises, truly confers the other sacraments."[27]

Luther's concept of justification by faith alone led to his denial of the intrinsic efficacy of the sacraments.[28] The Reformers followed Luther to a greater or lesser extent in their denial of sacramental causality. The Council of Trent affirmed against the errors of the Reformers: "If anyone says that through the sacraments of the New Law grace is not conferred by the performance of the rite itself (*ex opere operato*) but that faith alone in the divine promise is sufficient to obtain grace, let him be anathema."[29]

The expression *ex opere operato* means "from the work worked" or more specifically, from the sacramental sign

objectively performed. The efforts of man do not produce
the effects of the sacraments, but Christ's power. Thus the
sacramental causality is not *ex opere operantis*, "from the work
of the worker." Nevertheless, the intrinsic efficacy of the
sacraments does not mean that they are automatically fruitful for the recipient. Indeed the recipient of the sacrament
must place no obstacle in the way. Thus sacraments contain
the grace which they signify and signify the grace which they
contain.[30] Thus they are not merely signs, nor are they
intended merely to stimulate the faith as the Reformers
maintained.[31]

The intrinsic and objective efficacy of the sacraments is
Christ's guarantee that He will act in the sacraments independent of the worthiness of His minister. In this way,
Christ's faithful are not at the mercy of the holiness of minister for their own pursuit of holiness. The validity of sacraments celebrated in an essentially correct manner is to be
presumed; this concept has an immediate application in the
theology of marriage where the validity of that sacrament
enjoys the favour of the law.[32] The *opus operantis* (work of the
worker) does of course have a certain importance in that the
life of the minister and his worthiness are relevant for his
own spiritual growth and for that of his community as well as
for the avoidance of sacrilege and so that there is a coherence
between his life and his ministry, his handling of sacred
things. The *opus operantis* is also important in preaching and
sacramentals.

1.7   Matter and form of the sacraments

This formulation of the Aristotelian categories of matter and
form was first applied to the external sign of the sacraments
by William of Auxerre and by Stephen Cardinal Langton,
during the Middle Ages. The matter of each sacrament is
indeterminate until it is informed or given meaning by the
form, or the words spoken by the minister of the sacrament.
For example, pouring water over someone's head is not baptism unless accompanied by the form using the words "John,
I baptize you in the name of the Father and of the Son and of

the Holy Spirit." The intention of the minister to perform the sacrament is, as will be seen, also essential for the validity of the sacrament. A distinction is also made between the remote and the proximate matter. The remote matter is that which will be used in the sacrament, and the proximate matter is that which is actually used in the carrying out of a sacrament. For example, in baptism, the water is the remote matter and the actual pouring of the water is the proximate matter of that sacrament. The form of each sacrament consists of a prayer, the pronunciation of which determines the matter, and which together with the matter constitutes the external sign of the sacrament. Thus the form of words must be pronounced audibly, so that they are externalized. A purely interior recitation of the form would be insufficient. The matter and form of each sacrament will be examined in each respective chapter.

The external sign, or the rite of each sacrament, is composed of matter and form. This is the sacrament as such (*sacramentum tantum*) and according to classical theology it produces two effects, the first of which is the so-called *res et sacramentum* and the second effect is the 'effect as such' or *res tantum*. The sensible sign thus causes two effects, the first which is a sign and a cause of a further effect. The ultimate and principal effect (*res tantum*) is sacramental grace. It is signified and caused by the first two causes but is neither a sign nor a cause of any further sacramental effect.

This intermediate sign-effect known as the *res et sacramentum* is of a special significance in Baptism, Confirmation and Sacred Orders and is known as the sacramental character, as will be discussed below. In the Holy Eucharist, the *res et sacramentum* is the Body and Blood of Christ. In Holy Matrimony it is the union between the spouses arising from the matrimonial bond. In the sacrament of Penance, this sign-effect is considered to be interior penitence. In the Sacrament of the Sick, it is formulated to be spiritual Anointing (*spiritualis unctio*).

A distinction is also made between the substance of the sacraments (that which is needed for validity), a ceremonial part (required for liceity) and a disposition (needed for fruit-ful reception). The Church has the power to state what is necessary for the validity of the sacraments. She has also the power to determine what is required for the validity of the sacraments, but within limits. For example, in sacred orders, Pope Pius XII determined that the matter was the laying on of hands, rather than the handing of the instruments. On the other hand, it does not lie within the Church's power to change the fact that a male subject is required for priestly ordination.[33] Similarly, Pope Paul VI laid down that the mat-ter of the sacrament of Confirmation was the anointing with chrism. However, the Church does not have the power to change the matter from vegetable oil to some other sub-stance.[34] A further example is that the Church has the power to determine what is the sacramental and canonical form of Marriage, but she cannot dissolve a valid consummated mar-riage between Christians.[35]

Recent discussions between liturgists and theologians concern the relation between liturgy and dogma, in the interpretation of the expression "lex orandi, lex credendi", "the norm of prayer is the norm of belief".[36] The traditional interpretation of this axiom is that prayer must be based on true doctrine in order to be accepted as the prayer of the Church. On the other hand, modern liturgists sometimes imply that doctrine itself has evolved from liturgy, so invert-ing the traditional understanding. While liturgical loci have sometimes been foundational in doctrinal development, it is more often faith wishing to be expressed in prayer that is the determining factor. This implies that the sacraments cannot be changed arbitrarily, but only in obedience to the deposit of revelation.

1.8   The minister and the intention

Each sacrament is performed by its respective minister and this will be concretely elaborated in all the following chap-ters. Generally, a sacrament has an ordinary minister who is the one who carries out the sacred rite according to canonical and liturgical norms. It will be seen that some sacraments also have an extraordinary minister, who can perform the sacrament in cases of necessity. For example, in Baptism, the ordinary minister is a bishop, priest, or a deacon. The extraordinary minister is anyone who has the intention of doing what the Church does, even a non-Christian.

Apart from exceptional cases like the absolution of an accomplice in a sin against the sixth commandment, even an unworthy minister validly performs the sacraments, as was pointed out in the foregoing discussion of the intrinsic efficacy of the sacraments. The Reformers required that the minister had to be holy in order that a sacrament be valid. The Council of Trent made it clear that even a minister in mortal sin validly performs a sacrament.[37] The condition, on the part of the minister for the validity of a sacrament is that he has at least the intention of doing what the Church does.[38] In the course of the condemnation of the Jansenist heresy, the Church made clear that an external intention manifested in the performance of the rite is, of itself, insufficient. An interior intention is required.[39]

A closer look at the intention of the minister yields a classification into four possible categories. The actual intention is one which is present throughout the sacramental rite at every moment. The virtual intention is that which was made before the rite and under which the ceremony is carried out, but it is not constantly called to mind. The habitual intention was made at some previous time in the past and while not revoked does not exert any positive influence upon the rite. The interpretative intention has never been made either explicitly or implicitly and does not exist in the present, yet it is considered that the minister would have elicited it. Of these four possibilities, clearly, the actual intention is more than sufficient for sacramental validity. The virtual intention is necessary and sufficient because the sacrament is performed in virtue of the previous act of the will, which should not be too remote in the past. The habitual and interpretative intentions are insufficient.

The intention of the minister must be sufficiently determined. For example, the sacrament of Penance would be invalid if the priest says "I absolve you" but does not distinguish which of two individuals is to be absolved. Even a minister without faith, provided he has the intention of doing what the Church does, performs a valid sacrament.

1.9 The recipient

The recipient of the sacrament is also known as its subject, or the one who directly benefits from its reception. Reception of a sacrament should ideally be valid, licit and fruitful. While the validity of a sacrament does not depend on the disposition of the minister, provided he has the intention of doing what the Church does, the disposition of the recipient is important for the reception of divine grace does depend on this. The subject must prepare himself or herself for the grace which the sacrament objectively brings. The sacraments cause grace *ex opere operato* to those who place no obstacle in the way. However, the subject's preparation for the sacraments is not the effective cause of the grace of the sacraments, it only removes obstacles to their reception. Opening a window allows fresh air to enter a room, but does not produce the freshness; it is the breath of air which causes that. An obstacle on the part of the subject can invalidate the sacrament, such as the case in which a person is baptized or ordained against their will. For the validity of a sacrament, the intention to receive it is the basic condition in the adult subject. The habitual intention to receive a usual rite of the Church is considered a necessary and sufficient intention in this respect for all sacraments apart from Penance and Marriage. An implicit intention is sufficient, as exists in the case of an unconscious sick person who had at one time the desire to die as a Catholic; this desire includes of itself the wish to receive Anointing of the Sick. The freedom of the will and the notion of an obstacle are of particular importance in the sacrament of Marriage, where, according to the Western concept, the spouses are both ministers and recipients of the sacrament and conditions for the invalidity or nullity of a marriage must be clearly determined. Obstacles also exist at the level of liceity or legitimate reception of a sacrament, as in the case where ordination is conferred illicitly upon a candidate who has not been confirmed.[40] Finally, reception of a sacrament may be valid and lawful, but not fruitful. This occurs, for example, when a person receives a sacrament in a state of mortal sin. Although the sacraments do not depend for their validity on the faith of the minister, and are not merely signs to arouse faith, nevertheless faith is part of the fruitful reception of the sacraments. They are lived in the context of faith and they perfect faith. However, they also presuppose and nourish Christian hope, because the sacraments look forward to the perfection of the Kingdom. These sacred efficacious signs also presuppose and stimulate charity, as the bond of communion within the Church and the pledge of power of the Holy Spirit.

When the obstacle to fruitful reception of a validly performed sacrament is removed, in the case of five of the sacraments, it "revives". This is evident for Baptism, Confirmation and Ordination which impart a character that can never be lost. After receiving the sacrament of Penance, these three sacraments revive if they are received validly but unworthily. If someone is married in a state of mortal sin, they are validly married, but they receive the grace only after having confessed and done penance for their mortal sins. The bearer of this revival is considered to be the character of baptism and confirmation which has remained despite the sins. A similar argument holds in the case of the sacrament of Anointing of the Sick, where an unfruitful reception due to sin is revived at a later point. The complication here is that mortal sin is considered to be forgiven by this latter sacrament, if there is a sufficient disposition.[41] In the case of baptism without due disposition on the part of the recipient, as when a man continues to live in a polygamous union at the time he receives the sacrament, the grace revives after a conversion of life and sacramental confession. Nevertheless, the grace does not revive according to common opinion in the case of the remaining two sacraments, namely Penance and the Eucharist. In the case of an insincere confession, the subject would need to confess again sincerely, but does not receive grace for the former act which was an invalid sacrament. In the case of the Eucharist, revival does not take place. One reason given for the fact that revival does not take place in the Holy Eucharist is that while Baptism, Confirmation and Orders are never repeated and Marriage and Anointing are rarely repeated, the Eucharist is easily repeated. It would also appear incongruous that a person who had received sacrilegious daily communion during a lifetime could then receive all at once by one act of repentance the graces of those communions.

1.10   The effects

1.10.1   Sacramental grace

The sacraments are carried out in the power and by the invocation (*epiclesis*) of the Holy Spirit, who is the Gift of the Father through the Son. The Holy Spirit is also especially associated with the gift of grace bestowed upon the recipient of each sacrament. The specific grace proper to each sacrament will be considered under the respective heading of each chapter. In general, the grace imparted by the sacraments renders God's love, presence and power available in the present moment, in a way which is specific to each sacrament. It is tempting to live in the past, or in the future, or in both, and thus to miss out on the present. For the human being, for the Christian, one of the hardest but most necessary tasks is to embrace the present moment. It is necessary to keep one eye in the past, one eye in the future, but both feet firmly in the present. Nowhere is the full thrust of the present moment more keenly felt than in the sacraments of the Church. The Church herself, as the Sacrament of Christ, makes His presence available, by the power of the Holy Spirit today in this present moment. The Creation, Incarnation, and the Eschaton are favoured "times" according to the mercy of God, in His economy of salvation (Ep 1:9–10). The eschatological dimension of the Sacraments manifests our participation in His New Creation (cf. Ap 21:1–7); here the biblical concept of fulness also indicates an existing sharing, during the current pilgrimage though history, in Christ and His Life.[42]

Baptism is a new "today", the first day of Christian life; Confirmation is the power of the Holy Spirit helping the growing Christian to live today for Christ. Reconciliation is a new today in Christ after we fall. Ordination makes men ministers of Christ today and forever; Marriage is the commitment today and always of man and wife to each other and to Christ. The Anointing of the Sick supplies grace to the Christian to face sickness today, and gives help to make the final journey into the eternal Day. The sacraments focus God's grace on the present moment in which we live. Yet, in doing so, they take in the past and look to the future. The Holy Eucharist, the greatest of all the Sacraments, illustrates the relation of past, present and future in salvation history: "O sacred Banquet in which Christ is received, the memory of His Passion is renewed, our souls are filled with grace and the pledge of future glory is given us."[43] One of the memorial acclamations after the Consecration shows how Christ's Sacrifice embraces past, present and future: "Christ has died, Christ is risen, Christ will come again." Hence creation and human history are renewed and healed by the sacraments which bring about salvation history.

1.10.2 *The sacramental character*

Three sacraments, namely Baptism, Confirmation, and Orders each impart a specific permanent seal upon the recipient known as the sacramental character: these sacraments cannot be repeated. The expression is of Greek origin (*spragis*) and denoted a mark impressed on animals or soldiers. Gradually the Greek word, and its Latin equivalents *signaculum* and *character*, evolved to mean any distinguishing sign or image, especially those which set aside people or things for public functions. Legal documents and money in ancient Rome bore official seals called "characters": the emblems of public office were denoted by the same word. In the patristic period, Baptism and Confirmation were called a seal (stamp), rather like a seal in lead or wax upon a letter indicating the authority with which the missive was sent. The Fathers noted that in the Letter to the Hebrews, Christ is said to be the "perfect Copy " of the Father's nature which can also be rendered as "Character of the Father's substance" (Heb 1:3). As Christ is the likeness of the Father, so Christians are stamped, sealed with the likeness of Christ by the Holy Spirit (II Co 1:21–22). During the patristic period, some Fathers like St. Irenaeus and Tertullian referred to baptism and to confirmation as a "seal".

As was seen above, St. Augustine defended, against the Donatist heresy, the truth that Baptism and Confirmation could not be repeated. He established clearly the doctrine of a character which is conferred independently of grace and which is not lost even by mortal sin.[44] The medievals stated that the character designates grace, makes the person resemble God by consecration. St. Thomas Aquinas specifically stressed that the character gives a person the right and duty to participate in the cult of the Church.[45] More recently, M.J. Scheeben remarked that the sacramental character is a reflection of the Hypostatic Union, and thus flows from the Incarnation. The union between Christ and His spouse the Church is a type of primordial character. Each sacramental character which a person receives configures them ever more perfectly to the likeness of Christ, but in each sacrament in a different way. The character is a change in the being of the person, an ontological change which is the basis for action in various forms.

The sacramental character is thus a sign, sculptured by God within the person configuring them to Christ. It is also a distinguishing mark, so that the Christian by Baptism is consecrated and set apart from the rest of the world. Christ's faithful are distinguished among themselves by the various sacramental characters. The baptised person is consecrated and united with Christ as a confessor of the faith, the confirmed person is set apart as a defender of the faith and the ordained man is denoted as a servant of Christ (in the diaconal order) or mediator (in the presbyteral and episcopal orders) within the Church. The sacramental character is a sign which disposes towards grace, because it is a sign and cause of such grace. The sacramental character perfects human nature and is indelible in this life and in the life to come. According to many Fathers, the character lasts beyond death into all eternity.[46]

1.11   Sacraments and sacramentals

The discussion above on the number of the sacraments showed that during the Middle Ages some actions of the Church were thought to be sacraments, but were not in fact definitively accepted as such by the Church. Hugh of St. Victor referred to lesser sacraments, which were in fact sacramentals. Peter Lombard was the first to use the Latin expression *sacramentalia* corresponding to the word sacramentals. Blessings, indulgences and exorcisms are examples of sacramentals. Sacramentals do not function with the intrinsic efficacy of the sacraments. Yet their power does not simply depend upon the subjective disposition of the person carrying out the particular rite. Because the Church is the Bride of Christ and His sacrament, she enjoys a power which is not restricted to the sacraments; the sacramentals are also connected with her intercessory power. Therefore, it is possible to propose that the sacramentals work in a more powerful way than *ex opere operantis*, namely according to the action of the person who carries it out. The sacramentals can be said to function *quasi ex opere operato*, almost according to the work of the worker. While the sacraments are of divine institution, sacramentals are of ecclesiastical institution. They are bound up with sacramental life and often lead to the sacraments: "Holy Mother Church has, moreover, instituted sacramentals. These are sacred signs which bear a resemblance to the sacraments. They signify effects, particularly of a spiritual nature, which are obtained through the intercession of the Church. By them men are disposed to receive the chief effect of the sacraments, and various occasions in life are rendered holy."[47] The use of holy water, a sacramental employed upon entering a church is part of the remote preparation for the celebration of the Mass. Indulgences are sacramentals which are related with the sacrament of Penance. The sacramentals do not confer sanctifying grace immediately but dispose the subject to receiving it, and presuppose at least the existence of Christian baptism as a foundation on which to build. It is to Baptism, the first of the sacraments of Christian initiation, that we now turn.

Notes

1   See O. Semmelroth, *Die Kirche als Ursacrament* (Frankfurt am Main: Joseph Knecht, 1953).

2   Vatican II, *Lumen gentium* 1. See also *ibid.* 9, 48. See St. Cyprian, *Epistle* 69, 6 in *PL* 3, 1142.

3   This fact is illustrated by the fact that St. Ambrose wrote works involving both expressions, namely *De Mysteriis* and *De Sacramentis*. See St. Ambrose, *De Mysteriis* in *PL* 16, 389–410; see Idem, *De Sacramentis* in *PL* 16, 409–462.

4   Pope Stephen I, *Letter to Cyprian, Bishop of Carthage* in ND1401.

5   See A. Miralles, "Il tragitto patristico-medievale fino alla definizione classica di sacramento" in *Annales theologici* 10(1996) p.337.

6   Hugh of St. Victor, *De sacramentis christianae fide*, Liber I, pars IX, cap.2 in *PL* 176, 317. "...deffinire potest quod sacramentum est corporale vel materiale elementum foris sensibiliter propositum ex similitudine repraesentans, et ex intitutione significans, et ex sanctificazione continens aliquam invisibilem et spiritualem gratiam."

7   Peter Lombard, *Sententiae in IV libris distinctae*, lib. IV, dis 1, cap. 4. "Sacramentum proprie dicitur, quod ita signum est gratiae Dei et invisibilis gratiae forma, ut ipsius imaginem gerat et causa exsistat."

8   See St. Thomas Aquinas, *Summa Theologiae* III, q.60, a.2.

9   Council of Trent, Thirteenth Session *Decree on the Most Holy Eucharist*, Chapter III in ND 1516.

10   See *CCC* 1131, 1116.

11   See Council of Trent, Seventh Session *Decree on the Sacraments*, canon 1 in ND 1311.

12   See the condemned Modernist errors in the Decree *Lamentabili* of the Holy Office in the year 1907, ND (1326/39–40). In the same year, the encyclical of Pope St. Pius X, *Pascendi Dominici Gregis* (see ND 1327) condemned the error that the sacraments were signs which developed in the Church to evoke faith.

13   See K. Rahner, *Theological Investigations*. Volume IV (London: Darton, Longman & Todd, 1965), p.274.

14   See Pope Innocent I, *Letter to Decentius, Bishop of Gubbio* in ND 1603.
15   See *Pontificale Romanum* (Malines: Dessain, 1958), pp.850–871 for the rite of blessing and coronation of a monarch. The ceremony is in many respects similar to an ordination. It involves anointing with the oil of catechumens and the imposition of the crown by the officiating bishops.
16   The Second Council of Lyons, "Profession of Faith of Michael Palaeologus" in ND 28.
17   Council of Florence, *Decree for the Armenians* in ND 1305.
18   Council of Trent, Seventh Session, *Decree on the Sacraments*, Canon 1 in ND 1311.
19   See G.W. Leibniz, *Systema theologicum inscriptum* (Paris: Leclerc, 1845), chapter 41ff.
20   See articles 25 and 39 of the Thirty-Nine Articles.
21   Council of Trent, Seventh Session, Canon 3 in ND 1313.
22   St. Thomas Aquinas, *Summa Theologiae* III, q.65, a.3.
23   See J.-H. Nicolas, *Sintesi dogmatica. Dalla Trinità alla Trinità.* Volume II. *La Chiesa e i Sacramenti* (Città del Vaticano: LEV, 1992), p.203.
24   M. Dhavamony, *Phenomenology of Religion* (Rome: Gregorian University Press, 1973), p.31.
25   St. Augustine, *Contra litteras Petilliani*, Liber 3, cap. 55 in *PL* 43, 385.
26   See Pope Innocent III, *Profession of Faith prescribed to the Waldensians* in ND 1301.
27   Pope Martin V, Bull *Inter cunctas*, Question proposed to the followers of Wyclif and Hus in ND 1304.
28   See Pope Leo X, Bull *Exsurge Domine* in ND [1309].
29   Council of Trent, Seventh Session, *Decree on the Sacraments*, Canon 8 in ND 1318.
30   See Pope Leo XIII, Bull *Apostolicae curae* in DS 3315.
31   See Council of Trent, Seventh Session, *Decree on the Sacraments*, Canon 5 in ND 1315: "If anyone says that these sacraments are instituted only for the sake of nourishing faith, let him be anathema."
32   See *CIC* 1060.
33   See chapter seven, section 7.5, for more detailed treatment of this point.
34   See chapter three, subsection 3.3.1, for a more detailed treatment of this point.
35   See chapter eight, sections 8.6 and 8.7, for further clarification on this point.

36   Prosper of Aquitaine, *Liber in quo proferuntur auctoritates episcoporum* 8 in *PL* 51, 209.

37   See Council of Trent, Seventh Session, *Decree on the Sacraments*, Canon 12 in ND 1322.

38   See Idem, canon 11 in ND 1321.

39   See Decree of the Holy Office in the year 1690 under Pope Alexander VIII, which condemned, among others, the following Jansenist error: "Baptism is valid, when conferred by a minister who observes all the external rites and the form of baptising, but interiorly within his heart resolves: I do not intend what the Church does." From ND [1325].

40   See *CIC* 1033: "Only one who has received the sacrament of sacred confirmation may lawfully be admitted to sacred orders."

41   See chapter six, where this is discussed in greater detail.

42   For the Scriptural idea of "fulness" see for example the texts Jn 1:14, 16; Ep 1:23; Col 1:19; 2:9.

43   The Divine Office, Feast of Corpus Christi, Second Vespers, Magnificat Antiphon.

44   See St. Augustine, *De baptismo contra Donatistas*, Lib. 6, cap. 1, 1 in *PL* 43, 197.

45   See St. Thomas Aquinas, *Summa Theologiae* III, q.63, a.2.

46   St.Cyril of Jerusalem speaks of a "seal of the Holy Spirit which cannot be erased in all eternity." From *Procatechesis*, 17 in *PG* 33, 366.

47   Vatican II, *Sacrosanctum Concilium*, 60.

2

Baptism

Christ never operates without water! He Himself is immersed in water; invited to the wedding, He begins with water the first signs of His power; when He speaks, He offers to those who are thirsty His living water which springs up to eternal life; when He speaks of love, He indicates among the proofs of love the gift of a glass of water to one's brother; He rests near a well; He walks on water and often wades through the waters; He quenches with water the thirst of His disciples. And the sign of Baptism follows Him right to His Passion; condemned to death on the Cross, again there is water, as Pilate's hands know; pierced by the lance, water flows from His side.

Tertullian, *De Baptismo*

The sacrament of Baptism is the first to be treated since it forms the basis of sacramental life within the Church. All the other sacred rites presuppose its existence and build upon it. Baptism is the gateway to life with Christ in the Church, being the first sacrament of Christian initiation, followed by Confirmation and culminating in the Holy Eucharist.

2.1 Institution

2.1.1 Old Testament prefiguration and preparation

In the pre-Christian and non-Christian religions, rites involving washing and ritual purification have always had a fairly central place. For example in the religions of ancient Egypt, Greece, Persia, India and Babylon it was held necessary to undergo some kind of ritual ablution in order to remove moral or cultic impurity. Christian Baptism is radically different from these pagan rites, and cannot be seen as having evolved from them in some way. Thus baptism is not simply based on an intrinsic human desire for spiritual purification. The institution of the sacrament on the contrary derives from a divine initiative; the sacrament is also consonant with the human wish for purification. As will be seen, the Christian sacrament stems from a direct command of the Saviour to baptize in His Name. Certain forms of Old Testament purification, however, in some sense foreshadow the Christian rite of Baptism. Under the Jewish law, there were two types of "purification". The first was incurred after having contracted legal impurity: for example as a result of contact with unclean animals, or of sickness, or again because of sexual impurities.[1] The second form of purification was that of initiation. The non-Jew could also take part in the observance of the Jewish law (as seen in Lv 17:8–15) provided he had been circumcised. Later, the idea developed that the non-Jew was impure by definition and had to be purified in a rite that was called baptism (*tebila* in Hebrew). However it cannot be said that Christianity simply adopted from Judaism the rite of Baptism, since it is "questionable whether it still existed at the time of the early Christian Church."[2]

The Old Testament also contains *types* of Christian Baptism, or events which prefigure this sacrament. The first of these consists in the primordial waters over which the Spirit of God hovered (Gn 1:2). St. Peter affirms the waters of the Flood to be "a type of the Baptism" which saves us now. (1 Pt 3:20–21, cf. Gn 7). Circumcision as a rite of initiation and ritual purification is a type of Baptism as St. Paul proposes:

"This is circumcision according to Christ. You have been buried with Him when you were baptised; and by baptism, too, you have been raised up with Him through your belief in the power of God who raised Him from the dead" (Col 2:11–12). The Israelites' passage across the Red Sea is also a baptismal type in Pauline theology: "They were all baptised into Moses in this cloud and in this sea" (I Co 10:2). Tertullian sees Moses' striking of the rock in the desert (Nb 20:1–11) as a figure of St. Peter and his successors who, by means of the waters flowing from the Rock who is Christ, communicate life to the Christian people.[3] The episode in which Naaman, army commander to the king of Aram, was healed from leprosy by a sevenfold ritual bathing in the river Jordan is rich in typological significance (II K 5:8–14). The Old Testament also contains *prophecies* of baptism of which the most explicit is that of Ezekiel: "I shall pour clean water over you and you will be cleansed; I shall cleanse you of all your defilement and all your idols. I shall give you a new heart, and put a new spirit in you" (Ez 36:25–26). The prophets also regard ritual ablution as connected to the future restoration of Israel. Isaiah refers to the washing away of "the filth of the daughter of Sion" (Is 4:4), and Zechariah prophecies that "when that day comes, a fountain will be opened for the House of David and the citizens of Jerusalem, for sin and impurity"(Zc 13:1).

2.1.2   New Testament institution

The word baptism derives from the Greek expression *baptizei* which means "to immerse" or "to plunge". In Holy Scripture, this words has several senses, of which the principal one is that of a washing. Through Christ's institution of the sacrament of Baptism, the immersion into water came to symboize "the catechumen's burial into Christ's death, from which he rises up with Him, as a 'new creature'."[4]

While Old Testament ritual washings may be seen as a remote prefiguration of Christian baptism, the baptism of John is a proximate foreshadowing of the sacrament which Christ instituted. The Precursor of Christ stated: "I have baptised you with water, but He will baptise you with the

Holy Spirit" (Mk 1:8). Thus there is an essential difference between the baptism of John and that of Christ. John's baptism was not a sacrament as such, but rather a preparation for the Christian rite; it was a bridge between the Old and New Testaments. St. Thomas explained it in this way: "The baptism of John did not confer grace, but only prepared the way for grace; and this in three ways: first, by John's teaching, which led men to faith in Christ; second, by accustoming men to the rite of Christ's baptism; third, by penance, preparing men to receive the effect of Christ's baptism."[5] In a sense John's baptism can be considered as a sacramental preparing for the baptism instituted by Christ.[6]

Christ underwent Baptism in the Jordan, at the hands of John the Baptist (Mk 1:9–11) and He also applied the expression baptism to His Passion and Death (Mk 10:38; Lk 12:50). The significance of the Baptism of the Lord was a sign of hope for all men, but above all a theophany or manifestation of His divinity. The One who did not need Baptism received it in order to sanctify the waters of Baptism, as indicated by many Church Fathers like St. Athanasius, St. Ambrose, St. Augustine, St. Gregory Nazianzen and St. Bede. St. Thomas followed this tradition when he noted that "through contact with His flesh the regenerative power entered not only into the waters which came into contact with Christ, but into all waters throughout the whole world and during all future ages."[7]

The institution of Baptism by Christ can be seen from three instances in the Gospels. First, the prediction of John the Baptist that Christ would found a new and perfect baptism in the "Holy Spirit and fire" (Lk 3:16). Second, in His discourse with Nicodemus, Christ insisted on the absolute necessity for salvation of regeneration by means of the baptismal rite (Jn 3:5). On the day of His Ascension, Jesus Christ addressed these solemn words to His Apostles: "Go, therefore, make disciples of all the nations; baptise them in the name of the Father and of the Son and of the Holy Spirit" (Mt 28:19; cfr. Mk 16:16). Christ would not have given the universal command to use a new rite unless He had instituted it beforehand. The early Church administered baptism and taught its necessity for salvation.[8] St. Paul also attested the importance of Baptism for salvation (I Co 1:14ff; Ro 6:1–11). The fact that the primitive Christian community practised Baptism from the beginning and stressed its importance to such a great extent can only be explained if the institution of the sacrament can be attributed to Christ Himself. Clearly only God could have instituted a sacrament which would forgive sins and prepare the way for eternal life with Him.

Various opinions exist as to when Christ instituted Baptism. St. Ambrose and several Scholastics maintained that Christ instituted this sacrament when He was baptized by John in the Jordan. Saint Thomas Aquinas also held that Christ instituted Baptism when He was baptised by John in the Jordan because the water was then given sanctifying force by him. However, the Angelic Doctor added that Christ only imposed the obligation of receiving it after His Passion and Resurrection, because only then would man be capable of being configured to His Passion and Resurrection.[9] A minority of theologians, including Peter Abelard, held that the foundational moment was in the discourse of Jesus with Nicodemus. St. Bonaventure, Blessed John Duns Scotus and others held that the institution occurred when Christ sent out the Apostles and disciples to baptize (Lk 9:1–6; 10:1–16; Jn 3:22–26; 4:1–2). Baptism as the origin of the Church is symbolized by the water which flowed from the opened side of Christ as He hung upon the Cross.[10] Many modern theologians held that the institution took place just before His Ascension when Our Lord sent His Apostles out into the whole world to proclaim the Good News and baptize.

It is probable that a multiple institution of Baptism by Christ took place, in which He progressively revealed the mysteries and gradually determined the essential features of the sacrament. This is rather like the institution of the Church which occurred in a number of pre-Paschal and post-Paschal phases. The Baptism of the Lord revealed the characteristics of the sacrament in a theophanic context, which the miracle of the Wedding Feast at Cana did in a different manner for the Holy Eucharist. The Baptism of the Lord indicated that the matter is water in a spiritual washing. It also pointed to the Trinitarian form. In the dialogue with Nicodemus, Christ insisted on the necessity of the sacrament. Whether Christ Himself performed baptisms is a disputed question (see Jn 3:22 and 4:2). It would seem likely that He would have baptized His Apostles as a prelude to their own ministry of baptizing other people.[11] Moreover, the Apostles would need to have been baptized in order to receive validly later the fulness of the power of orders. Baptism would have been the normal way in which the Apostles would have been freed from the bonds of original sin. It was opportune that the Apostles who were a kind of first-fruits of the Church, should be baptized, since they were the first preachers of the Gospel of which Baptism is the profession.

When Jesus sent the Apostles out to baptize (Jn 3:22), He began to implement the use of the sacrament. This is a totally different rite than that of John the Baptist as can be seen by his response when asked about the significance of Jesus' baptism (Jn 3:25–36). The question also arises how Christian baptism could have been truly administered before the Paschal Mystery, from which all the sacraments derive their power. A possible explanation is that Christ's redemptive act has a retroactive power which also explains why the first Mass took place on the first Holy Thursday which was before the first Easter. Thus the efficacy of Baptism derives from the Passion of Our Lord, which it foreshadowed. As soon as a sacrament was instituted it was capable of producing its effect, and this also holds in the case of Baptism. Thus the Baptisms imparted by the Apostles and disciples during the period of Christ's public ministry were true sacraments; however the full ecclesial context was lacking. The promulgation of the sacrament was imposed on all peoples by Christ just before His Ascension (Mt 28:18). The Church has administered Christian Baptism since the sending of the Holy Spirit for the first time on the day of

Pentecost (Ac 2:38); at that point the full ecclesial context of the sacrament was realized.

2.1.3   Historical development

Several early Christian texts bear witness to the existence of Baptism in the early Church. The *Didache*, which dates from around 100AD, speaks of a rite of immersion in running water, but also of a triple pouring of water on the head of the candidate.[12] St. Hippolytus, writing around the year 215 gave a very detailed description of baptism as it was celebrated at Rome. A period of catechumenate, even as long as two or three years, prepared for the sacrament. The rite bore a remarkable resemblance to the ceremony as performed today, with the pre-baptismal anointings and exorcism, the profession of faith, the baptism by immersion and then a post-baptismal anointing. Account was taken also of infant baptism, in which the parents answered on behalf of their children. The whole of Tertullian's treatise on Baptism which is the oldest monograph on this sacrament, dating from the late second century, tacitly assumes that Christ instituted the sacrament.[13] St. Augustine clearly affirmed the Christ instituted the sacrament: "Baptism does not derive its value from the merits of the one who is baptized nor from the merits of the one who baptizes, but possesses its own holiness and power, by the merits of Him who instituted it."[14] Christ's institution of baptism was envisaged in terms of a gift by St. Gregory Nazianzen who highlighted the various aspects of this sacrament:

> Baptism is God's most beautiful and magnificent gift.... We call it gift, grace, anointing, enlightenment, garment of immortality, bath of rebirth, seal and most precious gift. It is called gift because it is conferred on those who bring nothing of their own; grace since it is given even to the guilty; Baptism because sin is buried in the water; anointing for it is priestly and royal as are those who are anointed; enlightenment because it radiates light; clothing since it veils our shame; bath because it washes; and seal as it is our guard and the sign of God's Lordship.[15]

The fifth century inscription on the marble work at St. John Lateran in Rome also indicates the divine origin of Baptism:

> With virginal generation the Church conceives her children by the power of the Holy Spirit and gives birth to them in water. If you wish to be innocent, be purified in this bath, whether you are burdened by personal or original sin. This is the font which bathes the whole world, and which takes the wounds of Christ for its origin. Hope in the Kingdom of Heaven, all you who are regenerated in this font.[16]

Ancient illustrated baptisteries as that of the Duomo in Florence, which depicts salvation history culminating in Christ, implicitly affirm the divine institution of Baptism.

It is a dogma of the faith that Christ instituted the sacrament of Baptism. The Council of Trent solemnly defined that all sacraments were instituted by Christ.[17] In particular the Council also defined that the Baptism of Christ was effectively separate from that of John.[18] The Church also declared against Modernism, that the sacrament of Baptism was not instituted by an evolutionary process in the early Church.[19]

2.2   The external sign

2.2.1   The matter

The remote matter of the sacrament of Baptism is real and natural water.[20] A first category includes materials which are considered as certainly valid. These include natural water in a liquid state as found in the sea, rivers, wells, springs, fountains, pools, baths, swamps, lakes, melted snow or ice or hail, mineral water, sulphur water, dew, condensed vapours, water from perspiring walls, water with a small quantity of foreign matter (as in the case of muddy water) as long as the water predominates, and putrid water if it still remains water in the common estimation. In the case of water which is not considered clean, it is permissible to treat the water chemically to render it free from bacteria. It is permissible to warm up the water, especially in cold climates and in the case of infant baptism.

A second category of materials is regarded as doubtfully valid. These include light tea or coffee, thin broth, light beer, thin ink, water produced from soapsuds, artificial water extracted by distillation from flowers (such as rose water). A little apocryphal story is told about a candidate for the cardinalate some centuries ago whose family had a tradition of being baptized in rose-water. At issue was whether the man concerned had been baptized or not! Saint Thomas Aquinas stated that "Rose-water is a liquid distilled from roses; consequently it cannot be used for baptism."[21] The question was whether water preponderates in this substance or not. In the case of necessity, such as danger of death, doubtfully valid material may need to be used. If there is a real doubt about validity, its use should be made conditional by adding to the form the words "If this material be valid, John I baptize you...." A final category involves materials which are certainly invalid. These are substances which have never been water or have become transformed from being water. These include wine, thick beer, thick coffee or tea, oil, milk, body fluids including saliva, thick soup or gravy, lard or grease, foam, water mixed with another substance which predominates so that the symbolism of washing is lost.

Water is an appropriate matter for the sacrament of Baptism because it symbolizes regeneration into spiritual life, just as it is a principle of generation in the natural life of men, animals and plants. By reason of its moistness, it symbolizes cleansing, because of its coolness it symbolizes the cooling of the passions of sin, by reason of its transparency it allows the light to pass, symbolizing the illumination of the faith. Water portrays a twofold symbolism in Baptism, that of the destruction of sin, and also that which bestows life through the Holy Spirit.[22] Since water is so common and abundant, it is opportune that it is the matter of this necessary sacrament for salvation.[23] The water for the sacrament of Baptism should be prepared by a blessing which is part of the rite itself, unless the water has already been blessed. Already by the middle of the second century the first traces of a blessing for baptismal water appeared. Then Tertullian wrote of a sanctification of the water through God's blessing.[24] St. Ambrose indicated an exorcism and a blessing of the waters prior to Baptism.[25]

The proximate matter is the actual way in which the water is used in the sacrament. The word "to baptize" implies immersion, as occurred in the Acts of the Apostles, when Philip baptised the chamberlain of the Queen of Ethiopia (Ac 8:36). The concept of baptism as a burial with Christ (Rm 6:1–11; Col 2:12), is also most consonant with baptism by immersion. Nevertheless, in the case of the baptism of the three thousand (Ac 2:41) and the instance of baptism in prison (Ac 16:33), it seems likely that the rite took place by pouring. Very early documents like the *Didaché* allowed for Baptism by pouring.[26] Tertullian, St. Cyprian and St. Augustine refer also to sprinkling as a rite of Baptism.

There are then traditionally three ways in which the sacrament can be carried out, by immersion, by pouring and by sprinkling. Of these three proximate matters, St. Thomas Aquinas seems to prefer immersion, because of its suggestive symbolism of Christ's burial; however since washing may also be carried out by sprinkling or pouring, then these are also acceptable.[27] Baptism by immersion remained the main way of carrying out the sacrament in the East until the thirteenth century and in the West it existed until the fifteenth or sixteenth centuries. To this day, the later Reformed Christian communities like the Mennonites, the Baptists, the Brethren and the Disciples of Christ regard Baptism by immersion as part of their practice. The Neo-catechumenate movement within the Catholic Church regularly uses total immersion as the standard practice for baptism. In any case, for a true washing the water should flow. Thus a moistened finger touched on the baby's head is insufficient, since the water must touch the skin. When talking of sprinkling, this does not mean that a spray from an aerosol would be sufficient. The problem is that in the latter case, there is insufficient water touching the skin to constitute the symbolism of washing.

In some places the immersion, pouring or sprinkling took place three times to signify the Trinity of Divine Persons or else of Christ's three days in the grave.[28] In the Spanish Church the practice of a single immersion evolved to express, against the Arians, the Unity of Substance of the Three Divine Persons. The Catechism recommends either a triple immersion or a triple pouring.[29]

2.2.2 The form

The form of words which must accompany the matter of the sacrament in order to give it the value of an external sign, consists of two kinds. The Western formula is in the indicative voice, and runs: "John, I baptize you in the Name of the Father, and of the Son, and of the Holy Spirit." In the Eastern rites a passive formulation is often used, namely: "The servant of God, Anastasia, is baptized in the Name of the Father, and of the Son, and of the Holy Spirit."[30] Some scholars trace this difference between East and West to a desire especially in the East to combat the Novatian heresy; this error proposed that the faith of the minister was necessary for the validity of baptism. In order to eliminate this false idea, the Eastern bishops decided to substitute the words "I baptize you" with the expression "the servant of God is baptized".[31] Thus the subjective role of the minister is somewhat placed to one side.

A further discussion concerning the form involved the question whether the only valid one is Trinitarian, or whether a Christological expression would be sufficient. Various expressions in the New Testament indicate baptism "in the name of Jesus Christ" (Ac 2:38), "in the name of the Lord Jesus" (Ac 8:16), "in Jesus Christ" (Rm 6:3) and "in Christ" (Ga 3:27). During the Patristic era and in the Middle Ages, the Christological formula was often recognized as valid. St. Ambrose regarded as valid a baptismal formula expressed in the name of the Lord Jesus.[32] In the year 559, Pope Pelagius I condemned the use of the form which was only in the name of Jesus, and stated that a Trinitarian formula was required.[33] But later, in 866, Pope Nicholas I seems to have indicated that the Christological formula was a valid one.[34] Some medieval theologians such as Peter Lombard and Hugh of St. Victor regarded this form as valid. Others like St. Albert the Great, St. Bonaventure and St. Thomas regarded it as valid only for the duration of the Apostolic period. In particular, the Angelic Doctor held that the baptismal form adopting only the invocation of Christ was valid exclusively during the Apostolic age and not later, specifically because of a particular revelation from the Lord.[35] Even if in the early period of the Church there were Christological liturgical formulae, nevertheless they were at least implicitly Trinitarian as a Trinitarian profession of faith was required from the baptized. Thus a profoundly Trinitarian context accompanied any possible Christological form. Moreover any form of Baptism "in the name of the Lord" can be taken to mean under Christ's authority, indicating that Christ instituted the sacrament; it does not necessarily mean that a Christological liturgical formula was in use in the Apostolic age. The Council of Florence in 1439 stressed the necessity of using a Trinitarian formula.[36] In present day ecumenical discussion, a Trinitarian formula is a necessary condition for the recognition by the Catholic Church of the Baptism of other denominations.[37]

The form must also express the act of baptism. Hence, it is necessary to state "John, I baptize you" or "John is baptised". This fact was affirmed by Pope Alexander III in the twelfth century as well as by the condemnation of Jansenist errors under Pope Alexander VIII. The mention of the act of baptism is also implicit from the Council of Florence.[38] If the act of Baptism is not mentioned, the baptism remains indistinguishable from a simple blessing, albeit involving the use of water.[39]

In conclusion, the form of Baptism is required to contain the following elements. The minister and act of Baptism is encapsulated in an expression like "I baptize." The person being baptized should be named to specify that he or she is the recipient. The Unity of the Divine Essence is indicated by the formula "in the Name of". Finally, the Trinity of the Divine Persons must be mentioned explicitly.

2.3 The minister

The ordinary minister of Baptism is a bishop, a priest or a deacon. Clearly, as with all the sacraments, the chief dispenser of the sacrament is the bishop in his diocese. In the Western Church this truth is expressed by the norm that the baptism of adults (at least those who have completed their fourteenth year) must be referred to the bishop.[40] The extraordinary minister of Baptism can be anyone, because of the necessity of Baptism on the one hand and because of God's universal salvific will on the other. Thus the sacrament is very easy to obtain. Even a non-Christian can baptise, but he or she must have the intention of giving Christian Baptism, or have the intention of doing what the Church does. There are clear provisions under which a Catholic lay person may be named a regular extraordinary minister of baptism.[41]

2.4 The recipient

The recipient must of course not already be baptized. Apart from that, the Church's tradition permits the baptism of both infants and adults. When whole families were baptized in the primitive Church, it seems that children would have been baptized as well, as in the case of the family of the centurion Cornelius (Ac 10:44–48), and the family of Stephanas (I Co 1:16). Tertullian in the Western Church of the late second century bore witness to the baptism of infants.[42] Towards the year 250, in the East, Origen referred to the baptism of infants as a practice dating from the time of the Apostles.[43] Ancient Christian grave inscriptions indicated the Christian practice of baptizing infants during that period. The necessity of infant baptism was reiterated several times in the Church's tradition. In the thirteenth century Pope Innocent III explained that babies should be baptized, even though they are not capable of making a decision. There are two kinds of sin, personal sin which is committed with our consent and original sin, incurred without our consent. This original sin is also forgiven of the child in baptism without his consent.[44] The Council of Trent rejected the errors of the Anabaptists who believed only in adult baptism, since they held that infants could not make a profession of faith.[45] The Church has more recently upheld its teaching concerning the immemorial tradition of baptizing children in the faith of the Church. The Church believes in infant baptism, because it believes in necessity of Baptism for salvation.[46] This reaffirmation is especially necessary at the present time when there is a tendency to delay Baptism and allow children to decide their religion for themselves once they have grown up. The Church holds rather that children should be baptised as soon as possible.[47] In order to carry out a baptism of an infant, the minister must obtain the consent of at least one parent or a person *in loco parentis*. For the baptism to be lawful, there must be a well-founded hope that the child will be brought up as a Catholic.[48] However, any infant in danger of death may be baptised even if the parents are opposed.[49] In the case of an adult candidate, he or she must desire to be baptized, and be given suitable preparation.[50] Conditional baptism should be administered if baptism is uncertain either in the sense of its existence or its validity, or if the minister is not sure whether a person is alive or dead.[51] In the case of an unconscious adult, some evidence should indicate that the person at least was not opposed to receiving baptism before he or she fell unconscious. In all cases of Baptism, the details must be carefully registered; this is of capital importance for freedom for marriage, religious life or ordination later on. The new name given in Baptism must not be foreign to Christian sentiment.[52]

2.5 Effects of Baptism

This section examines the salvific effects of Baptism, in terms of the forgiveness of sins, relationship with the Most Holy Trinity and membership of the Church.

2.5.1   Forgiveness of sins

Before the human person can become a partaker in the life of
the Most Holy Trinity, his or her sins must be forgiven. In
Baptism, original sin, all personal sins and the temporal punishment due to sin are remitted.[53] By being baptised into
Christ's death, the Christian is freed from the slavery of sin
and imitates the Lord's resurrection (Rm 6:1–11; cf. Col
2:9–15). Baptism changes the person at the depths of his
being. An adult upon receiving Baptism will be freed from
sin, but past history will remain' unchanged, so the evil
effects of the adult's sinful past remain. Nevertheless the
temporal punishment due to sin is remitted, hence a person
whether adult or child who is newly baptized and then dies
goes straight to their eternal reward. However, if there is a
lack of disposition in the adult then the full effect is not
received. For example, Baptism will not forgive venial sins if
there is still attachment to them. If there is a more serious
lack of disposition, namely the wish to continue living in
mortal sin, then the subject receives the sacramental character, but not the divine life. The divine life is "revived" when
the obstacle is later removed through a sincere reception of
the sacrament of Penance. If, on the other hand, the recipient is absolutely unwilling to receive the sacrament, he does
not receive even the character, because his obstacle has
impeded the sacrament as such: "express dissent is something more than the absence of consent."[54]

Baptism is therefore justification or the transition from
the state in which a person is born a son of the first Adam to
the condition of being made an adopted child of God by
Christ the second Adam.[55] Luther misinterpreted the passage from the letter of St. Paul to the Romans which runs:
"through Our Lord Jesus Christ, by faith we are judged righ-
teous and at peace with God" (Rm 5:1). Luther claimed that
it was by faith alone that we were justified, and this idea led
to his rejection of an objective efficacy of the sacraments.
However, in reality, human cooperation is required along
with the grace of justification, since God never forces our
wills, but wants our loving response.

If the state of grace is lost after Baptism, it can be regained through the sacrament of Penance. However, when grace is lost, contrary to what some of the Reformers maintained, faith is not lost.[56] Despite the fact that baptism removes original sin, there remain some of its consequences, including suffering, illness and human fragility, like weakness of character, and also an inclination to sin known as concupiscence.[57]

2.5.2   *Union with Christ*

Having been freed from the bondage of sin, the baptised person is capable of union with Christ, which also involves a relationship with the Church. The baptized person is configured to Christ as Priest, Prophet and King. This is not merely an external configuration, but an internal one, so that the mind and will are united to Christ. This leads to the idea of the conversion of the intellect and will as a response to Baptism. The analogy used in the Scripture is to "have put on Christ" like a new article of clothing: "All baptised in Christ, you have all clothed yourselves in Christ" (Ga 3:27). The baptized person already belongs to the new creation: "And for anyone who is in Christ, there is a new creation; the old creation has gone, and now the new one is here" (II Co 5:17; cfr. Ga 6:15). This reality is stressed by the symbolism of the white garment used in the liturgical rite: "Jane you have become a new creation, and have clothed yourself in Christ. See in this white garment the outward sign of your Christian dignity. With your family and friends to help you by word and example, bring that dignity unstained into the everlasting life of heaven." Clearly the baptismal garment may be of a colour other than white in cultures where white does not have the same significance.

The configuration to Christ is based on the reality of the *sacramental character* received in Baptism. The concept of the sacramental character of Baptism and by analogy also those of Confirmation and Orders is based on the episode of the Samaritan woman at the well: "Whoever drinks this water will get thirsty again; but anyone who drinks the water that I shall give will never be thirsty again: the water that I shall give will turn into a spring inside him, welling up to eternal life"(Jn 4:13-14; cf. Jn 7:39, Ps 36:9; Is 58:11). In other words, a dynamic idea of the sacramental character is presented here. The character can be compared to the structure of the fountain itself which is put in at baptism, while the life of grace is the water. Through mortal sin the life of grace (like the water) is turned off, but the fountain or the character remains. Through sacramental reconciliation the life of grace is then "reconnected". The sacramental character configures the baptized person to Christ, so that Christ dwells within him or her (Rm 6:1-11). Through Baptism we are formed in the likeness of Christ.[58] The Christian is thus intimately linked with the mystery of Christ in His Incarnation, in His life, in His Passion, Death and Resurrection and looks forward to His Second Coming. The baptismal character also unites the Christian to the Church: "Incorporated into the Church by Baptism, the faithful are appointed by their baptismal character to Christian religious worship."[59] The character also has an anthropological aspect and changes the state of being of the one baptized, so leading to an essential distinction between the Christian and the non-Christian. In this way any inter-religious indifferentism is avoided. This aspect is linked with the idea of conversion: "Your mind must be renewed by a spiritual revolution so that you can put on the new self that has been created in God's way, in the goodness and holiness of the truth" (Ep 4:23-24).

The baptismal character gives the baptised a share in the priestly, prophetic and kingly role of Christ. The basis of the priestly aspect of the baptismal character is to be found in the first letter of St. Peter (I Pt 2:2-10). The functions of the priesthood of the people of God include participation in the liturgy, the sacrifice and sanctification of everyday life, martyrdom, voluntary virginity, marriage, acceptance and offering of suffering, sickness and death.[60] Since a ministerial priest must be baptised before he can be ordained, the priesthood of all the faithful is the basis on which the ministerial priesthood is built, the ministerial priesthood differing in essence from the priesthood of the baptised.[61]

The prophetic or teaching role of the baptismal character is grounded in the words of St. Peter who described the Christian as "set apart to sing the praises of God who called you out of darkness into his wonderful light" (I Pt 2:9). The baptized are "powerful heralds of the faith."[62] The lay members of Christ's faithful, by reason of their Baptism and Confirmation, are witnesses to the good news of the Gospel, by their words and by the example of their Christian life. They can also be called upon to cooperate with bishops and priests in the exercise of the ministry of the word.[63]

The sacramental character of Baptism also involves a participation in the kingship of Christ. St. Paul indicates that the regal power of Christ is progressively made known and brought about (Col 1:15–20; Ep 1:3–23). The Christian contributes to the coming of the Kingdom, remembering that "not even in temporal business may any activity be withdrawn from God's dominion."[64] This participation in the regal office of Christ also involves a struggle and fight against secularising forces in society and with the world of evil (Ep 6:11–14). In this particular area of the coming of the Kingdom the tension between salvation as gift and as response is most keenly felt. This flows from the fact that the character of the sacrament of Baptism is received in order that the Christian be a builder of a Kingdom which is not of this world, but which nevertheless begins in this world.

2.5.3   Gift of the Holy Spirit

St. Paul laid the foundations for a consideration of the indwelling of the Holy Spirit through Baptism: "In the one Spirit we were all baptised, Jews as well as Greeks, slaves as well as citizens, and one Spirit was given to us all to drink" (I Co 12:13). The special kind of presence of the Holy Spirit in the baptized person is a particular and personal one, which must be distinguished from other forms of divine presence. First, God is present in the whole of creation, then man and woman are made in the likeness and image of God. Some remnant of this likeness remains in men and woman despite original sin, so there is some presence of God in the non-baptized. But what is it that distinguishes the presence of God in the Christian and in the non-baptized? In the non-baptized, God is present as the Creator of the person, and also as the One in whose image the person is created. But in the baptized person, the Holy Spirit dwells personally, and thus the Christian enters into a tri-Personal relationship with God. Grace is, however, given outside the Church; the Jansenists were condemned for denying this.[65] A balance is required between regarding the Holy Spirit as only restricted to the sphere of the Church on the one hand and a type of indifferentism on the other, which would place the Holy Spirit equally in all. That the Holy Spirit is especially associated with Baptism can be seen from the Acts of the Apostles: "they were baptised in the name of the Lord Jesus and the moment Paul had laid hands on them, the Holy Spirit came down on them" (Ac 19:5–6).[66]

The Holy Spirit given in Baptism is not just an impersonal power or force. Rather, the Christian is the temple of the Holy Spirit (I Co 6:19). The Spirit cries "Abba, Father" in the heart of the Christian, enabling him or her to invoke the Father (Gal 4:6; Rm 8:15). The Holy Spirit brings about union with Christ and sonship and daughtership of the Father. Hence the Holy Spirit is present in the baptized Christian in a Trinitarian perspective.[67] The Holy Spirit is especially associated with the conferral of sanctifying grace to the baptized person.

Referring to certain passages in the Acts of the Apostles (for example Ac 1:5, 11:6), charismatic renewal has coined the phrase "Baptism in the Spirit". There are two interpretations regarding this term in Catholic Charismatic Renewal. The first envisages baptism in the Spirit as an actualization of what has been received in Baptism and Confirmation. The second explanation speaks in terms of a new outpouring of the Holy Spirit. The danger of the second interpretation is that it has sometimes been set up in opposition to the sacramental system of the institutional Church. This is often associated with an elitism which regards as "real" Christians only those who have received the special extra-sacramental outpouring of the Holy Spirit. In fact according to St. Paul, there exists only one Baptism (Ep 6:4). However, it is of course possible for the Holy Spirit to act outside the strict confines of the sacraments with special charismatic gifts of grace, but this is always in relation to Christ and the Church and the baptised Christian. An extra-sacramental outpouring of the Holy Spirit cannot be guaranteed in the same way as the sacraments which are certain channels of grace to those who put no obstacle in the way. Furthermore, any visible manifestations of the Holy Spirit must be discerned to see that they truly come from Him.

2.5.4   Adopted child of God the Father

The key text for beginning a discussion upon the special relationship with God the Father achieved though Baptism is St. Paul's Letter to the Romans. The Apostle affirms that "everyone moved by the Spirit is a son of God" (Rm 8:14), that the Spirit makes us cry Abba, Father (Rm 8:15), He makes us children and heirs (Rm 8:17), and images of the Son (Rm 8:29). St. Paul also refers to the baptized as "adopted sons" (Ep 1:5). The adopted sonship of the Father brought about by baptism implies a sharing in the divine nature.[68] The baptismal character uniting the baptized to Christ and the sanctifying grace infused by the Holy Spirit constitute the Christian as adopted child of the Father.

Being chosen sons and daughters of God involves the concept of predestination, based on an interpretation of the words of St. Paul to the Christians of Ephesus: "Before the world was made, He chose us, chose us in Christ, to be holy and spotless, and to live through love in His presence, determining that we should become His adopted sons through Jesus Christ" (Ep 1:4). What must be stressed in the Catholic position on predestination is that on the one hand God wishes all to be saved.[69] On the other hand, no one should rashly presume they are destined for salvation.[70]

2.5.5 *Membership of the Church*

Once the recipient of Baptism has been freed from the bond of sin, both original and personal, he or she is also able to be united to the Church. This union with the Church is characteristic of Baptism and involves three elements: communion of faith, ecclesial communion and Eucharistic communion. Baptism in fact prepares for reception of the Holy Eucharist and is orientated towards this culmination of sacramental life.

Baptism constitutes the Christian as a member of the Church: In the Acts of the Apostles, baptism was seen as the reception into the Christian community (Ac 2:37–41). However, baptism is always connected with a context of faith, so that ecclesial communion is indissolubly bound to communion of faith, as well as to Eucharistic communion: "These remained faithful to the teaching of the apostles, to the brotherhood, to the breaking of bread and to the prayers" (Ac 2:42). Baptism constitutes the basis of communion among all Christians, including those not yet in full communion with the Catholic Church. Thus a certain real though imperfect communion exists between the Catholic Church and other Christian Churches and ecclesial communities whose members are incorporated into Christ through Baptism.[71]

The idea of the "anonymous Christian" is an unsatisfactory one, since Christ Himself "explicitly asserted the necessity of faith and baptism (cf. Mk 16:16; Jn 3:5), and thereby affirmed at the same time the necessity of the Church which men enter through Baptism as through a door."[72] The sacramental character of Baptism configures the recipient to Christ and therefore to the Church. The character is a Christological and Ecclesiological mark. Even if a person formally leaves the Church, the indelible character is still present and hence the possibility of repentance always remains.

Baptism creates a unity within the Church, so that all other distinctions fall away: "All baptised in Christ, you have all clothed yourself in Christ, and there are no more distinctions between Jew and Greek, slave and free, male and female, but all of you are one in Christ Jesus." (Gal 3:27–28)

Therefore the Church transcends and embraces every nationality, and overcomes every racial or cultural division. The Church is open to all nations and cultures, which also involves a conversion of culture so that elements which are against Christian faith, morals or culture may be removed. However, this does not mean that all are identical in the Church; for example, a distinction exists between the ministerial priesthood and that of all the baptized.[73] The common dignity of all the faithful deriving from baptism and "the true equality between all with regard to the dignity and to the activity which is common to all the faithful in the building up of the Body of Christ"[74] is not to be confused with modern political democracy.

The People of God share in Christ's priestly office, prophetic office, kingly office.[75] Thus all the baptized, holding communion with the Holy See are full members of the Church. The mistaken idea that only priests and nuns are "professional Christians" runs counter to the dignity of the baptized person, upon whom has been conferred a key role within the Church. Ecclesial movements derive their efficacy and force from the baptismal commitment of their members. Thus all movements must be seen in the light of baptismal membership of the Church, and so avoid all forms of elitism or closure to those who are not members of the said groups.

The Catholic Church generally accepts the validity of Baptism of other Christian denominations where it is evident that the matter, form and intention are correct. In particular, the validity of Baptism conferred in the Eastern Churches separated from the Holy See is not in doubt. As regards other Churches and ecclesial communities, the certainty that a baptism of an individual has been carried out validly is facilitated by the existence of an agreement on baptism made by the Churches and ecclesial communities of the region, and by the fact that the individual baptism has been carried out in accordance with this agreement. The absence of a formal agreement of this kind does not mean that Baptism is invalid. Generally, the validity of Baptism is presumed unless there is a doubt about the matter or the form or the intention of the minister or the intention of an adult recipient. In particular, attention should be given to the danger of invalidity in cases where baptism has been conferred by sprinkling, especially of several people simultaneously.[76] Where a serious doubt persists, conditional baptism may be carried out in private.[77] It is forbidden to confer Baptism into two denominations at the same time. Thus, the sacrament may not be carried out by two ministers belonging to different Churches or ecclesial communities.[78]

2.6   Gift and response

Having considered the effects of Baptism as consisting essentially in the remission of sins, the giving of grace and the conferring of the sacramental character, it is now opportune to mention the response to these gifts. Baptism involves both gift and response. It is not just a "ticket" to automatic salvation; a response is also involved to what has been received in Baptism. In the interplay between divine action and the appropriate human response, good works are required as well as faith (Jm 2:14–26). Baptism brings with it a change of life (I Pt 3:21–4:6). Thus baptism is a gift and also a task which looks toward the future. The Christian is baptised into the Paschal Mystery of Christ which took place once and for all in the past, yet there is a pledge of glory yet to be revealed. The baptismal gifts unfold in this life and are perfected in Confirmation and find their ultimate focus in the Holy Eucharist. However, the final fruition only occurs in the future glory. The dynamic fulfilment of the sacramental character is illustrated by St. Paul in the following terms: "and you too have been stamped with the seal of the Holy Spirit of the Promise, the pledge of our inheritance which brings freedom for those whom God has taken for his own, to make his glory praised" (Ep 1:13–14).

2.7   The necessity of Baptism

While Baptism is not a ticket to automatic salvation, it is certainly a necessary condition. This truth has been stated
against various historical heresies in the life of the Church.
The Pelagians, who undermined the value of grace and
denied the transmission of original sin, thought that Baptism
was not necessary at all. Man could achieve salvation purely
by his own efforts. Against the errors of Pelagius, the sixteenth Council of Carthage in the year 418 affirmed that
Baptism truly remits original sin.[79] Against the errors of the
Messalians and Manichaeans, who maintained that Baptism
was only optional, the Council of Trent affirmed its necessity
for salvation.[80] The Waldensian anti-sacramental tendency
regarded the baptism of infants as superfluous, and was also
uncertain about the remission of sins brought about by the
sacrament.[81] Among the reformers, Luther believed that
Baptism was a sacrament, and held the baptism of babies to
be a real means of salvation, but was unable to harmonize his
notion of justification of faith alone with the idea that Baptism saves. Therefore he did not regard Baptism as necessary
for salvation, because faith alone possessed salvific power.
Calvin firmly rejected the baptism of babies. The Calvinists
retained that the Holy Spirit aroused faith directly in the
hearts of believers and that this coincided with the rite of
baptism. Babies who were children of believers received an
infused gift of faith and this regenerated them. Therefore,
according to the Calvinist outlook, Baptism was not necessary, but was simply a token or symbol of the process of direct
regeneration. The Modernists held that the necessity of
Baptism depended on a purely ecclesiastical precept.[82]

    More recently, the Magisterium has stated that "Jesus'
words are so universal and absolute in form that the Fathers
employed them to establish the necessity of Baptism."[83]
Although the context of this statement was a re-affirmation
of the practice of infant baptism in an increasingly pluralistic
situation, where some parents wanted to wait until the children were teenagers to allow them to choose their religion, it

is also a valuable corrective against a type of indifferentism which proposes that all religions are equal. Similarly the current lack of distinction between the natural and supernatural leads to a reduction of religion to naturalism and a denial of the importance of purification from original and actual sin. In any case, the recent affirmation is one in a long line of positive statements by the teaching Church regarding the necessity of Baptism. In the year 385, Pope Siricius stated this truth.[84] Pope Innocent I reiterated the teaching in the year 417.[85] The Council of Florence taught this doctrine as did the Council of Trent.[86]

The Church's teaching on the necessity of Baptism for salvation is completed by a consideration of how, in certain circumstances, this necessity can be supplied also by baptism of desire or baptism of blood. While God has bound salvation to the sacrament of Baptism, "He Himself is not bound by His sacraments."[87]

The idea of baptism of desire (also known as baptism of charity) can be based on the episode in the Acts of the Apostles, where the gift of the Holy Spirit was poured out upon the family of the centurion Cornelius even before he had received baptism (Ac 10:1–48). A certain response of faith must precede baptism (see Ac 8:36–37), which implies a saving action of the Holy Spirit preparing the recipient for sacramental Baptism, even before it is received. Hence, in the hypothetical case that a catechumen dies before the actual sacrament, it is inconceivable that God would deprive him or her of salvation. Surely, instead the person concerned would be saved by desire for salvation. The concept must be correctly understood however. Christ's command is that all should be incorporated by Baptism into the Church. It is possible however, to gain eternal salvation by belonging to the Church in "desire and longing". This desire does not always have to be explicit, as in the case of a catechumen. When someone is, through no fault of their own, invincibly ignorant of the Gospel of Christ or His Church, an implicit desire is acceptable, which is "contained in the good dispositions of soul by which a man wants his will to be conformed to God's will." This desire involves seeking God with a sincere heart and living according to conscience, guided by grace.[88] God wishes to save all people (I Tm 2:4), but always through the Church, the sign and sacrament of salvation. Baptism of desire cancels original sin and personal grave sins, but does not cancel with certainty venial sins nor temporal punishment due to sin; it functions *ex opere operantis*. Above all, this substitute for Baptism does not impart the sacramental character.

Baptism of blood involves the voluntary acceptance of death or mortal injury caused by an external agent, suffered for love of religion or some Christian virtue.[89] The Scriptural basis for this is to be found in Christ's words: "Anyone who loses his life for my sake will find it" (Mt 10:39, cfr. 10:32). Baptism of blood confers justification even on children before the age of reason, a classic example being the Holy Innocents. This substitutive element for Baptism unto salvation does not impart the sacramental character, because it is not a sacrament. Nevertheless, unlike baptism of desire, it operates *quasi ex opere operato* because it involves an objective confession of faith.

2.8   The fate of children who die without Baptism

This thorny question is also one of great pastoral significance, because as well as the terrible tragedy of the loss of a child who has hardly lived at all, there is the additional worry about his or her salvation. In the Patristic period, the great and enlightened St. Gregory of Nyssa held there to be a salvation for children dying without Baptism.[90] This concept was salvation obtained through the vicarious desire of the parents. In this opinion, St. Gregory of Nyssa was later followed by St. Bonaventure, and Cardinal Cajetan. The difficulty lies in the fact that the salvation would depend on the will of the child's parents. On the other hand, St. Augustine, and others in the period following him, held the children would not be saved, and would endure the smallest possible positive punishment of hell,[91] but would suffer the deprivation of the vision of God.

St. Thomas started a new way of thinking of the problem, by stating that although these children would be deprived of the full supernatural gifts of heaven, they would attain a certain natural blessedness, which then was called Limbo from the Latin expression, *limbus puerorum*. This idea of Limbo was upheld by Pope Pius VI against the rigorism of the Jansenist synod of Pistoia in the year 1794.[92] Pope Pius XII in an address to Catholic midwives in 1951 asserted that a state of grace at the moment of death is necessary for the enjoyment of the beatific vision, hence the necessity of baptizing infants.[93] There is a fair consensus among theologians that Limbo is an appropriate way of treating the question.[94]

Modern theologians have extended the foregoing arguments by saying that God is not bound by the sacraments, He can act outside them.[95] Thus, by giving the command to baptise, God does not tie His hands. Man is ordained to salvation and just as those who were living before the time of Christ could be saved even without Baptism, so also provisions are made for those, who, through no fault of their own cannot be baptized. One solution along these lines, which can be applied both to the sad case of suicide as well as to the death of infants before Baptism, is the concept of illumination. This opinion, which has the support of Blessed John Duns Scotus, is that God gives the infant an illumination during the moment of death so that he or she can choose between a life in union with Him or otherwise. H. Klee held a variant of this thesis in which, at the moment of death, the infant who had died without Baptism acquired the use of reason in order to make an act of charity and so be justified. A further idea was offered by J. Galot who proposed that, while for an adult baptism of desire substituted sacramental Baptism, for infants on the other hand, the desire of the Church as a whole substitutes Baptism by water.[96] The formulation of the Catechism is a suitable summary of the Church's concern: "As regards children who have died without Baptism, the Church can only entrust them to the mercy of God, as she does in her funeral rites for them. Indeed the great mercy of God who desires that all men should be saved, and Jesus' tenderness toward children which caused Him to say: 'Let the children come to me, do not hinder them', allows us to hope that there is a way of salvation for children who have died without Baptism."[97]

Notes

1   Leviticus chapters 11–15 contain many examples of this kind of purification.
2   M. Schmaus, *Dogma 5. The Church as Sacrament* (London: Sheed and Ward, 1975), p.141.
3   See Tertullian, *De Baptismo* cap 9, 3 in *CCL* 1, 284.
4   *CCC* 1214.
5   St. Thomas Aquinas, *Summa Theologiae* III, q.38, a.3.
6   See St. Thomas Aquinas, *Summa Theologiae* III, q.38, a.1.
7   St. Thomas Aquinas, *Summa Theologiae* III, q.78, a.5.
8   This can be seen, for example, from the following passages: Ac 2:38,41; 8:12f, 16, 36, 38; 10:47f; 16:15,33; 18:8; 19:3–5.
9   See St. Thomas Aquinas, *Summa Theologiae* III, q.66, a.2.
10 See Jn 19:34, 1 Jn 5:6–8; Vatican II, *Lumen gentium* 3.
11 See St. Thomas Aquinas, *Summa Theologiae* III, q.38, a.6.
12 See *SW*, pp.1–2.
13 Tertullian, *De Baptismo* in *CCL* 1, 275–295.
14 St. Augustine,*Contra Cresconium* 4, 19 in *PL* 43, 559.
15 St. Gregory Nazianzen, *Oratio* 40, 3–4, in *PG* 36, 361.
16 See M. Schmaus, *Dogmatica Cattolica. IV/1 I Sacramenti* (Casale: Marietti, 1966), pp.133–134.
17 See Council of Trent, Seventh Session, *Decree on the Sacraments* Canon 1 in ND 1311.
18 See Council of Trent, Seventh Session, *Canons on the Sacrament of Baptism*, Canon 1 in ND 1420.
19 See Holy Office, Decree *Lamentabili* in ND [1437/42].
20 Council of Florence, *Decree for the Armenians* in ND 1413; Council of Trent, Seventh Session, *Canons on the Sacrament of Baptism*, canon 2 in ND 1421; Congregation for Divine Worship, *Rite of Baptism for Children* 21/2.
21 St. Thomas Aquinas, *Summa Theologiae* III, q.66, a.4.
22 See St. Basil, *De Spiritu Sancto* cap. 15, 35 in *PG* 32, 130.
23 Cf. St. Thomas Aquinas, *Summa Theologiae* III, q.66, a.3.
24 See Tertullian, *De Baptismo*, cap. 4 in *CCL* 1, 279–280.
25 See St. Ambrose, *De Sacramentis* Lib. 1, cap. 5 in *PL* 16, 422–423.
26 See *Didaché* 7,3, in *Sources Chrétiennes* 248 (Paris: Cerf, 1978), pp.170–173.
27 Cf. St. Thomas Aquinas, *Summa Theologiae* III, q.66, a.7.

28 See St. Cyril of Jerusalem, *Mystagogical Catecheses* 2, 4 in *SW* p.13.

29 *CCC* 1239

30 See Council of Florence, *Decree for the Armenians* in ND 1413, which cites a second possible Eastern form as "By my hands Anastasia is baptized in the Name of the Father, and of the Son, and of the Holy Spirit."

31 See A. Piolanti, *I Sacramenti* (Vatican City: Libreria Editrice Vaticana, 1990), p.284.

32 See St. Ambrose, *De Spiritu Sancto* Lib. 1, cap. 3, 42–43 in *PL* 16, 713–714.

33 Pope Pelagius I, Letter *Admonemus ut* in DS 445.

34 Pope Nicholas I, Response *Ad consulta vestra* in DS 646.

35 See St. Thomas Aquinas, *Summa Theologiae* III, q.66, a.6.

36 The General Council of Florence, *Decree for the Armenians* as found in ND 1413.

37 See *ED* 93 which enunciates that the requirement is "a formula which clearly indicates that baptism is done in the name of the Father, Son and Holy Spirit."

38 See letter of Alexander III (1159–1181) in DS 757; see also condemnation (DS 2327) by the Holy Office of the Jansenist error that there is a valid baptism without the phrase "I baptize you". See also Council of Florence in ND 1413.

39 See St. Thomas Aquinas, *Summa Theologiae* III, q.66, a.5.

40 See *CIC* 863

41 See *Instruction on certain questions regarding the collaboration of the non-ordained faithful in the sacred ministry of the priest* (1997), 11.

42 Tertullian, *De baptismo* cap. 18, 5 in *CCL* 1, 293.

43 See Origen, *Commentaria in Epistolam B. Pauli ad Romanos*, Lib. 5, 9 in *PG* 14, 1047, where he states: "Pro hoc et Ecclesia ab apostolis traditionem suscepit, etiam parvulis baptismum dare."

44 See Pope Innocent III, *Letter to Humbert, Archbishop of Arles* in ND 506.

45 Council of Trent, Seventh Session, Canons 11–13 on baptism in ND 1430–1432.

46 Sacred Congregation for the Doctrine of the Faith, Instruction *Pastoralis actio* 14, in ND 1444.

47 See *CIC* 867.

48 See *CIC* 868, §1.

49 See *CIC* 868, §2.

50 See *CIC* 865.

51 See *CIC* 869.

52 See *CIC* 855.

53   The General Council of Florence, *Decree for the Armenians* as found in ND 1415.
54   Pope Innocent III, *Letter to Humbert, Archbishop of Arles* in ND 1410.
55   See Council of Trent, Sixth Session, *Decree on Justification* Chapter IV in ND 1928.
56   See Council of Trent, Sixth Session, *Decree on Justification* Canon 28 in ND 1945, 1978. Lutheran views on justification have developed since the time of the Reformation.
57   See *CCC* 1264. For further discussion on the effects and consequences of original sin see my *Mystery of Creation* (Leominister: Gracewing, 1995), pp.117–128.
58   See Vatican II, *Lumen gentium* 7.2. Cfr. also 31.1.
59   Vatican II, *Lumen gentium* 11.1.
60   See Vatican II, *Lumen gentium* 10, 34.
61   See Vatican II, *Lumen gentium* 10.2.
62   See Vatican II, *Lumen gentium* 35.2.
63   See *CIC* 759.
64   Vatican II, *Lumen gentium* 36.4.
65   See Vatican II, *Lumen gentium* 4 and 12 for an idea of the presence of the Holy Spirit in the Christian and the Church. See condemned error of Pasquier Quesnel in DS 2429 which denied that grace was given outside the Church.
66   See also Acts 10:47: "Peter then said 'Could anyone refuse the water of baptism to these people, now that they have received the Holy Spirit just as much as we have?' " It is interesting that the Holy Spirit was given here before actual sacramental baptism, as a prevenient grace.
67   See Romans 8:1–27 for the central ideas of the indwelling of the Holy Spirit in the Christian.
68   See Vatican II, *Lumen gentium* 40.1 and I Peter 1:4.
69   See I Timothy 2:4: "God wants everyone to be saved and reach full knowledge of the truth." See also the condemnation of an error of Cornelius Jansen in ND [1989/5], an error which implied that Christ did not die for all men without exception.
70   See Council of Trent, Sixth Session *Decree on Justification* in ND 1941. Also, no-one is predestined to evil as seen in ND 1967.
71   See *CCC* 1271 and Pope John Paul II, Encyclical Letter *Ut unum sint* (1995), 11.
72   Vatican II, *Lumen gentium*, 14.1.
73   See Vatican II, *Lumen gentium* 10.2, which states that "though they differ essentially and not only in degree, the common priesthood of the faithful and the ministerial or hierarchical priesthood are none the less ordered one to another."

74 *Ibid.*, 32.3.
75 *Ibid.*, 11–13.
76 *ED* 95 (c), note 105.
77 ED 99.
78 *ED* 97.
79 See Sixteenth Council of Carthage, canon 2 in DS 223.
80 Council of Trent, Seventh Session, canon 5 on baptism in ND 1424.
81 See Profession of Faith prescribed to the Waldensians in ND 1411.
82 See Holy Office, Decree *Lamentabili*, which condemned the following Modernist article as cited in ND [1437/42]: "The Christian community introduced the necessity of baptism by adopting it as a necessary rite and attaching to it the obligation of Christian profession."
83 Sacred Congregation for the Doctrine of the Faith, Instruction *Pastoralis actio* on infant baptism, 12 in ND 1443.
84 Pope Siricius, *Letter to Himerius, Bishop of Tarragona* in ND 1405.
85 Pope Innocent I, Letter *Inter ceteras Ecclesiae Romanae* to Silvanus in DS 219.
86 See Council of Florence, Decree for the Armenians in ND 1412. Council of Trent, Seventh session, Canon 5 in ND 1424: "If anyone says that Baptism is optional, that is, not necessary for salvation, let him be anathema."
87 *CCC* 1257 and see *CCC* 1260.
88 See Vatican II, *Lumen gentium* 16. See also Holy Office, Letter to the Archbishop of Boston (1949), in ND 855.
89 See St. Thomas Aquinas, *Summa Theologiae* I–II, q.124, a.1.
90 St. Gregory of Nyssa, *De infantibus qui praemature abripiuntur*, in *PG* 46, 161–192.
91 See St. Augustine, *Contra Julianum* 5, 11, 44 in *PL* 44, 809.
92 See condemned error of the pseudo-synod of Pistoia in DS 2626.
93 See Pope Pius XII, *Address to Catholic midwives*, in *AAS* 43 (1951), p.841.
94 See W.A. Van Roo, "Infants Dying Without Baptism" in *Gregorianum* 35(1954), pp.406–473.
95 See St. Thomas Aquinas, *Summa Theologiae* II, q. 68, a.2.
96 See J. Galot, "La salvezza dei bambini morti senza Battesimo" in *La Civiltà Cattolica* 122/2 (1971), pp.228–240; idem, "La salvezza dei bambini per mezzo del voto del Battesimo" in *La Civiltà Cattolica* 122/2 (1971), pp.336–346.
97 *CCC* 1261.

3

Confirmation

By the chrism of Confirmation new strength is infused into believers that they may uphold and defend vigorously the Church, their mother, and the faith which they have received from her.

Pope Pius XII, *Mystici Corporis*

Confirmation is the second sacrament of initiation. In most treatises on sacramental theology, less is said about Confirmation than about Baptism. Sometimes the sacrament has been neglected theologically, but it is nevertheless powerful and important.

3.1 Baptism and Confirmation

One issue which needs to be faced is that of the difference between Baptism and Confirmation. As has been seen in chapter two, the Holy Spirit is already imparted in Baptism, so it is interesting to ask what Confirmation adds to the baptized Christian.

The sacrament of Confirmation is intrinsically linked with the whole economy of Christian initiation.[1] Baptism and Confirmation are connected with one another and yet are distinct and different: "Incorporated into the Church by Baptism, the faithful are appointed by their baptismal character to Christian religious worship; reborn as sons of God, they must profess before men the faith they have received

59

from God through the Church. By the sacrament of Confirmation they are more perfectly bound to the Church and are endowed with the special strength of the Holy Spirit. Hence they are, as true witnesses of Christ, more strictly obliged to spread to spread the faith by word and deed."[2] At the same time, Baptism and Confirmation are both orientated to Christian apostolate: "The apostolate of the laity is a sharing in the salvific mission of the Church. Through Baptism and Confirmation all are appointed to the apostolate by the Lord Himself."[3] Baptism and Confirmation, in their turn, find their fulfilment and culmination in the Holy Eucharist: "As members of the living Christ, incorporated into Him and made like Him by Baptism, Confirmation and the Eucharist, all the faithful have an obligation to collaborate in the expansion and spread of His Body, so that they might bring it to fullness as soon as possible."[4] The connection between Baptism and Confirmation can be seen as analogous to the relation between Easter and Pentecost. The sending of the Holy Spirit at Pentecost puts a seal on the Paschal Mystery; in just this way, Confirmation puts the seal on the baptized person.

3.2   Institution and existence of Confirmation

Confirmation contains two ritual actions, a laying-on of hands and an anointing with perfumed oil, called chrism, and a set of significant words go with each. Here a look is taken at the existence of this rite according to the Scriptures, the Fathers, and the teaching of the Church.

3.2.1   Scripture

In the Old Testament, some prefigurations of Confirmation can be highlighted. From earliest times, the hands were used to call down a blessing on specially chosen people (Gn 48:13–16) and to designate individuals for some special role (Nb 8:10). Anointing with oil, especially perfumed oil, was one of the rituals of joyous celebration of the Old Covenant (Am 6:6). As well as prefigurations, there were also prophecies of a future outpouring of the Holy Spirit, such as that of Joel: "After this I will pour out my Spirit on all mankind. Your sons and daughters shall prophesy, your old men shall dream dreams, and your young men will see visions." (Jo 3:1) The prophet Isaiah foretold a future gift of the Holy Spirit: "For I will pour out water on the thirsty soil, streams on the dry ground. I will pour out my Spirit on your descendants, my blessing on your children." (Is 44:3)

In the New Testament, Christ fulfilled His mission in the power of the Spirit (Mk 1:10), and proclaimed: "The Spirit of the Lord is upon me" (Lk 4:17–21). Christ promised the Holy Spirit to the Apostles so they might bear fearless witness to Him (Lk 12:12, cfr Jn 14–15). After His Resurrection, Christ once again promised the Holy Spirit: "You will receive power when the Holy Spirit comes down on you; then you are to be my witnesses" (Ac 1:8; cf. Lk 24:49). The fulfilment of Christ's promises took place at Pentecost when the Holy Spirit came down mightily upon Our Lady and the Apostles. Early believers were baptized and received the Holy Spirit (Ac 2:38). The language of anointing is used in connection with the Baptism of Jesus to describe how He was filled with the Holy Spirit (Ac 10:38) and also in reference to His divine Sonship (Hb 1:9). The expression is then also applied to describe how Christians share through Christ in the messianic gift of the Spirit (I Jn 2:20–27). The Acts of the Apostles describe a rite imparting a gift of the Holy Spirit which was connected with Baptism yet distinct from it, involving a laying-on of hands: "When the apostles in Jerusalem heard that Samaria had accepted the word of God, they sent Peter and John to them, and they went down there, and prayed for the Samaritans to receive the Holy Spirit, for as yet He had not come down on any of them: they had only been baptized in the name of the Lord Jesus. Then they laid hands on them and they received the Holy Spirit" (Ac 8:14–17). Around thirty years later, St Paul carried out the same rite at Ephesus (Ac 19:1–8). The Letter to the Hebrews cites a laying of hands which is distinct from Baptism (Hb 6:2).

From what has been outlined, it emerges that the rite carried out by the Apostles Peter and John has all the characteristics of a sacrament. It was conferred with a tangible sign,

namely the imposition of hands. The rite produced grace (Ac
8:18), and was distinct from Baptism. It was permanently
instituted by Christ. Since the Lord promised to impart the
Holy Spirit to all the faithful, it must be assumed that He
laid down clear instructions about how this Gift was to be
communicated. Since the Apostles regarded themselves as
simply Christ's ministers and stewards of the divine mysteries (I Co 4:1) and not initiators of the same means that since
they administered this rite of the gift of the Holy Spirit, then
this sacred act must have been founded by Christ Himself.
Nothing is certain about the precise moment in which the
Lord instituted Confirmation. Some theologians hold that
He founded it before the Resurrection, others maintain that
it was instituted afterwards. Other scholars again propose
that Christ set up Confirmation at the Last Supper, when
He spoke at great length about the gift of the Holy Spirit (Jn
16:5–15). Some theologians have stated that the sacrament
was prefigured when Christ laid his hands on the children
(Mt 19:13), while at the Last Supper He founded it more
clearly, instructing the Apostles to administer it after
Pentecost.[5]

3.2.2   Church Fathers

The very early Christian liturgies of initiation included a
post-baptismal laying-on of hands and anointing, but it is not
always clear whether this was a sacrament separate from Baptism. Even today in the current rite of Baptism of children,
there is an anointing with chrism after Baptism, and this
foreshadows the later Confirmation of the child. This
anointing is a vestige of Confirmation from the rite of initiation of adults when all three sacraments of initiation were
given together, and is applied with the following prayer:
"God the Father of Our Lord Jesus Christ has freed you from
sin, given you a new birth by water and the Holy Spirit, and
welcomed you into His holy people. He now anoints you with
the chrism of salvation. As Christ was anointed Priest,
Prophet, and King, so may you live always as members of His
body, sharing everlasting life." However, the distinction

between the two sacraments became clear by the time St. Hippolytus in his Treatise on the Apostolic Tradition, dating from about 215 AD, referred to the Roman rite of initiation, in which two post-baptismal anointings took place. After baptism, the candidates came out of the font and were immediately anointed with the oil of thanksgiving by the priests who used the following words: "I anoint thee with holy oil in the Name of Jesus Christ."[6] Then, afterwards, the second anointing with consecrated oil clearly seems to be Confirmation. After everyone had been dried and dressed, all went into the church, where the bishop laid hands upon the candidates, and prayed over them. He then poured the consecrated oil on each candidate and laid his hand on the head of each one, reciting the formula: "I anoint thee with holy oil in God the Father Almighty and Christ Jesus and the Holy Ghost."[7] The bishop then sealed every candidate on the forehead and gave him a kiss of peace. This very early description of Confirmation is very similar to what occurs today. Tertullian referred to three distinct phases in the rite of Christian initiation, so that Confirmation was seen as a sacrament in its own right: "The flesh is washed that the soul may be made spotless: the flesh is anointed so that the soul may be consecrated: the flesh is signed with the cross that the soul may also be protected; the flesh is overshadowed by the imposition of the hand that soul also may be enlightened by the Spirit: the flesh feeds on the Body and Blood of Christ so that the soul as well may be replete with God."[8]

In the Christian East, around the middle of the fourth century, St. Cyril of Jerusalem treated of the sacrament of Confirmation in his catechetical lectures: "Now just as Christ was truly crucified, and buried, and raised again, and through Baptism, in virtue of a kind of likeness, you were accounted worthy of being crucified, and buried, and raised again, so too it is with the unction. He was anointed with the spiritual oil of gladness, that is with the Holy Spirit, who is the Oil of gladness since He is the Author of spiritual joy. But you were anointed with ointment, having been made partakers and associates of Christ."[9] In the West, at the end of the fourth century, St. Ambrose dealt with all the sacraments of initiation including references to Confirmation: "Now after Baptism you went up to the bishop. Consider the anointing that followed. Was it not what David says: 'It is like precious oil upon the head, running down upon the beard, running down upon Aaron's beard.'... You have received the spiritual seal.... God the Father has sealed you, Christ has confirmed you, and the Spirit has given you the pledge in your heart."[10]

Thereafter, the theological development of Confirmation was greatly influenced by the thought of certain Faustus who was Abbot of Lérins and then bishop of Riez in Southern France during the second part of the fifth century. One of his homilies had a great impact on the later medieval sacramental theology of Confirmation. His idea was that Confirmation equipped the Christian to be a soldier of Christ:

> Military proceedings require that when a commander receives a man into the number of his soldiers, he should not only put his mark upon him, but also equip him with arms suitable for fighting with.... So the Holy Spirit, who descended upon the baptismal waters bearing salvation, gave at the font all that is needed for innocence: at Confirmation He gives an increase of grace, for in this world those who survive through the different stages of life, must walk among dangers and invisible enemies. In Baptism we are born again to life, after Baptism we are confirmed for battle.[11]

Then, in the ninth century, Rabanus Maurus archbishop of Mainz, referred to two anointings which the Christian received after Baptism. The first anointing on top of the candidate's head was carried out by the priest; the second was effected on the candidate's forehead by the bishop. The first anointing signifies the descent of the Holy Spirit to consecrate a worthy dwelling for God, while the second confers the sevenfold grace of the same Holy Spirit upon man with all the fullness of sanctity. At the second anointing, Confirmation, the Holy Spirit comes upon the Christian to fill him with heavenly gifts, and to strengthen him by His grace to bear the name of Christ fearlessly before the kings and rulers of this world and preach Him with a free voice.[12]

The Angelic Doctor developed these ideas on Confirmation which he regarded as "a certain spiritual growth bringing man to perfect spiritual age."[13] In another formulation, St. Thomas described Confirmation as "the sacrament of the fulness of the Holy Spirit."[14]

3.2.3 Church teaching

The term Confirmation was used for the first time at the Council of Riez in 439. The Council of Florence, one thousand years later, defined Confirmation to be a sacrament in which the Holy Spirit is "given for strength."[15] The Council of Trent stated, against the Reformers, that Confirmation is a true sacrament.[16] That this sacrament was instituted by Christ was taught by the Tridentine decree on sacraments in general, in contrast to the Lutheran Augsburg Confession which had professed that Confirmation was only of apostolic institution.[17] Later, at the turn of the twentieth century, the Modernists went even further than the Reformers and denied that the rite of Confirmation was used by the Apostles, maintaining that "the formal distinction between the two sacraments, Baptism and Confirmation, has nothing to do with the history of primitive Christianity."[18] In 1971, Pope Paul VI stressed that after Pentecost the Apostles, "in fulfillment of Christ's wish, imparted the gift of the Holy Spirit to the newly baptized by the laying-on of hands to complete the grace of Baptism." Paul VI made it clear that "this laying-on of hands is rightly recognized by the Catholic tradition as the beginning of the sacrament of Confirmation."[19] These affirmations teach the divine institution by Christ of the sacrament of Confirmation.

3.3 The external sign

3.3.1 The matter

The matter of Confirmation has undergone an historical evolution in the various rites of East and West. Seemingly, during the period of the Acts of the Apostles, Confirmation was imparted by the laying on of hands and a prayer (see, for example Ac 19:1-7). However, the idea of sacred anointing is implicit in the New Testament conception of the giving of the Spirit, as St. John pointed out: "But you have not lost the anointing that He gave you, and you do not need anyone to teach you; the anointing that He gave teaches you everything; you are anointed with truth, not with a lie, and as it has taught you, so you must stay in Him" (I Jn 2:27). Sometimes in the first century of the Church's life, the rite of Confirmation was so linked with the concluding ceremonies of Baptism, that it is difficult to discern what was the essence of Confirmation.

In the oldest Roman rite, that of Hippolytus dating from the first half of the third century, Confirmation was administered as follows. After Baptism, when the candidates had dried and dressed, all went into the church, where the Bishop laid hands upon them with a prayer. Then, the Bishop anointed them with holy oil on the head, saying : "I anoint you with holy oil in the Father Almighty, in Jesus Christ and in the Holy Spirit." Thus both an anointing and a laying-on of hands were employed. In all the subsequent Latin liturgies, the anointing with chrism *and* the laying-on of hands have been present in all the rites. However, in the Oriental Liturgies of the Byzantine, Armenian Orthodox, Syro-Antiochene rites only chrismation is used. On the other hand, the Chaldean-Nestorian liturgy has only a laying-on of hands. The Coptic and Ethiopian rites present both chrismation and imposition of hands. In the Latin rites of the West, the anointing grew in importance from the fifth century onwards. Then from the thirteenth century onwards, the anointing was given still further importance, without forgetting however the laying-on of hands. Pope Innocent III regarded the anointing as an expression of the laying-on of hands.[20]. The First Council of Lyons and the Council of Florence reduced the laying-on of hands to the anointing of the candidate's forehead with the hand, while the Council of Trent did not treat this particular question.[21] The idea therefore developed that the laying-on of hands was included within the symbolism of the signing with chrism on the forehead. Pope Benedict XIV (1740–1758) was the first to stress anew the laying-on of hands as a ritual element in its own right, while making clear that the matter of the sacrament was anointing. In the present-day Orthodox Church, the laying-on of hands is tending to lose its importance.

As regards the relationship between the laying-on of hands and the anointing with chrism, there are several interpretations. One approach considers that the laying-on of hands mentioned in the Acts of the Apostles evolved into an anointing. Another position affirms that even in the Acts of the Apostles chrismation was used as well as imposition of hands, but this anointing with chrism was simply not mentioned. In any case, Paul VI clarified any doubt concerning the future understanding of the matter of the sacrament of Confirmation, when he reformed the rite: "Therefore, in order that the revision of the rite of Confirmation may fittingly embrace also the essence of the sacramental rite, by our supreme apostolic authority we decree and lay down that in the Latin Church the following should be observed for the future. The sacrament of Confirmation is conferred through the anointing with chrism on the forehead, which is done by the laying on of the hand, and through the words: 'Accipe Signaculum Doni Spiritus Sancti' (Be sealed with the Gift of the Holy Spirit)."[22] The definition of Pope Paul VI applies to the Latin Church. The document also makes it clear that the laying-on of hands with the prescribed prayer before the anointing is not part of the essence of the sacrament and so is not required for validity, but "is to be held in high esteem" because it contributes to the integral perfection of the rite and a clearer understanding of the sacrament. Paul VI also specified that the extension of hands over all the candidates as a group before the anointing differs from the laying-on of the hand by which the anointing is carried out on the forehead of each candidate. A clarification has more recently been issued to the effect that during the actual gesture of Confirmation it is sufficient for the minister to apply the chrism with his thumb, and he need not impose his hand at the same time on the candidate's head.[23] In the preparation

of the chrism, generally olive oil is employed, which is mixed
with perfume and then blessed by the bishop on Maundy
Thursday at the Chrism Mass. Vegetable oil other than
obtained from olives may be adopted, but it is not admissible
to use animal or mineral oil as the remote matter for the sacrament of Confirmation.[24]

3.3.2   The form

The form of Confirmation, the prayer which accompanies
the matter, has also known great variety of expression during
its history. The Scriptures simply speak of a prayer which
accompanied the laying-on of hands (Ac 8:15). Some of the
Fathers like Tertullian and Saint Cyprian describe the
administration of the sacrament with a crismation and an
invocation of the Holy Spirit. St. Ambrose and St. Augustine
regarded as important the invocation of the Holy Spirit with
His sevenfold gifts. In the Eastern Church, from the fourth
century onwards, a simple formula was employed involving
the expression "seal of the gift of the Holy Spirit." This
expression was also used in the West until the tenth century,
but in the Middle Ages, the form underwent many varia-
tions, until the twelfth century. At that point in the West, the
following form became normative: "I sign you with the sign
of the Cross and confirm you with the chrism of salvation. In
the Name of the Father and of the Son and of the Holy
Ghost." This formula lasted until 1971, when Pope Paul VI
renewed the rite of Confirmation with the new form: "Jane,
be sealed with the Gift of the Holy Spirit." The name of the
candidate mentioned in the rite is either that which he or she
received in Baptism, or else a new Confirmation name chosen for the occasion. The new form resembles the ancient
formula of the Byzantine Rite, by which the Personal Gift of
the Holy Spirit on the day of Pentecost is recalled (Ac 2:1–4,
38). The Syro-Malabar rite adopts the formula "Chrism of
the Gift of the Holy Spirit", while the Chaldean rite has "Be
perfect in the name of the Father, and of the Son, and of the
Holy Spirit." The Coptic Ethiopian rite uses the form:
"Anointing of grace of the Holy Spirit." In all these cases, it is

significant that the formulations express either directly or indirectly the double effect of Confirmation, namely the character and grace.

3.4   The minister

In New Testament times, those baptized by Philip were confirmed by higher authorities, namely the Apostles John and Peter, not by Philip himself (Ac 8:14f). In the West, the Confirmation part of the rite of Christian initiation was always administered by a bishop, as was seen above in the rite of Hippolytus. When Confirmation was separated from Baptism, it was always performed by the bishop. A significant reason for this is that the public aspect of the Church is manifested in Confirmation and therefore the bishop is the competent minister. St. Thomas Aquinas ascribed the conferral of Confirmation to bishop, because this sacrament is a completion which involves a supreme act of power. While in Baptism man is built into a spiritual dwelling, in Confirmation he is consecrated to be a temple of the Holy Spirit. This act of perfection is reserved to a more perfect minister, namely the bishop.[25] The Councils of Florence and of Trent say that the *ordinary* minister is a bishop.[26] However, in the East from the fourth century onwards a different practice emerged in which priests were the regular ministers; however the oil always had to be previously blessed by the bishop. Since that time, in the Eastern tradition the sacraments of initiation have always been conferred together. Thus, Confirmation is administered immediately after Baptism, even to infants, and so, since normally the priest is minister of Baptism, he is also minister of Confirmation.

In the West however, Confirmation could also be imparted by priests under special circumstances, so that they were regarded as extraordinary ministers of this sacrament.[27] Papal authority extended the necessary permission. From the time of St. Gregory the Great onwards, many Popes gave the faculty of administering Confirmation to priests of the Latin rite, including missionaries, abbots and cardinals. When the Councils of Florence and Trent spoke of the bishop as the ordinary minister of the sacrament, this implied that there could be an extraordinary minister, namely the priest. According to the present discipline, a priest may now confirm if, without episcopal orders, he holds rank equivalent in law to a diocesan bishop, for example if he is a prefect apostolic, a prelate or abbot nullius, an apostolic administrator, or a diocesan administrator. A priest who, with a mandate from the bishop, baptizes an adult or receives him into full communion receives the faculty to confirm him. It is evident that converts to Catholicism from the Oriental Churches not in full communion with Rome, are not to be confirmed as they have already received the sacrament validly along with Baptism. The only question may arise in the case of those oriental rites which have no anointing such as those of the Chaldean-Nestorian liturgies. The third situation in which a priest has the power to confirm is the case of a person in danger of death.[28]

The theological significance of the permission given to a simple priest, as an extraordinary minister, to administer Confirmation, has been expressed as the "unlocking" of a power which he already possesses by virtue of being a priest. This is not simply a matter of jurisdiction, since a bishop can confirm validly outside his own diocese, even without permission. For liceity, a bishop requires the permission "at least reasonably presumed, of the diocesan bishop."[29] Nor is the power simply part of presbyteral orders, since a priest cannot confirm validly everywhere like bishops. Nevertheless, since, in the East, the priest is also the ordinary minister of Confirmation, this power would seem to be more easily shared with the presbyteral order than is the power to ordain, where the instances of a priest being the extraordinary minister have been extremely rare.[30]

3.5   The recipient

The subject of Confirmation is any baptized Christian, who has not yet received the sacrament. Much discussion has taken place as regards a suitable age for Confirmation. First of all, it is best not to regard Confirmation as sacrament of

Christian maturity, because this may be seen to imply Baptism belongs to immaturity; also the Oriental Churches administer Confirmation directly after Baptism. The question of age is also connected with the order in which the sacraments of initiation are carried out. In the case of the traditional order, namely Baptism, Confirmation and the holy Eucharist, Confirmation would be administered earlier so that the child would not be deprived of holy communion beyond the age of seven or eight. In the case of the order which has prevailed in much of the West in recent times, namely, Baptism, First Communion and Confirmation, a greater flexibility of age has been possible. In some cases, Confirmation has been regularly imparted in the late teens, around eighteen years. The Council of Trent suggested seven as a suitable age for Confirmation and this has also been indicated by the post-conciliar documents after the Second Vatican Council, but for pastoral reasons it may be given at a more mature age.[31] It seems appropriate in any case that Confirmation should be administered before the onslaught of the teenage years, so that the young person may have the grace to face the challenges which these years bring, both physically and spiritually.

3.6   The effects

The sacrament of Confirmation completes the sacrament of Baptism. It confers grace beyond that already received in Baptism and also imparts a new sacramental character. It perfects what has been bestowed in Baptism; but both Baptism and Confirmation are completed in the Eucharist. The character of Confirmation is connected with the specific nature of the sacrament. What Confirmation adds may be seen by comparing the nature of the sacramental character of Baptism, Confirmation and Ordination. Baptism confers upon the Christian union with Christ and His Church. Confirmation endows the baptized person with mission within the Church, as a lay Christian. Ordination to the presbyteral and episcopal orders gives a share in Christ's role as mediator between God and man. In more detail, the character received in Confirmation entrusts the person with the public nature of his or her being Christian. While Baptism focuses more on the individual life of the member of the Church, Confirmation places a stress on the communal aspect. This explains in part why the sacrament is connected with growth towards Christian maturity. Part of this growth includes the struggle to do good and to fight evil, from which flows the analogy that the confirmed Christian is a soldier of Christ. Confirmation endows the recipient with the power to proclaim the Christian faith publicly by words and deeds.[32]

The sacramental character bestowed in Confirmation is the basis for the increase in divine life, in terms of a closer union with Christ, and a deeper indwelling of the Holy Spirit, in a closer adopted sonship of God the Father. Nevertheless, it should be stressed that the Holy Spirit is not given for the first time in Confirmation; He has already been conferred in Baptism. Rather Confirmation puts the seal on Baptism as Pentecost completes Easter. The chrism symbolizes the outflowing of the Holy Spirit who proceeds from the Father and the Son. The prayer before Confirmation speaks of the sevenfold Gift with which the candidates will be endowed, the spirit of wisdom and understanding, the spirit of right judgment and courage, the spirit of knowledge and reverence, the spirit of wonder and awe in God's presence. These gifts are already enumerated by the prophet Isaiah (Is 11:2). The gift of wisdom enables the Christian to consider the eternal truths and to judge all things by them, to cherish salvation and the means necessary to obtain it, and to relish the things of God. Understanding is the power of penetrating the deepest meaning of the truths of revelation, and also teaching others these truths. Right judgment or counsel is the power of deciding prudently about the concerns of God and of salvation, involving also a strengthening of the will to make choices for the better. The gift of courage or fortitude enables the Christian to possess firmness of soul in professing the faith and in persevering in the life with Christ. It involves strength in adversity during the struggles with the world, the flesh and the devil. The gift of knowledge enables the confirmed person to view and utilize temporal things in the light of eternal life. Reverence or piety is the gift which disposes the person to serve God the Most Holy Trinity with tender love and devotion, and to practise what the Church teaches. The gift of wonder and awe in God's presence (or fear of the Lord) enables the confirmed Christian to have the correct reverence for the majesty and sovereignty of God, not only in the religious sphere but in all aspects of life, remembering that God is present everywhere.

Confirmation is important for salvation and while it is not absolutely necessary in the same way as Baptism, nevertheless care should be taken to ensure that this precious means of salvation is readily available. During the Carolingian period some theologians held that the sacrament would augment the degree of heavenly happiness after death. St. Thomas Aquinas pointed out that while Baptism is necessary for salvation in the sense that there is no salvation without it, Confirmation is necessary for the perfection of salvation. Those who omit the sacrament of Confirmation out of contempt put their salvation at risk.[33] The practice of the Church also highlights the salvific importance of this sacrament, by conferring Confirmation upon a child who is below the age of reason and in danger of death, so that he or she "should not be deprived of the benefit of this sacrament."[34] It is recommended (though not absolutely required) that candidates for the sacrament of matrimony should be confirmed first.[35] The sacrament of Confirmation is required for the lawful reception of ordination.[36]

Notes

1   See Vatican II, *Sacrosanctum Concilium*, 71.
2   Vatican II, *Lumen gentium* 11.1.
3   *Ibid.*, 33.2.
4   Vatican II, *Ad gentes* 36.1.
5   See St. Thomas Aquinas, *Summa Theologiae* III, q.72, a.1.
6   St. Hippolytus, *The Apostolic Tradition* 21, 19 as in *SW*, p.8.
7   St. Hippolytus, *The Apostolic Tradition* 22, 2 as in *SW*, p.8.
8   Tertullian, *De Resurrectione Carnis*, cap. 8, 3 in *CCL* 2, 931.

9   St. Cyril of Jerusalem, *Mystagogical Catecheses* 3, 2; in *PG* 33, 1089–1090.

10   St. Ambrose, *De Mysteriis*, 6, 29; 7, 42; in *PL* 16, 398, 402–403.

11   St. Faustus of Riez, *Homily for Pentecost* in L. G. Walsh, *The Sacraments of Initiation* (London: Geoffrey Chapman, 1988), p.141.

12   See Bd Rabanus Maurus, *De Clericorum Institutione*, Lib. 1, cap. 30 in *PL* 107, 314.

13   St. Thomas Aquinas, *Summa Theologiae* III, q.72, a.5; see also a.1.

14   St. Thomas Aquinas, *Summa Theologiae* III, q.72, a.1.

15   See Council of Florence, *Decree for the Armenians* in ND1416–18.

16   Council of Trent, Seventh Session, Canon 1 on the Sacrament of Confirmation in ND1434.

17   See *ibid.*, Canon 1 on the Sacraments in General in ND1311.

18   See decree *Lamentabili* of the Holy Office (1907), condemning the articles of modernism in ND[1437/44].

19   Pope Paul VI, Apostolic Constitution on the sacrament of Confirmation, *Divinae consortium naturae* (1971).

20   See Pope Innocent III, Letter *Cum venissit* DS 785.

21   See First Council of Lyons in DS 831; Council of Florence in ND 1416.

22   Pope Paul VI, Apostolic Constitution on the sacrament of Confirmation, *Divinae consortium naturae* (1971).

23   See Pontifical Commission for the Interpretation of the Decrees of Vatican II, *Response* of 9th June 1972 in *AAS* 64 (1972) p.526.

24   See Rite of benediction of the oils and for the consecration of chrism in *EV* 3(1968–1970) N. 2858.

25   See St. Thomas Aquinas, *Summa Theologiae* III, q.72, a.11.

26   See Council of Florence, Decree for the Armenians in ND 1417; also Council of Trent, Seventh Session, canon 3 on Confirmation in ND 1436.

27   See First Council of Toledo in DS 187, which gave permission for priests to administer Confirmation in the absence of the bishop.

28   See *CIC* 883.

29   *CIC* 886 §2.

30   See chapter 8, section 7.4.

31   Congregation for Divine Worship, General Introduction to the Rite of Confirmation, 11.

32   See St. Thomas Aquinas, *Summa Theologiae* III, q.72, a.5.

33   See St. Thomas Aquinas, *Summa Theologiae* III, q.72, a.1.

34   Congregation for Divine Worship, *General Introduction to the Rite of Confirmation*, 11.

35   See *CIC* 1065 §1.

36   *CIC* 1033.

4

The Holy Eucharist

It is at one and the same time a Sacrifice-Sacrament, a Communion-Sacrament, and a Presence-Sacrament.

Pope John Paul II, *Redemptor Hominis*, 20.4.

Among the seven sacraments, the Eucharist is the central one because Christ is rendered present in His Paschal Sacrifice, whole and entire. From the earliest days of the Church, the Eucharist was regarded as the highest mystery, the climax of the celebrations of Baptism and Confirmation which preceded in the sacraments of Christian initiation. The celebration of the Mass is the most perfect representation of the Church, the action in which the Church on earth is most perfectly herself. In the most blessed Eucharist "is contained the whole spiritual good of the Church."[1] The Eucharist is the "Sacrament of sacraments" and all the other sacraments are ordered to it as their end.[2] It is the greatest sacrament because it contains Christ Himself substantially; while the other sacraments sanctify only when a recipient makes use of them, in the Eucharist, "the Author of sanctity Himself is present before the sacrament is used."[3] The Eucharistic Sacrifice is the "source and summit of the Christian Life."[4] The Eucharist renders Christ present both as regards His Incarnation and His Redemption, in His Being and in His sacrificial action.

75

4.1   The institution of the Eucharist

The institution of the Holy Eucharist by Christ was prepared and prefigured both in the Old and in the New Testaments.

4.1.1   Prefigurations in the Old Testament

Several episodes and events in the Old Testament prefigure the sacrament and Sacrifice of the Eucharist. The sacrifice of Melchizedek, priest and king, involved an offering of bread and wine (Gen 14:18). The manna with which God nourished His people in the wilderness (Dt 8:3) pointed forward to the Eucharist in which Christ feeds His Church with His own Body and Blood as she makes her journey towards the heavenly banquet. The Passover celebration involved a feast of unleavened bread, and was an annual commemoration of the event in which God freed His people from the Egyptians: "This day is to be a remembrance for you, and you must declare it as a feast in the Lord's honour. For all generations you are to declare it a day of festival for ever" (Ex 12:14). This memorial, or *zikkaron* in Hebrew, brought to mind the past in an objective way, with the aim of finding once more its permanent relevance. This memorial of God's wonders was expressed in blessing (*berakah* in Hebrew), which has a sense of rendering thanks to God. The word Eucharist traces its Greek origins from this idea of thanksgiving. The new Passover, the celebration of Christ's death and resurrection, is made present in the Sacrifice of the Mass, in which is celebrated Christ's victory over sin and death. The ratification of the covenant (Ex 24:1–11) involved the use of bull's blood which was sprinkled over the people. In the new and eternal Covenant, the Precious Blood of Christ was shed for all, and is made present in the Eucharist. Bread and wine are seen as staple foods in the Old Testament, bread which strengthens man's heart and wine which gladdens it (see. Ps 103:15). The inebriation of wine is interchangeable with that of love in Semitic thought: "Your love is more delightful than wine" (Sg 1:2). The banquet which is mentioned in the book of Proverbs (Pr 9:1–6) is prepared by Wisdom personified, namely the Eternal Word. The house built by Wisdom can be seen as an allusion to the Incarnation of Christ, and the invitation "Come and eat my bread, drink the wine I have prepared!", as an allusion the Eucharist. In the Jewish tent of meeting and in the temple which succeeded it, a golden altar was set up, upon which was set the bread of the Presence (Ex 35:13; I Sam 21:6; I K 7:48) which seems a clear prefiguration of the Eucharist and of Eucharistic reservation.

4.1.2 Prefigurations in the New Testament:

In His words and actions, Jesus Christ prepared His followers for the Paschal sacrifice which took place in the fullness of time. Two particular miracles of Christ foreshadow the institution by Him of the Most Holy Eucharist. The Wedding Feast at Cana can be seen in the context of the Christmas theophanies, along with the epiphanic visit of the Magi with their presentation of the gifts to the new born Christ, and the Baptism in the Jordan. These theophanies express the divinity of Christ and His salvific mission. However, the Wedding Feast of Cana in which Christ changed water into wine (Jn 2:11) also prefigured the far greater wonder in which wine would be changed into His Precious Blood. In the earlier occasion, the water is changed into wine at the wedding feast at Cana; the Last Supper, in which wine is changed into Christ's Blood is like the wedding feast in which is celebrated the marriage of Christ to His Church. This is supported by Christ's words at the Last Supper "From now on, I tell you, I shall not drink wine until the day I drink the new wine with you in the kingdom of my Father" (Mt 26:29). Jesus' words indicate that the Eucharist is a participation in the definitive Wedding Feast of the Lamb. The miracle of the multiplication of the loaves (Mt 14:13–21) is also a New Testament prefiguration of the Eucharist. The miracle of the multiplication of this staple human food, bread, foreshadows the far greater event in which Christ changes bread into His own Body.[5]

4.1.3 Institution by Christ

Scholars have discussed whether the Eucharist was instituted in the context of the Jewish Passover meal, or whether it was a radically new meal which had some elements in common with the Passover. There seems to be a tension between the synoptics which call to mind the Paschal meal and the Gospel of St. John which links the beginning of the feast of Passover with the evening of the death of Jesus.[6] The Council of Trent indicated that "after He celebrated the old Pasch, which the multitude of the children of Israel offered to celebrate the memory of the departure from Egypt, Christ instituted a new Pasch, namely Himself to be offered by the Church."[7] Therefore whatever opinions one may take concerning the timing of the Last Supper in relation to the Passover meal, Jesus gave the Passover its definitive meaning.[8] The Gospel accounts transmit a liturgical tradition, but at the same time affirm an historical event, namely the Last Supper, so intimately connected with the climax of salvation history. From the synoptic Gospel accounts of the institution by Christ of the Eucharist (Lk 22:7–20; Mt 26:17–29; Mk 14:12–25), several themes become clear. First, Jesus told His disciples that His sacrificial death was imminent. His Blood which will be outpoured for all mankind, seals the New and Eternal Covenant. The accounts indicate that Jesus offered Himself as food and drink to His disciples. Jesus Christ ordered His disciples then to repeat this sacred action by His choice of words "Do this in memory of Me."

While St. John's Gospel does not contain the account of the institution of the Eucharist, nevertheless in many ways it can be said that the whole of the Fourth Gospel is Eucharistic. St. John recounts the miracle at Cana (Jn 2:1–12) and the multiplication of the loaves (Jn 6:1–15) which prefigure the Eucharist. Moreover, the discourse in the synagogue at Capernaum (6:22–71) is an extremely clear affirmation of the Holy Eucharist. This discourse contains three parts: in the first, Jesus is presented as the Bread of Life to Whom the believer comes close through faith (vv.22–48); the second part invites the believer in very realist terms to eat the Body of Christ and drink His Blood (vv.49–59); the third section portrays the negative reaction of some of those who heard the discourse, and reaffirms the

importance of the discourse and the truth of Jesus' words as
spirit and life (vv.60–70). The account of the Last Supper is
very extensive in the fourth Gospel and contains much
Eucharistic allusion. The episode when Jesus washed His
disciples' feet (Jn 13:1–16), can be interpreted in many
ways. One approach is the more moral one which contains an
invitation to imitate what Jesus did. However, a deeper look
is helpful, at the very being of the act. Jesus, by washing the
feet of the disciples, was offering them a symbol of His
self-abasement, not for the sake of humiliation in itself, but
in terms of self-offering or sacrifice. This symbolizes at one
time the Sacrifice of Calvary and the Sacrifice of the Mass.
When Christ says "I have given you an example so that you
may copy what I have done to you" (Jn 13:15), He is not
merely asking us to copy a washing of the feet, but rather
commanding His Apostles to repeat the sequence of the
Last Supper, namely to celebrate the Mass. The phrase is
simply another way of saying "Do this in memory of Me."
The handing of a piece of bread to Judas the traitor (Jn
13:26) is connected with the Eucharist, as indicated in the
discourse at Capernaum where Jesus had foretold His
betrayal (Jn 6: 64, 70). Furthermore, the parable of the Vine
and the branches (Jn 15:1–17) indicates the vine as a symbol
of the Kingdom of God and the fruit of the vine is the matter
for the sacrament of the New Covenant. Moreover, the vine
which symbolizes the union between Christ and His Church
in Johannine thought is the equivalent of the image of the
Body in Pauline thought. The priestly prayer of Jesus (Jn
17:1–20) is inseparable from the Eucharist, since the perpetuation of this Sacrifice depends on the institution of the
priesthood with which it is intimately united.

St. Paul presents two accounts of the Eucharist, one of its
institution (I Co 11:23–32) and the other in the context of
the prohibition for Christians to take part in pagan sacrificial
meals (I Co 10:14–21). The realism of St. Paul's Eucharistic
doctrine is striking. St. Paul's parallel between eating the
pagan sacrificial victims and the Eucharist (I Co 10:21)
would make no sense unless we were really consuming the

Victim of the Sacrifice of Calvary. Similarly, the remark about recognising the Body of Christ (I Co 11:29) involves a highly realist interpretation of Christ's presence in the sacrament.

The Letter to the Hebrews deals with the radical novelty of the Sacrifice of Christ and His Priesthood with respect to the Old Covenant which prefigured and prepared the Paschal Mystery. The New Covenant is sealed in Christ's Blood (Heb 9:15–28), and the Christian has a "supreme high priest" (Heb 10:21). In this context the fact that the Christian has his "own altar" (Heb 13:10) could well refer to the Eucharistic sacrifice, but the opinions of theologians are divided upon this point. The practice of the primitive Church in its Eucharistic celebrations is clear from the New Testament writings and not least from the words: "These remained faithful to the teaching of the Apostles, to the brotherhood, to the breaking of the bread and to the prayers" (Ac 2:42). This passage is of great importance since it illustrates the consciousness right from the early days of the Church of the indissoluble link between Eucharistic communion ("the breaking of the bread"), communion of the faith ("the teaching of the Apostles") and ecclesial communion ("the brotherhood"). From these various New Testament sources, it emerges as Christ's intention to institute the sacrament of the Holy Eucharist, as it was for Him to found the Church, the Papacy, and the other sacraments.[9]

4.2   The external sign

As can be seen from the scriptural accounts, Christ's institution of the Holy Eucharist indicated the essential external sign of this most august sacrament, in terms of its matter and form.

4.2.1   The matter

The bread to be used for the Eucharist must be made from wheat, which has been mixed with water and baked. Any variety of wheat is acceptable, but bread made from other types of grain would constitute invalid material. Similarly invalid would be bread made with milk or oil instead of water. The matter of the Eucharist is thus that which in common estimation is bread made from wheat, without a notable admixture of other materials to render it no longer wheat. By the same token, nothing must be taken away from the wheat, which would change the nature of the bread. For this reason, gluten-free hosts are not seen as valid matter for the Eucharist, as that essential component of wheat has been taken out. In the case of communicants with coeliac disease, it is possible to communicate avoiding the Host and receiving only from the chalice. Low-gluten hosts are valid matter, provided that they contain a sufficient quantity of gluten to make bread, that there is no addition of foreign materials and that the procedure for making these hosts does not change the nature of the substance of bread.[10] Altar breads should be fresh and in good condition, and not corrupted or mouldy. The Council of Florence affirmed that the Eucharist is validly celebrated with either leavened or unleavened wheaten bread.[11] The tradition of the whole Church until the ninth century lay in the use of leavened bread in the Eucharist. Then, the first clear witness to the use of unleavened bread in the Eucharist was Rabanus Maurus. Thereafter, in the Latin Church, the tradition has been to use unleavened bread for the Eucharist; this absence of yeast represents purity, according to St. Paul's words: "Christ, our Passover, has been sacrificed; let us celebrate the feast then, by getting rid of all the old yeast of evil and wickedness, having only the unleavened bread of sincerity and truth" (I Co 5:7–8). The Greek Church persevered in its use of leavened bread, in which, for Eastern theology, the yeast symbolizes the vivifying action of the Holy Spirit. For the Greeks, unleavened bread in the Eucharist would be like a body without a soul, and would smack of the heresy of Apollinaris of Laodicaea who denied that Christ had a human soul.

The wine used in the Mass must be naturally fermented and made from the fruit of the grape, to which a small amount of water is added at the offertory. The wine cannot be made from any other fruits or from the stems and skins of the grapes after the juice has been pressed out. In regions where fresh grapes cannot be obtained, it is permissible to make the wine from raisins. However, wine from which the alcohol has been completely extracted, or which has more than 20% alcohol, is invalid material. Similarly invalid is wine to which foreign substances have been added, so as to change its character. It is permissible to fortify the wine with a little spirit made from the grape, in order to prevent its corruption; this fortification must be carried out in the manner approved by the Holy See.[12] Water is added to the wine at the offertory. This symbolizes our participation in the divinity of Christ, just as He participated in our humanity. It also indicates the Passion of Christ, in which water flowed from His side after it was pierced with the lance. Some Fathers also saw in the mixture of water and wine a symbolic portrayal of the union in Christ of the divine and human natures. The addition of water is therefore important. As regards the quantity, a few drops are sufficient. About one fifth or one quarter (if the wine is stronger) is not an unlawful quantity of water to add. A quantity of water in excess of one third would render the matter doubtful. In this latter case, the celebrant should add more wine, or else start afresh.

The matter for use in the celebration of the Mass must be physically and morally present to the celebrant, who joins the matter and the form. In other words, the prescribed form uses the word "this" for both the consecration of the bread and of the wine, and the word indicates that the matter must be nearby.

4.2.2   The form

The Catholic Church regards the words of institution as the form of the Eucharist, namely, for the bread: "Take this, all of you, and eat it: this is my Body which will be given up for you." Over the chalice, the words are "Take this, all of you, and drink from it: this is the cup of my Blood, the Blood of the new and everlasting Covenant. It will be shed for you and for all, so that sins may be forgiven. Do this in memory of Me." Saint Anselm of Canterbury made the distinction between the essential elements in the Canon of the Mass and the incidental features, and this paved the way for describing the words of institution as efficacious in bringing about transubstantiation. The Council of Trent implied that the words of institution are efficacious in bringing about transubstantiation, when it affirmed that the Body and Blood of Christ are present after the Consecration.[13]

In the Eastern Churches, with a stress on the dynamic presence of the Holy Spirit, the *epiclesis* is also seen to play a determining role in the transformation of the species. The expression epiclesis signifies a "calling down" in Greek. When St. Irenaeus wrote that the bread receives the invocation of God and becomes the Eucharist, he seemed to have attributed consecratory power to the epiclesis.[14] St. Basil claimed that the invocation of the Holy Spirit has a great importance in the Mysteries (the Eucharist), and that while the words of institution are handed down in the written tradition, the epiclesis is part of unwritten tradition.[15] Among the Oriental rites, the epiclesis follows the words of institution. In the Divine Liturgy of St. John Chrysostom and that of St. Basil, the priest recites the following epiclesis: "Make this bread the precious Body of Christ. And that which is in this chalice the Precious Blood of Your Christ. Changing them by Your Holy Spirit. Amen. Amen. Amen." As regards the importance of the epiclesis, there are two positions in Eastern Christendom. The more radical idea places the efficacy of the Eucharistic Sacrifice in the epiclesis alone while the more balanced approach regards as necessary the words of Institution together with the epiclesis. Present day Orthodox theology sees the words of institution and the epiclesis as woven into a seamless necessary whole within the context of the Anaphora (Eucharistic Prayer). Within this picture, Eastern theology holds the words of institution in very high regard. For instance, Nicholas Cabasilas compared the words of institution to the words of the Creator "go forth and multiply" given to our first parents: "Just as those words once pronounced by the Creator are not sufficient for the generation of children, but are effective only through the union of man and woman, so also the words of Christ, pronounced once upon a time by Him at the Last Supper,... are not sufficient for the consecration of the gifts, but only take effect through the prayer of the priest."[16] Even in the West, the epiclesis is considered to hold a certain importance, and it occurs before the words of institution, when the celebrant extends his hands over the offerings. In the Second Eucharistic Prayer, the formulation runs: "Let Your Spirit come upon these gifts to make them holy so that they may become for us the Body and Blood of Our Lord Jesus Christ." The Third Eucharistic Prayer has the following epiclesis: "We ask you to make them holy by the power of your Spirit that they may become the Body and Blood of Your Son Our Lord Jesus Christ." The Fourth Eucharistic Prayer adopts the following formulation: "Father, may this Holy Spirit sanctify these offerings. Let them become the Body and Blood of Our Lord Jesus Christ." The Roman Canon has an implicit epiclesis, in the words "Bless and approve our offering; make it acceptable to You, an offering in spirit and in truth. Let it become for us the Body and Blood of Jesus Christ, Your only Son, our Lord." The reference in the prayer is to the Father and the Son, and the Holy Spirit is also present, as the One who blesses.

In all cases, the celebrant of the Eucharist must pronounce externally the words constituting the form.[17] This is especially necessary for concelebrants and those who celebrate Masses without the people, where a misconception may have arisen regarding a silent recitation of the Eucharist Prayer. A quiet recitation of the words of institution would constitute a valid Mass, while a purely internal formulation would not. Thus the intention in itself does not suffice for validity.[18]

4.3   The Eucharistic Presence of Christ

When a dearly loved human friend departs he or she leaves behind a token or symbol, a photograph or precious object reminding us of them. When the Eternal Word made Man left us and ascended to the Father, He bestowed infinitely more upon His friends. He left us Himself in His Sacrifice veiled under the appearances of bread and wine. This act of love clearly lies within His divine power. It would have been merely human to leave us symbols of His presence, but since He is Divine He gave us His very Self. After all, which human being in love with another would choose a merely symbolic contact instead of a flesh and blood relationship, if it lay within their power? Thus since it lies within God's power to change bread and wine into the Body and Blood of His Son, and mindful of His Son's promise "I am with you always; yes, to the end of time" (Mt 28:20), is it not consonant with God's same power that He entrusted to His Church the power of consecrating the Body and Blood of His Son? In the *kenosis* of the Incarnation, the Word took flesh and dwelt among us. This self-emptying continued in the Redemption, when Christ's sufferings hid his divine beauty and finally in the Eucharist, where Christ further veiled His glory under the appearances of bread and wine.

4.3.1 *Patristic belief*

In continuity with the realism concerning the Eucharist professed in the New Testament, the early Fathers expressed their faith in the real and substantial presence of Christ in this sacrament. In the first centuries, St. Ignatius of Antioch, St. Justin and St. Irenaeus argued the real presence of Christ in the Eucharist against the Docetists, who did not believe in the reality of the Incarnation. It is highly significant also for the later history of theology that belief in the doctrine of God made Man is closely connected with Eucharistic faith. For when the Reformers denied the substantial presence of Christ in the Eucharist, that error was but a step away from denying the very dogma of the Incarnation. At the beginning of the second century, St. Ignatius of Antioch taught that the Eucharist is the Flesh of our Saviour Jesus Christ, which suffered for our sins and which the Father raised from the dead.[19] About fifty years later, St. Justin Martyr also affirmed, against the Docetists, the reality of Christ's presence in the Eucharist: "We call this food the Eucharist.... Not as ordinary food and drink do we partake of them, but just as, through the word of God, our Saviour Jesus Christ became incarnate and took upon Himself Flesh and Blood for our salvation, so, we have been taught, the food which has become the Eucharist by the prayer of His word, and which nourishes our flesh and blood by assimilation, is both the Flesh and Blood of that Jesus who was made flesh."[20] About thirty years later, St. Irenaeus took for granted the reality of Christ's presence in the Eucharist:

> Just as a cutting from a vine, planted in the earth, bears fruit in due season, and a grain of wheat, falling on the ground therein dissolves, and rises again with large increase by the Spirit of God who sustains all things, and thereafter, by the Wisdom of God, becomes fit for man's food, and at last receives the Word of God and becomes a Eucharist, which is Christ's Body and Blood, so too our bodies, nourished by the Eucharist, and laid in the earth there to suffer dissolution, will in due season rise again.[21]

In the middle of the fourth century, St. Cyril of Jerusalem clearly taught that the bread and wine are changed into the Body and Blood of Christ. Nevertheless he was unclear as to when this change took place, linking it rather with the epiclesis.[22] St. Gregory of Nyssa on the other hand, towards the end of the fourth century, taught the doctrine of the change in the elements of bread and wine and also indicated that the moment of consecration was linked with the words of institution: "Rightly then do we believe that now also the bread which is consecrated by the word of God is made over into the Body of God the Word."[23] During the same period, St. John Chrysostom wrote about the Eucharistic change, which in some of his works he associated with the epiclesis, and in others with the words of institution: "Christ is present, and He who arranged that table (of the Last Supper) the very same even now arranges this table. For it is not man who brings about that the gifts which are set forth become the Body and Blood of Christ, but Christ Himself who was crucified for us."[24] In the early part of the fifth century, St. Cyril of Alexandria also taught the reality of the Eucharistic change, and also gave reasons why the appearances of bread and wine remain: "For lest we be stunned with horror on seeing flesh and blood set out on the holy tables of the churches, God condescends to our weakness and sends the power of life into the elements and transforms them into the power of His own flesh, that we may have and partake of them as a means of life, and that the Body of life may become in us a life-giving seed."[25]

In St. Augustine's writings on the Eucharist, two tendencies are to be found. One of these highlighted the realism of continuity between Christ's flesh which hung upon the Cross and the Eucharistic Christ: "From Mary's flesh He took flesh. And because in His very flesh He walked on earth, and because His very flesh He gave us to eat for our salvation — and no one eats that flesh unless he has first adored it — we find how...not only do we not sin by adoring, but we sin by not adoring."[26] On the other hand, St. Augustine also emphasized the spiritual and sacramental manner in which Christ's flesh is to be eaten: "Then it shall come to pass that the Body and Blood of Christ will be life to each one, when that which is received visibly in the sacrament is in very truth spiritually eaten, spiritually drunk."[27] Both aspects of St. Augustine's thought are necessary to make up the full Catholic vision of the Holy Eucharist. The danger was that, in the later development, some thinkers exaggerated the spiritual aspect of the Eucharist, so drifting into mere symbolism.

4.3.2   Theological development

There were then two tendencies in both Western and Eastern thought, the realist and the symbolist approaches. While St. John Chrysostom and St. Ambrose stressed the identity between the Christ of history, born of the Virgin Mary and the Eucharist, Origen highlighted the more symbolic side. So long as the tendencies were held together, as in St. Augustine, the integrity of the faith was maintained. In the Middle Ages, however, there arose two controversies concerning the relationship between the real and the symbolic in the Eucharist. In the first situation, around the year 844, Paschasius Radbertus, Abbot of the Benedictine Monastery of Corbie wrote the first monograph on the Eucharist, entitled *De Corpore et Sanguine Domini*. He stressed the complete link between the flesh and blood of Christ born of the Virgin Mary, crucified and risen from the dead, and the Eucharist. He did not delineate any difference in the two modes of being of Christ, not distinguishing between the historical and sacramental dimensions. Radbertus' approach was opposed by those who took a more symbolic line, such as a monk of the same monastery, Ratramnus (d.868) and Rabanus Maurus, Archbishop of Mainz (d.856).

The controversy surfaced again in the eleventh century. Lanfranc of Bec (d.1089) took Paschasius' ideas a bit further, saying that Christ's Body and Blood were subject to the laws of digestion. Then Berengar of Tours (d.1088) reacted against a naturalist view of the Eucharist, making a sharp distinction between the historical mode of existence of Christ and His sacramental mode of existence in the Eucharist. But Berengar exaggerated this distinction, and emptied the sacrament of real meaning, falling into the error of pure symbolism. Hence he was condemned, and had to submit several times to the Church's teaching. Pope St. Gregory VII instructed that Berengar take an oath which included the concept of substantial change:

> I... believe that the bread and wine which are placed on the altar are, by the mystery of the sacred prayer and the words of the Redeemer, substantially changed into the true and proper and life-giving Body and Blood of Jesus Christ our Lord; and that, after consecration, they are Christ's true Body, which was born of the Virgin and hung on the Cross, being offered for the salvation of the world, and which sits at the right hand of the Father; and Christ's true Blood, which was poured forth from His side; not only by way of sign and by the power of the sacrament, but in their true nature and in the reality of their substance.[28]

The expression transubstantiation (*transsubstantiatio*) appeared for the first time around the year 1140 in the writings of a theologian by the name of Roland Bandinelli, who later became Pope Alexander III and reigned from 1140 to

1142. It was then first used in an official document of Innocent III in the year 1202, in which the Pope asserted that Christ "transubstantiated" the bread and wine into His Body and Blood. Innocent III condemned the error of those who maintained that in the sacrament of the altar there was only "an image, an appearance or a symbol" of the Body and Blood of Christ.[29] The Fourth Lateran Council in the year 1215 formulated the Church's belief in the Eucharistic change in terms of transubstantiation.[30] The dogma of transubstantiation was then found in the profession of faith of the Second General Council of Lyons.[31]

St. Thomas Aquinas further developed the theology of the Eucharistic presence of Christ involving transubstantiation, which he regarded as a suitable expression for this marvellous transformation.[32] He taught that the bread and wine are changed into the Body and Blood of Christ at the Consecration, and that thereafter only the accidents (that which the senses discern) of bread and wine are left.[33] The whole Christ is present under each species of this Sacrament. By transubstantiation, the bread is converted into the Body of Christ and the wine into His Blood. However, since Christ is now risen and dies no more, His Blood and Soul must be present by natural concomitance or connection along with His Body under the appearances of bread and similarly His Body and Soul must be present along with His Blood under the appearances of wine. The Godhead of Christ is united with His Body, Blood and Soul by the hypostatic union. Therefore Christ is present under every part of the species of bread and wine.[34] The Angelic Doctor trod a very careful line between ultra-realism and symbolism, and retained both the realist and sacramental aspects of the mystery. This is exemplified when he considers what happens when the Eucharist is consumed: "What is eaten under its own species, is also broken and masticated under its own species; but Christ's Body is not eaten under its proper, but under the sacramental species.... Consequently, Christ's very Body is not broken, except according to its sacramental species."[35] In the Holy

Eucharist, the accidents of bread and wine remain without their own natural substance in which to inhere.

4.3.3   The Reformation

In the Middle Ages, the Church reacted against the errors of the Waldensians and later against those of Wyclif and Hus which denied the reality of the presence of Christ in the Eucharist.[36] However, a widespread denial of the Church's doctrine only occurred at the Reformation. The Council of Trent proposed Catholic teaching concerning the presence of Christ in the Eucharist, by declaring that after the consecration of the bread and wine, "our Lord Jesus Christ, true God and true Man, is truly, really and substantially contained under the appearance of those perceptible realities."[37] The Council condemned the error of Luther who professed consubstantiation, namely that the bread and wine continue to exist together with the Body and Blood of Christ. Similarly rejected was the idea of Osiander, who maintained the concept of impanation in which Christ was hypostatically united to the substance of bread and wine.[38] The Tridentine teaching clearly also excluded the idea of Zwingli who thought that Christ was present in the Eucharist merely in sign, and that of Calvin who held that Christ was solely present in dynamic power.

4.3.4   Recent reaffirmations

Far from being an outmoded concept, transubstantiation is an ever appropriate way of expressing the Church's faith in the change which takes place in the Eucharist. On several occasions after the Council of Trent, the Church has once more declared her faith in this mystery of the Eucharistic presence of Christ. In the year 1794, Pope Pius VI reaffirmed the doctrine of transubstantiation against the Jansenist errors of the Pseudo-Synod of Pistoia.[39] In the year 1950, Pope Pius XII repudiated the error of those who proposed that the doctrine of transubstantiation is based "on a philosophical notion of substance which is now out of date" and which "must be corrected in such a way that the presence of Christ in the most holy Eucharist is reduced to some sort of symbolism."[40] Pope Paul VI also pointed out the danger of exaggerating the symbolic aspects of the Eucharist and reaffirmed the value of the concept of transubstantiation. He regarded as insufficient some recent approaches to the question in which the change has been described in terms of transignification or transfinalisation, because in any case it is the change of substance which should lie at the basis of any discussion of the new meaning and finality of the Eucharistic species. [41] Elsewhere, the Pope solemnly affirmed that the mysterious change taking place in the Eucharist is "very appropriately called by the Church *transubstantiation*." The Pope added that "every theological explanation which seeks some understanding of this mystery must, in order to be in accord with the Catholic faith, maintain that in the reality itself, independently of the mind, the bread and wine have ceased to exist after the Consecration, so that it is the adorable Body and Blood of the Lord Jesus that from then on are really before us."[42] The Catechism of the Catholic Church has restated the formulation of the Council of Trent: "This change the holy Catholic Church has fittingly and properly called *transubstantiation*."[43]

The doctrine of transubstantiation was developed in the Scholastic philosophical framework, involving a distinction between substance and accidents. The doctrine does not, however, depend on Aristotelian philosophy. The distinction between substance and accidents is accessible to the common-sense realism of every age. The idea of substance refers to the underlying reality. Consider the example of a person, who in his or her substance remains the same all through life, although their appearance changes, such as the hair colour, the weight, the look. We would say that the substance of the person remains the same, but the accidents change. Accidents are those qualities which we experience empirically. In the Eucharist, on the other hand, it is the substance which changes, but the accidents remain the same. The substance is the fundamental essence of a thing, whose nature is to sustain and gather into a unity the accidents. The expression substance is used in a metaphysical way here, not a physical way. The distinction between substance and accidents is real, not just imaginary. In the case of the person, the distinction between the person and his or her accidental features is after all real. Therefore, even though the notion of substance and accidents originated from Aristotelian philosophy, the distinction between substance and accidents is also independent of philosophical and scientific development; it is not an idea which is tied to any philosophical current so that it stands or falls with it. The expression *transubstantiation* applied to the Eucharistic change must take its place alongside others like *consubstantial* applied to the doctrine concerning the Most Holy Trinity. The formulation was developed after a long period of reflection in order to describe the faith which already existed in the mode of transformation taking place in the Mass. It is a word which is normative for the life of faith.

Moreover, there is no contradiction in the fact that Christ sits at the right hand of the Father in heaven and is also present in innumerable hosts reserved throughout the world. The one body of Christ, without change of its ontological content and without local movement, makes new particular relations with a determined place, in that He becomes present without extension in the place where before transubstantiation there was the bread. The Eucharist is thus an extension of the Christ's Incarnation and an application of His redemptive act. Furthermore, when the sacred Host is broken, Christ is present in each part of the broken Host. In the words of the Angelic Doctor:

> Nor a single doubt remain,
> When they break the Host in twain
> But that in each part remain,
> What was in the whole before.[44]

The presence of Christ in the Eucharist is perpetual, which means that it remains so long as the species continue as such. Thus, Christ is not only present in the reception or use of this sacrament as some Reformers maintained.[45] The early Church brought Holy Communion to the sick and to prisoners who could not attend the Mass. St. Cyril of

Alexandria taught that the Sacred Host which was conserved after the Mass in which it was consecrated was still Christ's Body: "For Christ is not altered, and His holy Body is not changed, but the power and capacity of the blessing and of the life-giving grace exist in it for ever."[46] Therefore the Holy Eucharist needed to be reserved in a worthy place. Once the period of persecution was over, and Christians could build churches, it was possible to move further towards Eucharistic reservation. The artistic decoration of the tabernacle and monstrances started in the early Middle Ages. Devotion to Christ in the Blessed Sacrament increased, and this is a practical example of the development in understanding of doctrine. Pope Paul VI re-echoed the Church's teaching on this matter: "It is not only while the sacrifice is being offered... that Christ is truly Emmanuel, 'God with us'. He is so after the offering of the sacrifice, the making of the sacrament, as long as the Eucharist is kept in churches and oratories... as the spiritual centre of the universal Church and the whole of humanity."[47] The Blessed Sacrament in the tabernacle is "the living heart of each of our churches."[48] Pope John Paul II stated how "adoration of Christ in this Sacrament of love must also find expression in various forms of Eucharistic devotion."[49] This devotion starts from worthy and noble reservation of the Blessed Sacrament, so encouraging visits during the course of the day. Exposition and benediction of the Blessed Sacrament are also occasions when the Christian can focus on the central act of love which redeems him. Sometimes exposition is extended for a long period, as in the forty hours devotion or in perpetual exposition. Processions of the Blessed Sacrament are a tangible and public way of expressing the Church's belief. Holy Thursday celebrates the institution of the Eucharist in the context of the Paschal Triduum and the Solemnity of Corpus Christi, instituted by Pope Urban IV in 1264, celebrates the nature of this Sacrament.

4.3.5   Greek idea

Greek Orthodox theology took over the expression for transubstantiation after the Second Council of Lyons and rendered it with the word *metousiosis*. The latter Greek expression came into greater use in Orthodoxy only in the seventeenth century in the struggle against the unorthdoxy of Patriarch Cyrillus Lukaris. Lukaris had studied in Germany and in Switzerland and had absorbed Lutheran and Calvinist doctrines, and rejected the traditional doctrine of the substantial presence of Christ in the Eucharist, implying that Christ was only present in the use of the Sacrament.[50] Although Lukaris was Patriarch of Constantinople his heterodoxy was rejected by the Orthodox Church and her theologians. In particular, in 1640 Peter Mogila, Metropolitan of Kiev wrote a defence of the true doctrine of each sacrament in which he defended *metousiosis*.[51] The expression rapidly became widespread in the Eastern Churches. Modern Orthodox theology does not closely define the nature and manner of the Eucharistic presence of the Body and Blood of Christ.

4.4   The Eucharistic Sacrifice

In the Eucharist, both being and action are important, but as elsewhere it is being that grounds action (*agere sequitur esse*). Hence it is that transubstantiation which makes present the Body and Blood of Christ also renders present Christ's Sacrifice upon the Cross.

4.4.1   Patristic concept

The teaching of the Letter to the Hebrews on the Priesthood and on the Sacrifice of Christ stimulated Christian thought on the Eucharist as a Sacrifice.[52] From human religious experience, from the Scriptures and from Christian reflection, it can be seen that there are many elements contained in the idea of Sacrifice. The basic theme is that of making something or someone holy, and this comes from the Latin root of the words sacrifice and consecration. This action of making holy involves an offering to God, in terms of a sacrificial victim. However, someone must offer the victim and that person is the priest. The priest offers upon an altar of sacrifice, which is located in a holy place or a temple. The appropriate response in the sacrificial action is worship and adoration of God, in a context of commemoration and memorial, involving forgiveness of sins, expiation and atonement. The sacrifice is concluded with participation, union and communion.

Already in the *Didaché* (Teaching of the Twelve Apostles) which dates from around the year 100, the idea of the Sacrifice of the Mass can be found, though not of course in its fully developed form: "On the Lord's own day, assemble in common to break bread and offer thanks; but first confess your sins so that your sacrifice may be pure."[53] In his dialogue with Trypho around the year 150, St. Justin Martyr regarded the Sacrifice of the Eucharist as the fulfillment of the prophecy of the prophet Malachi (Ml 1:10–12): "God has therefore announced in advance that all the sacrifices offered in His name, which Jesus Christ commanded to be offered, that is, in the Eucharist of the Bread and of the Chalice, which are offered by us Christians in every part of the world, are pleasing to Him."[54] St. Irenaeus also referred to the Eucharist as the fulfilment of Malachi's prophecy: "Therefore the oblation of the Church, which the Lord taught was to be offered in the whole world, has been regarded by God as a pure sacrifice, and is acceptable to Him."[55] Tertullian, in his Catholic phase, referred to the Eucharist as a Sacrifice, and is one of the oldest witnesses, around the beginning of the third century, to the offering of Mass for the dead.[56]

In the East, St. Gregory Nazianzen developed the connection between the Sacrifice of the Mass and the spiritual sacrifice of the participant: "No-one is worthy of the great sacrifice and of the great High Priest of God, unless first he has made of himself a living and holy offering pleasing to God and offered to God a sacrifice of praise and a contrite heart."[57] St. John Chrysostom expressed the link between the Sacrifice of Calvary and the Sacrifice of the Mass: "For

Christ is everywhere one complete Body. Just as He is one Body and not many bodies even though He is offered in many places, so too there is but one sacrifice. It is our High Priest who offered the sacrifice which cleanses us. So we offer now that which was then offered, and which cannot be exhausted."[58]

St. Cyprian referred to the Eucharist as the memorial of the Lord's Passion: "If our Lord and God, Jesus Christ, is Himself the High Priest of God the Father, and commanded this to be done for a memorial of Himself, certainly that priest truly performs his office in the place of Christ who imitates that which Christ did, and then offers in the Church to God the Father a real and complete sacrifice."[59] St. Augustine maintained that Christ was mystically offered in the Mass: "The whole redeemed city, that is to say, the congregation and community of the saints, is offered as a corporate sacrifice through the great Priest, who also offered Himself in His Passion for us, in the form of a servant, that we might be the body of so glorious a Head...This is the sacrifice which the Church continually celebrates in the sacrament of the altar."[60] In his many writings, Augustine developed both the spiritual-dynamic and realist-objective ideas of the Sacrifice of the Eucharist. Sometimes he emphasized one aspect and sometimes the other, so that at times he has been misinterpreted especially by those who over stress the spiritual aspect at the expense of the objective element. Pope St. Leo the Great clearly indicated that it was our Saviour's wish to found the Mass as a Sacrifice: "Christ instituted the Sacrament of His Body and Blood and taught that this sacrifice must be offered to God."[61] Faustus of Riez deepened further this theme that the Lord instituted the sacrament of His Sacrifice : "And since Christ wished to remove His Body from our eyes and ascend to the heavens, it was necessary that He consecrate... the Sacrament of His Body and Blood, so that what was sacrificed once and for all as our Ransom, may be constantly worshipped in the mystery constantly renewed."[62] Pope St. Gregory the Great stressed the fact that the sacrifice of the Mass renews the Paschal Mystery in a salvific way: "Every time that we present to Him the sacrifice of His Passion, we renew His Passion for our redemption."[63]

The Greek Fathers highlighted the relationship between the Incarnation and the Eucharist. The school of Antioch identified the real Body of Christ, born of the Virgin Mary, crucified and risen, with the Eucharistic Christ and thus put more stress on the Redemption, the saving action of Christ. On the other hand, the school of Alexandria saw the dignity of the Eucharist in terms of the Body and Blood of the Word which create union with Him, and hence put more stress on the Incarnation.

In general, in the First Millennium of the Church the stress was on the event-character of the Eucharist, while in the Second Millennium the emphasis has been more on the objective content aspect. Both the aspects of being and of action have always been present in the Mass. Sometimes the Fathers adopted the expressions spiritual sacrifice or memorial for the Eucharistic Sacrifice, but this does not mean that they thought that the Eucharist was not the real Sacrifice of Calvary; it was only later, especially with the Reformers, that there was a denial of the Sacrifice of the Mass.

4.4.2   Further development

The Patristic ideas on the Sacrifice of the Mass were further developed in the Middle Ages. Increasing clarification on how the Mass is a Sacrifice is found especially in St. Thomas Aquinas. The Angelic Doctor stated that the sacrament of the Eucharist is a representative image of Christ's Passion, which is His Sacrifice. "Accordingly the celebration of this sacrament is called Christ's sacrifice."[64] The separate consecration of the Body and of the Blood of Christ symbolizes the Passion of the Lord. The sacrificial essence of the Mass consists in the separate consecration of the Body and Blood of Christ, so that the state of victim is mystically represented on the Altar.[65] Nevertheless, Christ is present whole and entire under each of the species, because of the natural union of the Body and Blood of Christ in His risen state. Hence the immolation is mystical, because Christ is made present on the Altar in the state of His Passion and Death in which there was separation between His Body and Blood. The Mass is thus the unbloody representation of the Sacrifice of the Cross. Pope Pius XII endorsed this understanding of how the Mass is a Sacrifice: "The Eucharistic species under which He is present symbolise the violent separation of His Body and Blood, and so a commemorative showing forth of the death which took place in reality on Calvary is repeated in each Mass, because by distinct representations Christ Jesus is signified and showed forth in the state of victim."[66]

While the leading figures in the Protestant Reformation differed in their understanding of the mode of Christ's presence in the Eucharist, they all rejected the concept of the Mass as a Sacrifice. The Reformers denied the link between the Sacrifice of Calvary and the Last Supper, and they attempted to remove from the Eucharistic celebration every allusion to oblation, offering or sacrifice. For Luther, Calvary was a Sacrifice but the Eucharist was seen merely as a promise or testament sealed by the Blood of Christ shed on Calvary.[67] Zwingli and Calvin, for whom the Eucharist was but a fellowship meal, went even further in rejecting any sacrificial element in this celebration. Cranmer, in the English Reformation, imported Lutheran and Calvinist elements into Anglicanism. He wished to eradicate the idea of "the sacrifice and oblation of Christ made by the priest for the salvation of the quick and the dead."[68] Article thirty-one of the Anglican Thirty-Nine Articles from the Book of Common Prayer is a clear rejection of the sacrificial character of the Mass. Recent dialogue between Catholics and Anglicans has resulted in an agreement that "Christ instituted the Eucharist as a memorial (*anamnesis*) of the totality of God's reconciling action in him. In the Eucharistic prayer the Church continues to make a perpetual memorial of his death" and enters "into the movement of his self-offering."[69] However, this statement is incomplete as it does not express the truth that the Sacrifice of Christ is really present in the Mass and that the Church participates by offering the Sacrifice in

Christ and with Christ. Also "the propitiatory value that Catholic dogma attributes to the Eucharist is not mentioned."[70]

The Council of Trent reaffirmed Catholic doctrine concerning the Holy Sacrifice of the Mass, teaching that it was divinely instituted by Christ. The Council proposed as a matter of faith that the Mass is a visible Sacrifice which is propitiatory for the living and the dead. It upheld the practice of Masses in honour of the Saints, but clarified that the Sacrifice is offered to God alone. The Council of Trent taught, against the Lutheran notion, that the sacrificial character of the Eucharist cannot simply be reduced to the Communion, nor is the Sacrifice of the Mass merely spiritual. Trent affirmed the basic unity between the Sacrifice of Calvary and the Sacrifice of the Mass.[71]

Present-day attempts to propose a tension between the sacrifice element and the meal element in the Eucharist are unhelpful. These approaches include a deformation of the altar of sacrifice into the table of a fellowship meal, in the manner of the Reformers who destroyed altars and replaced them with tables in keeping with their rejection of the Catholic doctrine of the Sacrifice of the Mass. Pope John Paul II reaffirmed the importance of the sacrificial character of the Mass by stating that "the Eucharist is above all else a Sacrifice."[72] The Mass is the same Sacrifice as that as Calvary represented in an un-bloody manner. Thus the Eucharist makes present the Paschal Mystery of Christ at all times and in all places, in the Church. This one sacrifice which is made present across history and across the entire face of the earth requires that the one priesthood of Christ is shared with the ordained priests who act in His person in the Eucharist.

4.5   The minister

Only an ordained bishop or priest is the valid celebrant of the Eucharist. This truth has been reiterated several times in the history of the Church. As a protest against the sometimes worldly lifestyle of clerics in the Middle Ages, the Waldensians maintained that the basic requirement in the celebrant of the Eucharist was holiness, therefore even a lay person could celebrate it, if he was sufficiently holy. In their error, the Waldensians fell into the trap of confusing the person and the office; in any case how could the holiness of a person be judged by anyone apart from God?[73] More recently the Church has reaffirmed that only a validly ordained priest or bishop can celebrate a valid Eucharist.[74] The context of this restatement is a current error which seeks to make the power of the ministerial priest derive in some way from the community of the faithful. Thus, in the absence of the priest, the community could designate a celebrant for the Eucharist. This erroneous solution has been proposed for the case of faithful who are deprived of the Eucharist for a considerable time. However, insufficient account has been taken of the axiom that in these cases God can supply His grace outside of the sacraments.

As regards the intention which the minister must have, the basic condition is that of "at least of doing what the Church does." The celebrant must make a general intention to celebrate Mass, which must be either explicit and actual, or at least virtual. If the intention is virtual, it is made before Mass so that the celebration is carried out under its influence, but it does not explicitly always remain during the action.[75] Furthermore, the celebrant also formulates a particular intention, which can be to apply the Mass for one person or a group of persons, living or dead. The custom of Masses for the dead is very ancient and was already mentioned by St. Augustine.[76] The Mass can also be offered for a desire such as the beatification of a particular person, or else in honour of Christ, Our Lady or a particular saint. The general and particular intentions must be made at least before the words of Consecration, but it is desirable that they be made much earlier, namely before the celebration of Mass.

The custom of Mass intentions is fully in keeping with the tradition of the Church.[77] However, even without a particular offering, there should be an application for those in need. By making an offering, the faithful contribute to the good of the Church. Any appearance of trading in Mass offerings must be avoided. Separate Masses must be said if they have been requested as separate, even if the offering is small. A priest may retain the stipend only from one Mass each day, apart from Christmas Day when he may keep three stipends. Mass offerings are of different types. The most common kind is the *manual* offering given to the priest to celebrate one or several Masses. The *Gregorian* Mass is celebrated for a particular intention on thirty consecutive days. The *foundation* Mass is set up according to a fund which allows the yearly celebration of Mass, usually for a deceased person, for a given number of years.

4.6   Eucharistic Communion

The Eucharistic Sacrifice is celebrated in the form of a banquet and so the link between the sacrifice aspect and the meal aspect of the Mass is important. The Eucharist unites many facets, not as elements which simply lie side by side, but rather which are gathered into an organic unity. The uniting factor is the Sacrifice of Christ. The communion aspect is the fulfilment of the sacrifice, so that the Sacrifice culminates in Holy Communion. Holy Communion is a participation in the Sacrifice of Christ. Since Communion is an integral part of the Sacrifice it is necessary for the sacrificing minister, and is also highly recommended to the faithful who participate in the Mass.[78] By receiving Holy Communion, the faithful are strengthened and "they manifest in a concrete way that unity of the People of God which this holy Sacrament aptly signifies and admirably realizes."[79] This concept of ecclesial communion which is nourished by Eucharistic Communion is not to be confused with superficial ideas about community. In recent years there has been a tendency to stress the community aspect of the liturgy at the expense of the individual aspect. Also the very notion of community has often had more in common with psychological or sociological concepts than with that mystical ecclesial communion which is essentially a divine gift. In other words, the horizontal aspect of community has been highlighted to the detriment of the vertical God-given way.

4.6.1   The recipient

In the past, exaggerated severity and scrupulosity have sometimes prevented the faithful from communicating at Mass. Jansenism, a heretical system of thought which exaggerated the woundedness of the human person as a result of the Fall, discouraged people from going to Holy Communion; some Jansenists boasted of staying months or even years away from participation in Christ's Body.[80] In the early years of this century, Pope St. Pius X encouraged frequent and even daily communion, provided the right dispositions were met.[81] In more recent times a new tendency is to be found. Sometimes "everyone participating in the Eucharistic assembly goes to communion; and on some such occasions,..., there has not been due care to approach the Sacrament of Penance so as to purify one's conscience."[82] The basic conditions for receiving Holy Communion involve ecclesial communion, that is being in good standing with the Church, thus being free from schism. Communion of faith is also required, a freedom from formal or material heresy. A state of grace is a further precondition and this involves freedom from mortal sin. Finally a correct disposition is needed, which includes fulfilment of the Eucharistic fast which, in the present Latin rite legislation, involves abstaining from food and drink, apart from water, for an hour before the reception of Holy Communion.[83] Medicine also does not infringe the fast, and the sick and elderly and those who care for them are dispensed from the hour limit. A certain bodily disposition and reverence is also needed, expressed by a genuflection before reception of the Blessed Sacrament. Such gestures as well as suitable dress "ought to convey the respect, solemnity and joy of this moment when Christ becomes our guest."[84] If these conditions are fulfilled, frequent and even daily Holy Communion is to be encouraged. On occasions, participation at more than one Mass in the course of a single day raises the issue of receiving Holy Communion more than once a day. A Catholic who has received the blessed Eucharist may receive it again on the same day only within the context of a Eucharistic celebration in which that person participates.[85] The meaning of "again" in this context would seem to be on a second occasion, rather than many times on the same day.[86]

If a Christian is unable to fulfil the necessary conditions for receiving Holy Communion, it is still possible to participate in the Mass through spiritual communion. Thus a Mass without reception of Holy Communion should not be deemed fruitless. St. Thomas Aquinas drew a parallel between baptism of desire and sacramental Baptism, arriving at the idea that spiritual communion involved a desire to unite oneself with the offering of the Sacrifice and to receive Holy Communion. While some effects of the sacrament could be obtained in this way, the actual receiving of Holy Communion "produces more fully the effect of the sacrament than the desire thereof."[87] The concept finds its pastoral application to people who are unable to go to communion, because they cannot fulfil the conditions mentioned above; at the same they have a genuine and great hunger for the Eucharist.

In the West, Holy Communion was administered under both kinds until the thirteenth century. At that time, given the doctrinal and theological awareness that Christ is fully present under either species, communion under one kind only started to spread. St. Thomas Aquinas pointed out the practical difficulties which occurred in distribution under both kinds: "On the part of the recipient the greatest reverence and caution are called for, lest anything happen which is unworthy of so great a mystery.... Because the multitude of the Christian people increased, in which there are old, young, and children, some of whom have not enough discretion to observe the due caution in using this sacrament, on that account it is a prudent custom in some churches for the Blood not be offered to the reception of the people, but to be received by the priest alone."[88] Then with the Reformation, it was necessary to assert against the errors of the time that Christ was received "whole and entire" under each species.[89] The practice of communion under one kind became general in the West until after the Second Vatican Council which once again encouraged the possibility for the faithful of receiving both the Host and from the chalice under certain circumstances. In the Christian East, Communion under both kinds has always been the more usual form of reception.

4.6.2   Ecclesial Communion

The bond of Ecclesial Communion in the Church transcends space and time. A bond exists between the members of the Church in heaven whose intercession we invoke in the Eucharist, the members of the Church in purgatory for whom we offer Mass and the Church on earth gathered together in its Eucharistic celebration. An indissoluble link holds between Eucharistic Communion and Ecclesial Communion, as seen from the earliest times in the Church: "These remained faithful to the teaching of the apostles, to the brotherhood, to the breaking of the bread and to the prayers" (Ac 2:42). Eucharistic Communion expresses and builds Ecclesial Communion. Our Blessed Lady participates in the Eucharistic celebration in a special way:

> Her motherhood is particularly noted and experienced by the Christian people at the Sacred Banquet — the liturgical celebration of the Mystery of the Redemption — at which Christ, His true Body born of the Virgin Mary, becomes present. The piety of the Christian people has always very rightly sensed a profound link between devotion to the Blessed Virgin and worship of the Eucharist: this is a fact that can be seen in the liturgy of both the West and the East, in the traditions of the Religious Families, in the modern movements of spirituality, including those for youth, and in the pastoral practice of the Marian Shrines. Mary guides the faithful to the Eucharist.[90]

The angels and saints are also involved in the Eucharist, which is a foretaste of paradise. The Roman Canon expresses the reality of angelic participation in the Mass: "We pray that Your angel may take this sacrifice to Your altar in heaven and then as we receive from this altar the sacred Body and Blood of Your Son, may we be filled with every grace and blessing." The Eastern rites express this sharing in the heavenly liturgy in the Cherubic Hymn: "We who mystically represent the cherubim, who sing to the life-giving Trinity the thrice-holy hymn, let us lay aside all earthly care." In most of the liturgies of the East and West, both the Holy Virgin Mother of God and the Saints are venerated in the Eucharistic Prayer, indicating once more the living bond of love which unites the Church militant to the Church triumphant in the Mass.

The bond of communion thus expressed has important consequences for the so-called community dimension of the Eucharist. The tendency today is the regard this dimension in a purely empirical or emotional way, rather than the organic and ontological way in which it should be seen. The Mass then becomes a celebration of the "togetherness" of the people present rather a gathering together by God the Father through His Son in the power of the Holy Spirit of God's people. In reality, the Eucharistic initiative comes from God, and the Sacred Mysteries lead back to the Most Holy Trinity. Thus every celebration of the Mass has an essentially ecclesial character. Pope Paul VI affirmed that every Mass "even if celebrated by a priest in private, is not private; it is the act of Christ and the Church."[91] He also made it clear that it is incorrect to exaggerate the community Mass to the detriment of Masses which are celebrated privately.[92]

4.6.3 Ecumenical issues

The concept of Ecclesial Communion and its relationship with Eucharistic Communion is the principle for dealing with the question of whether other Christians may share in the Catholic Eucharist and also clarifying the problem of Catholics sharing in the Eucharist celebrations of other Christians. The underlying idea is that there is a limited Eucharistic reciprocity between Catholics and other Christians belonging to Churches which have preserved the Apostolic Succession, generally all Christians of the East.[93] Those Churches with the Apostolic Succession are truly deserving of the name Church and owing to the validity of all seven sacraments are in a relatively close but imperfect bond of communion with the Catholic Church. In this category are to be found all the Orthodox Churches and the ancient Oriental Churches. Thus in the case where members of the Eastern Churches ask for the Eucharist of their own free will and are properly disposed, they may receive Holy Communion in the Catholic Church.[94] However, it is not envisaged that a member of a Church in partial communion would receive Catholic Holy Communion on a permanent basis, but is rather seen as a temporary measure during a situation of need. By the same token, a Catholic who finds himself physically or morally without access to a Catholic minister and is in need, or stands to gain genuine spiritual benefit, may receive Holy Communion at a celebration of the Eastern Churches. Care must be taken in this case to avoid the dangers of error and of indifferentism; the Catholic who receives Holy Communion in this way must also respect Eastern usage and avoid given scandal to Eastern Christians.[95]

The possibility of intercommunion with those Christian denominations which have not maintained Apostolic Succession is very limited, because their degree of communion with the Catholic Church is more distant. These bodies are generally known as ecclesial communities and include most Christians of the West who are separated from full communion with Rome. Only very exceptionally can the Catholic Eucharist be given to a member of an ecclesial community. A precondition which must be met in this case is danger of death or other grave and pressing need, of which the local Ordinary is the judge. Also, the person must be unable to have recourse to his or her own minister. Furthermore, the Christian of an another denomination must freely ask for the Eucharist. Clearly he or she must manifest Catholic faith in the Eucharist and be properly disposed.[96] On the basis of the same considerations of communion, a Catholic may not communicate at those denominations which do not have valid Orders and a valid Eucharist. An exception is the Old Catholic Church which is generally regarded as having valid Orders; where this reality can be assured, then a Catholic who finds himself in danger of death or grave and pressing need, and with no possibility of getting access to the

Catholic Eucharist, may approach a validly ordained minister for the Eucharist.[97] Holy Communion may not be given to the unbaptized under any circumstances.

Eucharistic concelebration symbolizes full communion in faith, worship and community life within the Catholic Church. Therefore, ecumenical concelebration by Catholic priests at Eucharistic celebrations of other Christians is completely excluded as it presupposes a degree of ecclesial communion which is at present lacking between the Catholic Church and other Churches or ecclesial communities. It is likewise forbidden for priests or ministers of other denominations to concelebrate at a Catholic Mass.[98]

4.6.4 The effects

The effects of receiving the Holy Eucharist are manifold. The special grace of this sacrament consists in a spiritual nourishment of union with Christ corresponding to the effect which material food produces upon bodily life. This fruit involves sustaining, stimulating growth, renewing, repairing and giving joy to the life of grace received at Baptism and Confirmation. Furthermore, the Eucharist brings about an increase in sanctifying grace, and also weakens concupiscence, the inclination to sin. It also remits venial sins and renews charity so as to prevent serious sins in the future. Reception of Holy Communion effects a partial remission of the temporal punishment due to sins; the degree of this remission depends upon the fervour and devotion with which the Eucharist is received.

The consequences of receiving Holy Communion can be summarized as ecclesiological, soteriological, social, and eschatological. The Holy Eucharist unites more closely with Christ all those who receive Him. Since Christ and His Church are inseparable, therefore, the Blessed Eucharist binds all the faithful more intimately in the one Mystical Body of Christ which is His Church.[99] Holy Communion is also necessary for salvation, for unless the Christian "eat the flesh of the Son of Man and drink His blood" he will have no life. Participating in the Flesh and Blood of the Saviour in this way gives the communicant a share in the life of Christ crucified and risen, and so the Christian delights in his or her own hope of rising again.[100] For this reason the Church stipulates as a minimum requirement that after making their first Holy Communion, each Christian must receive the Eucharist at least once a year. The obligation must generally be fulfilled during the Easter cycle, between Ash Wednesday and Pentecost, indicating the indissoluble bond between the Eucharist and the Paschal Sacrifice.[101] In this context, Holy Communion given to the dying, known as Viaticum, has a special significance, that of nourishment on the last journey with Christ to the Father. In recent years, the social implications of the Eucharist have been drawn out. Nevertheless the idea is not new. St. John Chrysostom pointed out the inconsistency between the divine mercy expressed in the Eucharist and human reluctance to help the poor: "You have tasted the Blood of the Lord, yet you do not recognize your brother.... You dishonour this table when you do not judge worthy of sharing your food someone judged worthy to take part in this Meal....God freed you from your sins and invited you here, but you have not become more merciful."[102] Since the Eucharist is the source of charity, an authentic sense of this sacrament makes it a school of active love for one's neighbour.[103] In the present era of ecological awareness, many would affirm that celebrating the Mass also implies a commitment to one's neighbour in terms of safeguarding the environment. Thus the Eucharist is "a thanksgiving which embraces the whole of creation."[104]

Finally, Holy Communion is a pledge of future glory with the Most Holy Trinity. This eschatological aspect is encapsulated in the memorial acclamation at Mass: "Christ has died, Christ is risen, Christ will come again". At the institution of the Eucharist on the first Maundy Thursday, Christ directed His Apostles attention to the fulfilment in glory of the Eucharistic Banquet: "From now on, I tell you, I shall not drink wine until the day I drink the new wine with you in the Kingdom of my Father " (Mt 26:29). In this way, the Holy Eucharist anticipates the Wedding Feast of the Lamb.[105]

While the Holy Eucharist is the culmination of the sacraments of Christian initiation, it is also seen along with Penance and Anointing in the group of sacraments which complete the earthly pilgrimage. It is to these two sacraments of healing which we now turn.

Notes

1   Vatican II, *Presbyterorum ordinis*, 5.2. See St. Thomas Aquinas, *Summa Theologiae* III, q.65, a.3.
2   See St. Thomas Aquinas, *Summa Theologiae* III, q.65, a.3.
3   Council of Trent, Thirteenth Session, *Decree on the Most Holy Eucharist*, Chapter III in ND 1516.
4   Vatican II, *Lumen gentium*, 11.1.
5   See *CCC* 1335.
6   Cf. Jn 19:14, 31, 42. See also J.-H. Nicholas, *Sintesi Dogmatica. Dalla Trinità alla Trinità* Vol. II *La Chiesa e i Sacramenti*. (Città del Vaticano: Libreria Editrice Vaticana, 1992), p.308.
7   Council of Trent, Twenty-Second Session, *Doctrine on the Most Holy Sacrifice of the Mass*, in ND 1546.
8   See *CCC* 1340.
9   See Council of Trent, Thirteenth Session, *Decree on the Most Holy Eucharist* in ND 1514–1515. Idem, Twenty-Second Session, *Doctrine on the Most Holy Sacrifice of the Mass*, in ND 1546. See also condemnation of a modernist error in DS 3449.
10   See Congregation for the Doctrine of the Faith, *Response to doubts* in *AAS* 74 (1982) pp.1298–1299. See Idem, Circular Letter *Questo dicastero* (19 June 1995) in *EV* 14(1994–1995) N. 2886.
11   Council of Florence,*Decree for the Greeks* in ND 1508.
12   See the Responses of the Holy Office in DS 3264, 3312, 3313.
13   See Council of Trent, Thirteenth Session, Canon 4 on the Most Holy Sacrament of the Eucharist in ND 1529.
14   See St. Irenaeus, *Against the Heresies* Lib. 4, cap. 18, 5 in *PG* 7, 1028–1029.
15   See St. Basil, *De Spiritu Sancto* cap. 37, 66 in *PG* 32, 188.
16   Nicholas Cabasilas, *Liturgiae expositio*, 29 in *PG* 150, 429–430.
17   It was mentioned in chapter one, section 1.7, that the form of each sacrament must be pronounced externally.
18   The rubrics in the current missal indicate that the words of institution "should be spoken clearly and distinctly, as their meaning demands." See also Pope Pius XII, *Discourse to international convention on the Liturgy* 22 September 1956 in *AAS* 48

(1956) p.718. Also Holy Office, *Response to dubium* in *AAS* 49 (1957) p.370.

19   St. Ignatius of Antioch, *To the Smyrnaeans*, 7 in *SW* p.133.

20   St. Justin, *The First Apology* as found in *SW* p.133.

21   St. Irenaeus, *Against the Heresies* Lib. 5, cap. 2, 3 in *PG* 7, 1127.

22   See St. Cyril of Jerusalem, *On the Mysteries* 1,7 in *SW* p.137.

23   St Gregory of Nyssa, *Catechetical Oration*, 37 in *PG* 45, 95–96.

24   St. John Chrysostom, *Homily 1 on the Betrayal of Judas*, 6 in *PG* 49, 380.

25   St. Cyril of Alexandria, *Commentary on Luke 22:19* in *PG* 72, 911–912.

26   St. Augustine, *Commentary on Psalm 98*, 9 in *PL* 37, 1264.

27   St. Augustine, *Sermon 131*, cap. 1 in *PL* 38, 729.

28   See Council of Rome, *Oath prescribed to Berengar of Tours* in ND 1501.

29   Pope Innocent III, Letter *Cum Marthae Circa* to John, Former Archbishop of Lyons in ND 1502.

30   See Lateran IV, Symbol of Lateran, in ND 21.

31   See Lyons II, *Profession of Faith of Michael Paleologus* in ND 28.

32   See St. Thomas Aquinas, *Summa Theologiae* III, q.75, a.4.

33   St. Thomas Aquinas, *Summa Theologiae* III, q.75, a.5.

34   See St. Thomas Aquinas, *Summa Theologiae* III, q.76, aa.1–3.

35   See St. Thomas Aquinas, *Summa Theologiae* III, q.77, a.7.

36   See Pope Innocent III, *Profession of faith prescribed to the Waldensians* (1208), in ND 1504; See also Pope Martin V, Bull *Inter cunctas*, Questions proposed to the followers of Wyclif and Hus (1418), in ND 1507/16 and 1507/17.

37   Council of Trent, Thirteenth Session, *Decree on the Most Holy Eucharist*, Chapter 1 in ND 1513 and canon 1in ND 1526.

38   Council of Trent, Thirteenth Session, *Decree on the Most Holy Eucharist*, canon 2 in ND 1527.

39   See Pope Pius VI, Constitution *Auctorem fidei*, 29 in DS 2629.

40   Pope Pius XII, Encyclical Letter *Humani generis* (1950) in ND 1571.

41   See Pope Paul VI, Encyclical Letter *Mysterium Fidei* (1965) as found in ND 1577–1580.

42   Pope Paul VI, *The Creed of the People of God* (1968), 29.

43   *CCC* 1376; See Council of Trent, Thirteenth Session, *Decree on the Most Holy Eucharist* in ND 1519.

44   St. Thomas Aquinas, Hymn "Lauda Sion Salvatorem": "Fracto demum sacramento, ne vacilles, sed memento, tantum esse sub fragmento, quantum toto tegitur." See also Council of Trent, Thirteenth Session, *Decree on the Most Holy Eucharist*, Canon 3 in ND 1528.

45   See Council of Trent, Thirteenth Session, *Decree on the Most Holy Eucharist*, Canon 4 in ND 1529.
46   St. Cyril of Alexandria, *Epistula ad Calosyrium* in *PG* 76, 1075–1076.
47   Pope Paul VI, Encyclical Letter *Mysterium fidei*, 67–68.
48   Pope Paul VI, *Credo of the People of God*, 26.
49   Pope John Paul II, *Dominicae Cenae* 3.5.
50   See the Protestant Confession of Cyrillus Lukaris as found in *SW* pp. 175–176.
51   See the Orthodox Confession of Peter Mogila as found in *SW* pp. 176–177.
52   See Heb 8:6–13 which deals with the themes of covenant and sacrifice and Heb 10:11–18 which treats of sacrifice, purification from sins and sanctification.
53   The *Didache* 14,1 as found in *SW* p.39.
54   St. Justin Martyr, *Dialogue with Trypho*, 117 as found in *SW* 117.
55   St. Irenaeus, *Adversus haereses* Lib. 4, cap. 18, 1 in *PG* 7, 1024.
56   See Tertullian, *On the Crown* in cap. 3, 3 in *CCL* 2, 1043.
57   St. Gregory Nazianzen, *Oratio* 2, 95 in *PG* 35, 498.
58   St. John Chrysostom, *Homily 17 on Hebrews*, 3 in *PG* 63, 131.
59   St. Cyprian, *Epistle* 63, 14 in *SW* p.186.
60   St. Augustine, *The City of God* Lib. 10, cap. 6 in *PL* 41, 284.
61   Pope St. Leo the Great, *Sermon* 58, cap. 3 in *PL* 54, 333.
62   St. Faustus of Riez, *Sermon on the Body and Blood of Christ* in *PL* 30, 272.
63   Pope St. Gregory the Great, *Homilia 37 in Evangelia*, 7 in *PL* 76, 1279.
64   St. Thomas Aquinas, *Summa Theologiae* III, q.83, a.1.
65   St. Thomas Aquinas, *Commentary on St. John's Gospel*, VI, 7. See also Idem, *Summa Theologiae* III, q.76, a.2.
66   Pope Pius XII, Encyclical Letter *Mediator Dei* (1947) in ND 1566.
67   See M. Luther, *The Babylonian Captivity of the Church* as cited in *SW* p.198.
68   T. Cranmer, *Defense of the True Catholic Doctrine of the Sacrament* as found in *SW* p.203.
69   Anglican-Roman Catholic International Commission, *Windsor Statement*, 5.
70   Congregation for the Doctrine of the Faith, *Observations on the ARCIC Final Report* in *AAS* 74 (1982), p.1066.
71   Council of Trent, Twenty-Second Session, *Doctrine on the Most Holy Sacrifice of the Mass*, in ND 1546–1548, 1555–1558.
72   Pope John Paul II, *Dominicae Coenae* (1980), 9.
73   See Pope Innocent III, Profession of Faith prescribed to the Waldensians as found in ND 1504, 1703.

74   See Congregation for the Doctrine of the Faith, Declaration *Mysterium ecclesiae* in defence of the Catholic doctrine on the Church against certain errors of the present day (1973) part 6.6; Idem, *Letter to all Catholic Bishops concerning the Minister of the Holy Eucharist* (1983) in *AAS* 75(1983) pp.1001–1009.
75   See chapter one, section 1.8.
76   See St. Augustine, *Sermon 172* cap. 2, 2 in *PL* 38, 936–937.
77   For the canonical aspects of Mass offerings see *CIC* 945–958.
78   See Pope Pius XII, Encyclical Letter *Mediator Dei* in ND 1570.
79   Vatican II, *Lumen gentium* 11.1
80   See R. Knox, *Enthusiasm* (Oxford: Oxford University Press, 1950), pp.215–217.
81   See Pope St. Pius X, *Sacra Tridentina Synodus* in DS 3375–3383.
82   Pope John Paul II, *Dominicae cenae*, 11.5.
83   See *CIC* 919.
84   *CCC* 1387.
85   See *CIC* 917.
86   See Pontifical Commission for the Authentic Interpretation of the Code of Canon Law, *Reply* (26 June 1984) in *EV* 9 (1983–1985), N.862.
87   St. Thomas Aquinas, *Summa Theologiae* III, q.80, a.1.
88   St. Thomas Aquinas, *Summa Theologiae* III, q.80, a.12.
89   Council of Trent, Twenty First Session, *Doctrine on Communion under Both Kinds and on Communion of Little Children*, canon 3 in ND 1543.
90   Pope John Paul II, Encyclical Letter *Redemptoris Mater*, 44
91   Pope Paul VI, Encyclical Letter *Mysterium fidei*, 32.
92   Cf. *Ibid.*, 11.
93   See *ED* 122.
94   See *ED* 125.
95   See *ED* 123–124.
96   See *ED* 130–131.
97   See *ED* 132.
98   See *ED* 104e and *CIC* 908.
99   See I Cor 10:16–17; 12:13.
100 See Jn 6:53–54.
101 See *CIC* 920.
102 St. John Chrysostom, *Homily 27 on I Corinthians*, 5 in *PG* 61, 230–231.
103 See Pope John Paul II, *Dominicae Coenae*, 5–6.
104 See A. Hough, *God is not 'Green'* (Leominster: Gracewing, 1997), p.181. See also I. Zizioulas, *Il creato come eucaristia* (Magnano: Edizioni Qiqajon, 1994).
105 See *CCC* 1329.

5

Penance

The literature and history of the human race bear witness to
a general interest in the most empirical fact of moral evil. At
the beginning of human existence, there occurred the tragedy which is known as the Fall, and this primordial act of dis-
obedience left its mark on human beings in original sin
transmitted throughout the race. A propensity for wrongdoing remained and throughout history men and women, rec-
ognizing that objective value of right and wrong, have sought
somehow to set right the account of sin and guilt. In most
religions there are rites which convey a sense of penance and
reparation for wrongdoing. These, in their imperfect way,
indicate man's initiative in trying to find God once more, and
make peace. However, in the Old Testament, it is essentially
God the Father who takes the initiative to find man lost in his
sins, and this economy of Redemption culminates in the
coming of His Son, who makes the definitive act of Atonement upon the Altar of His Cross. Even the Christian, who
has been cleansed of original sin by the sacrament of Baptism, still has to struggle against the concupiscence or the
inclination to sin which remains, as well as the temptations
which the world and the devil proffer. This redemptive

action of Christ is made available through the sacrament of Penance. While all the sacraments derive their power from the Paschal Mystery, it is the sacrament of Penance which is most especially intended for the forgiveness of sins.

5.1   Scriptural data

5.1.1   Old Testament

The phenomenon of the Fall as described in the third chapter of the book of Genesis is expounded in most theology books dealing with creation or Christian anthropology.[1] This primordial tragedy of the first parents of mankind had repercussions in the original sin passed on to all men and women apart from Our Lady. It also left echoes in the cosmos as a whole. The Fall was rapidly succeeded by a series of other sins, of various kinds. The first murder, the sin of Cain (Gn 4:1–16), marked only the beginning of many acts of violence among men. Even among God's chosen people, many acts of infidelity towards God occurred, not least the sin of idolatry committed by the people of Israel with golden calf (Ex 32:1–14). Even specially chosen men of God fell into grave sins; a case in point was David with his double grave sin of adultery and murder (2 Sam 11).

The Covenant which God made with His people was closely bound up with sacrifices for sin (see Lv 4–5), and ritual sacrifices were offered on behalf of the people by the priests (Lv 6). The idea of a confession of sins was present in the Old Testament ritual when Aaron had to declare all the people's faults upon a goat (the scapegoat) which then bore all those sins into the wilderness (Lv 16:20–22). The sins of individuals, like David, were often rebuked by the prophets. The individual concerned was required to perform a penance and was forgiven by God, but not without some punishment, which in David's case was constituted by the death of Bathsheba's child (1 Sam 12:1–25).

Nevertheless, the Old Testament idea of the forgiveness of sins was different from the New Testament picture. The priest of the Old Law could *declare* that sins were forgiven but actual interior forgiveness only became fully developed in the New Testament. The writer of the Letter to the Hebrews highlighted this fundamental difference between the Old and the New Covenants: "The blood of goats and bulls and the ashes of a heifer are sprinkled on those who have incurred defilement and they restore the holiness of their outward lives; how much more effectively the blood of Christ, who offered himself as the perfect sacrifice to God through the eternal Spirit, can purify our inner self from dead actions so that we do our service to the living God" (Heb 9:13–14). Nevertheless the Old Testament was a preparation for and a prefiguration of the redemption brought by Christ. In particular, the Old Covenant wisdom literature and the prophets gradually interiorized the vision of sins and repentance. The penitential psalm commonly known as the *miserere* expressed repentance in terms of a new creation: "A pure heart create for me, O God, put a steadfast spirit within me" (Ps 50:10). The prophet Joel also proposed a conversion in terms of newness of heart: " 'But now, now — it is the Lord who speaks — come back to me with all your heart, fasting, weeping, mourning.' Let your hearts be broken, not your garments torn, turn to the Lord your God again, for He is all tenderness and compassion" (Jl 2:12–13). The prophet Ezekiel spoke of an interior idea of repentance: "Shake off all the sins you have committed against me, and make yourselves a new heart and a new spirit!" (Ez 18:31). The forgiveness extended to David after his sin seemed to be at a profound and interior level (see 1 Sam 12:13). Daniel linked repentance with good works: "By virtuous actions break with your sins, break with your crimes by showing mercy to the poor, and so live long and peacefully" (Dn 4:24).

5.1.2   New Testament

The basic idea of repentance and divine forgiveness is graphically portrayed in the parable of the prodigal son (Lk 15:11–32). The keynote of the Christian vision of forgiveness is its Trinitarian nature. It is offered by the Father through Christ His Son by the gift of the Holy Spirit. In the parable of the prodigal son, it is the father who forgives, and also makes the first move in this dynamic: "While he was still a long way off, his father saw him and was moved with pity. He ran to the boy" (Lk 15:20). In His love, God makes the first move in the process of reconciliation, but invites the sinner to collaborate. In the parable of the prodigal son, outward signs of inner forgiveness are offered in the best robe and the ring offered to the younger son, symbolizing the restoration of his dignity. Thus reconciliation is a sacramental process, because it involves an invitation to the sinner to collaborate in this encounter by contrition, confession and satisfaction. The feast offered to the younger son symbolizes the Eucharist to which the reconciled sinner is once more invited to participate. This outward sign of the inward grace cf reconciliation was instituted by Christ.

One instance of the divine institution of the sacrament of Penance lies in the promise of the power of the keys and the power of binding and loosing: "I will give you the keys of the kingdom of heaven" (Mt 16:19a). This power of the keys was prefigured in Old Testament prophecy: "I place the key of the House of David upon his shoulder; should he open, no one shall close, should he close, no one shall open" (Is 22:22). The keys of the kingdom denote the supreme authority (of teaching, governing and sanctifying) on earth over the kingdom of God, and the person who has this power can allow a person to enter this kingdom or exclude him from it.[2] However, since it is precisely sin which hinders entry into the kingdom, the power to forgive sins must also be included in the power of the keys. In this way, the power of the Cross of Christ is actualized today through Christ's minister. Immediately after the promise of the power of the keys, Jesus said to St. Peter "Whatever you bind on earth shall be considered bound in heaven; whatever you loose on earth shall be considered loosed in heaven" (Mt 16:19b). "Binding and loosing" signifies exclusion from the community by the imposition of a ban, or the re-acceptance by the removal of the ban. As sin is the ground for the exclusion, the power to forgive sins is included in the power of binding and loosing.

The power which St. Peter and his successors enjoy fully with regard to binding and loosing, was extended on similar terms to all the Apostles: "I tell you solemnly, whatever you bind on earth shall be considered bound in heaven; whatever you loose on earth shall be loosed in heaven" (Mt 18:18). The bestowing of this gift of divine forgiveness occurred in the context of instructions how a sinner should be corrected, and thus the passage has an immediate reference to the forgiveness of sins.

As is the case with most of the sacraments, the power of sacramentalized forgiveness only became fully actualized after the first Easter. Sacramental Penance had a pre-Paschal foundation and a post-Paschal actualization. Christ promised the power before Easter and bestowed it fully after His Redemptive Act was accomplished. On the evening of the day of His Resurrection, Jesus Christ appeared to the Apostles and said to them: "Peace be with you. As the Father sent me, so am I sending you" (Jn 20:21). Then, He breathed on them, indicating a giving of power, and said: "Receive the Holy Spirit. For those whose sins you forgive, they are forgiven; for those whose sins you retain, they are retained" (Jn 20:22–23). The parallelism of structure relating binding and loosing on the one hand and forgiving and retaining on the other is notable. With these words; Jesus extended His own mission of seeking out and saving what was lost to the Apostles (Lk 19:10). The expression which Jesus uses "to forgive sins" asserts a real eradication of sin, not a mere covering of the guilt of the sin or a mere remission of punishment. Our Lord knew that, given the weakness of fallen humanity, the Apostles would immediately need the power to forgive sins. Thus, the power bestowed upon St. Peter and the Apostles was not just a personal charisma given to them alone, but it was the will of Christ that His power of the remission of sins should continue in the Church as a permanent institution, like the Papacy and the Most Holy Eucharist and the other sacraments.

Other New Testament texts also indicate the existence of a divinely-instituted sacrament of Penance. One instance is provided by Christ's instructions about how to deal with grave sinners in the community: "If your brother does something wrong, go and have it out with him alone, between you two selves. If he listens to you, you have won back your brother. If he does not listen, take one or two others along with you: the evidence of two or three witnesses is required to sustain any charge. But if he refuses to listen to these, report it to the community; and if he refuses to listen to the community, treat him like a pagan or a tax collector" (Mt 18:15–17). This text also forms the basis for the penitential practice of the early Church. The concept of excommunication lies in the idea of a medicinal period of reflection (like the prodigal son had) so as to allow a space for true repentance.

St. Paul mentioned a number of sins which exclude the sinner from the kingdom of God: "When self-indulgence is at work the results are obvious: fornication, gross indecency and sexual irresponsibility; idolatry and sorcery; feuds and wrangling, jealousy, bad temper and quarrels; disagreements, factions, envy; drunkenness, orgies and similar things. I warn you now, as I warned you before: those who behave like this will not inherit the kingdom of God" (Gal 5: 19–21). This passage leads to the distinction between sins which exclude from God's Kingdom and those which do not. A further step in the distinction between mortal and venial sin was provided by St. John: "If anybody sees his brother commit a sin that is not a deadly sin, he has only to pray, and God will give life to the sinner — not those who commit a deadly sin; for there is a sin that is death, and I will not say that you must pray about that. Every kind of wrong-doing is sin, but not all sin is deadly" (I Jn 5: 16–17). On this Scriptural basis and in the light of Tradition, the Church developed the difference between mortal and venial sin such that mortal sin involves grave matter, directly known and willed.[3] Several interpretations have been offered of what constitutes "the unforgivable sin" mentioned in St. Matthew's Gospel: "Everyone who says a word against the Son of Man will be forgiven; but let anyone speak against the Holy Spirit and he will not be forgiven either in this world or in the next" (Mt 12:32; see also Lk 12:10). The unforgivable sin is often linked with the idea of "hardness of the heart" or "final impenitence", which is the ultimate sin of refusing God's forgiveness for sins, or refusing to repent.[4]

Nevertheless, right from the time of the early Church all concrete serious sins could be forgiven. It is worth remembering that St. Peter committed the grave sin of denying Our Lord three times and yet he was forgiven, following his repentance. The man who committed the very grave sin of incest in Corinth and was excommunicated (I Co 5:1–5), seems later to have been forgiven (II Co 2:6–10). Despite this established tradition of forgiveness, nevertheless in the early Church some misinterpreted a passage in the Letter to the Hebrews as implying that if one had fallen away seriously one could not be readmitted to the fold a second time: "As for those people who were once brought into the light, and tasted the gift from heaven, and received a share of the Holy Spirit, and appreciated the good message of God and the powers of the world to come and yet in spite of this have fallen away - it is impossible for them to be renewed a second time" (Heb 6:4–6). However, this text should be regarded as referring to hardness of the heart, not to the impossibility of forgiveness for lapses after Baptism. St John referred to an acknowledgment of sins in order to obtain forgiveness (I Jn 1:9) and St. James instructed the faithful in these terms: "Confess your sins to one another" (Jm 5:16). While these passages refer to a confession of sins but do not necessarily mean sacramental confession, nevertheless, from the beginning in the Church, the possibility existed of a forgiveness of sins after baptism.

5.2   Historical and theological development

5.2.1   Patristic period

On the basis of the well-known Gospel texts (Mt 13:16–19; 18:15–20 and Jn 20:21–23) as well as of the practice of the primitive community in excluding and re-admitting the

sinner, there developed the Catholic doctrine of the sacrament of Penance. In the post-apostolic age as in the apostolic
one, there was a clear distinction between everyday sins and
grave ones. Perhaps in the early Church very grave sins were
not that common, and it is in this context that the severe
penitential practice of early Christianity must be evaluated.
Theologically, according to ecclesial and theological tradition, for a Christian who is in a state of grace and participates
in the normal sacramental life of the Church, the power of
grace is such that he is not easily exposed to grave sin and this
does not normally enter into Christian life.[5]

In the early Church, for serious sins, the penitential practice involved an exclusion from the Church community and a
readmission; this period of exclusion can be seen as fostering
a "nostalgia" for the Church. Hence the sacrament of Penance was applied to those sins which we would call mortal or
grave. There was no obligation to sacramental Penance in the
case of venial sins. It was held by the Church that every sin,
without exception, could be forgiven if the sinner was repen-
tant. The question was how often could one be forgiven.
Certain rigorist heretics opposed this position of the Church.

An early second century document, the *Didaché* or
Teaching of the Twelve Apostles, taught that everyday or
venial sins could be expiated by prayer, fasting, and
almsgiving. All serious sins could be forgiven, by a process
which seemed to have involved confession and also a period
of separation from the community of the Church until repentance took place.[6] St. Ignatius of Antioch drew attention to
the same process, in which the bishop with his priests determined the penance which the penitent must perform: "The
Lord forgives all those who mend their ways and return to
union with God and to communion with their bishop."[7] The
Shepherd written by Hermas (around the year 180) furnished
the clearest description of the penitential practice of the
Roman Church in the second century. The Church did not
wish to publicise too readily the existence of a second chance
of obtaining forgiveness for serious sins committed after baptism as this might have been seen as a loophole allowing

people to sin. However, if Christians did fall aside, all sins could be forgiven, even apostasy and adultery. In the *Shepherd*, Hermas stated that only one chance of repentance should be allowed to a Christian who has fallen into mortal sin; the fact that he opposed the offering of many chances, seems to imply that the Roman practice at that time was to allow more than one chance. Hermas' reason for allowing only one chance of repentance after baptism was also connected with his belief that Christ would soon come again. St. Irenaeus described confession for serious sins in which the sinner went to the bishop or a priest, who possess a type of judicial power. They must bring the sinner to conversion, inflicting a penance which could involve excommunication in certain cases. Public confession also included a public penance.

In the third century Christian East, the work known as the *Didascalia Apostolorum* maintained that all sins could be forgiven. A period of penance (a fast of two to seven weeks) was imposed after excommunication, followed by a reconciliation conveyed by the imposition of hands by the bishop.[8] Clement of Alexandria (who died before 215) explained that the difference between Baptism and later reconciliation lies in the fact that in Baptism God forgives sins through His pure divine mercy, while the baptized person who becomes a sinner again must make expiation for his sins before God will forgive him. In brief, in the East, the tendency was to follow Origen (of the Alexandrine school) for whom Penance had a pastoral and educational aspect, as a healing from sin. Nevertheless, the period of penance was longer than the baptismal catechumenate.[9]

In the Western Church of the third century, Tertullian (who died after 220) contributed writings which can be divided into two periods, one as a Catholic and the other as a Montanist. During his Catholic phase, Tertullian traced a clear description of the penitential life of the church. For him and for other Fathers the sacrament of Penance was the "second plank after the shipwreck of the loss of grace."[10] It is not clear from Tertullian's writings whether the confession of sins was public (namely, in front of the whole community) or only in front of the priests. However, the penance was always public, so that it was clear who was performing it. Tertullian in his period as a Montanist (from the year 205 onwards) became very severe, and considered that the three sins of murder, apostasy and adultery could not be forgiven. The Catholic bishops, on the other hand, admitted that such serious sins as murder and apostasy could only be forgiven on the sinner's death bed after lifelong penance.

A great crisis which also led to clarification concerning penitential discipline was provided by the Novatian schism. The Roman priest Novatian joined forces with a rigorist minority in Rome and became the second anti-Pope. He maintained that the Church could not pardon certain sins even at the moment of death, but this error was condemned by the First General Council of Nicaea in the year 325, which also stated how reconciliation was to be offered to the Novatians. The Council also insisted that reconciliation was not to be denied to the dying.[11] The Novatian schism continued to plague Christendom for at least three centuries. St. Cyprian (who died in 258) was one of many bishops who opposed the heresy of Novatian. In one of his letters, he stated that "the Church, crowned with so many virgins, flourishes and chastity and modesty keep the glorious tenor of their way, nor has the vitality of continence been destroyed because penance and pardon are allowed the adulterer."[12] More than any other Church Father of this period, St. Cyprian taught the sacramentality of Penance, which involved three stages. The first part started with a private confession made to the bishop. A period of penance was then imposed upon the contrite sinner, which would include prayer, fasting, acts of charity and other renunciations. The second stage involved the request by the sinner to the bishop, clergy and the community to be readmitted to communion with the Church. The third and final phase consisted of the reconciliation which occurs through the laying-on of the hands by the bishop. Those who were gravely ill could enjoy a less strict penitential discipline.[13] In the West, following St. Cyprian, there followed a tendency to see Penance as expiation, satisfaction and ecclesiastical reconciliation.

Donatism, a further rigorist heresy was opposed by St. Augustine in the fifth century. The Donatist heresy included the false notion that the Church was only for the perfect so that if a Christian sinned gravely, he could not return back to the Church. On the other hand, St. Augustine maintained that a grave sinner need not be excommunicated in every case, but only if his sin aroused scandal. Nevertheless, every grave fault excluded the sinner from the Eucharist. Against the Donatist heresy, St. Augustine also asserted that any bishop could forgive sins, not just a holy one, because the bishop does so in virtue of the power of orders. It is considered that St. Augustine introduced private confession or at least paved the way for it. Further progress against rigorist tendencies came about during the same period when Pope Celestine I insisted that all those who so requested should have easy access to reconciliation at the moment of death.[14]

In the fifth century, St. Leo the Great did not introduce private confession, but rather confirmed the existing practice of private confession for private sins: "I order that all measures be taken to eradicate the presumptuous deviation from the apostolic rule through an illicit abuse of which I have learned of late. In the procedure of Penance... there should be no public confession of sins in kind and number read from a written list, since it is enough that the guilt of conscience be revealed to the priests alone in secret confession."[15] From this declaration, it is clear that the safeguarding of the reputation of the penitent is of Apostolic tradition. However, Pope Leo did not say that penance had to be private; he was advocating private confession with a public penance in cases of sins which were not generally known. Even if people knew that someone was expiating a sin, they did not know what the offence was. Leo the Great also insisted on the necessary role of the priest in confession acting on behalf of Christ. Already in Leo's thought can be found the idea that confession, contrition and satisfaction are necessary components of the sacrament of Penance.[16]

In the East, a development away from public confession also took place but for different reasons. At the end of the fourth century, the public confession of a lady of the upper classes who had been involved in a sexual relationship with a deacon gave great scandal to the populace, so that Bishop Nectarius of Constantinople suppressed the office of priest penitentiary (who had previously supervised the procedure for public penance) and decreed that each member of the faithful had to decide whether they were worthy to come to communion or not. Other local churches followed suit, and so the penitential apparatus of the primitive Church was gradually dismantled.

In conclusion, the penitential practice of the first six centuries can be summarized in the following terms. The first stage generally involved confession of the sin or sins which could be public or private. The general tendency was that confession became increasingly private in the West after St. Leo the Great and in the East after Bishop Nectarius of Constantinople. The second phase consisted of a period of separation from the Church of varying length, during which the penitent was required to perform acts of mortification. The length of this period of penance depended on the gravity of the offence. St. Basil stipulated twenty years penance for wilful murder, fifteen for adultery, seven years for fornication, two years for theft and lifelong penance for apostasy. The bishop enjoyed a certain discretion in reducing these penances especially for the fervent.[17] The special penitential practices which took place during the penitential period could involve prayers (especially the penitential psalms), fasting from meat or wine, the wearing of red clothes, almsgiving to the poor and abstinence from marital relations. The final stage involved the absolution of the penitents and this was often carried out on Holy Thursday. Generally this absolution took place after the period of penance, though it sometimes took place beforehand. In either case, the penance had to be completed before Holy Communion was received.

5.2.2 The Middle Ages

Between the time of Hermas' *Shepherd*, dating from around the year 180, and the Third Council of Toledo in the year 589, the practice of the Church often did not allow for a repetition of ecclesiastical penance for grave sins. This was clearly connected with the considerable length of time required to complete the penance. In the fifth century, some authors had proposed that the monastic life could substitute for public penance. As a monk, the penitent could receive Holy Communion even before his full period of penance was completed, lest on the pretext of excessive humility he prolong his separation from Christ's Body and Blood to Whom he had united himself to be made one body.[18] In the early sixth century, St. Caesarius of Arles stipulated that lesser sins and hidden crimes could be expiated by private penance, yet he also spoke highly of public penance. Just as a man needs "to enlist the aid of his neighbours and relatives when his vineyard has become a wilderness through neglect" so the public penitent with the help of the whole community of the faithful "can uproot the thorns and thistles of his sins, that with God's help a harvest of good works may spring up, and the vineyard of his heart, which used to yield not grapes but thorns, may begin to show forth the sweetness of spiritual wine."[19]

By the early part of the sixth century, a new penitential discipline had arrived from Ireland and England to France and thence to Spain. This new concept permitted reconciliation to penitents as often as they asked for it. The Third Council of Toledo reacted severely against the new approach, but it was only a regional council and the new way prevailed.[20] The new approach solved the problem of many Christians, who having fallen into grave sin, because of the heavy and disabling public penance, felt that they must wait until there was a danger of death before being reconciled. As a matter of fact, in the English and Irish Churches, the practice of "once-only" reconciliation and public penance never really became established. In the penitential book of Bishop Theodore of Tarsus who was made Archbishop of Canterbury in 668, there was no ceremony of public reconciliation in the English Church because there was no public penance. Either Theodore imported into England the more lenient practices of his Greek Church of origin or he simply developed his system according to the Celtic approach which was already in force.[21] Hence, since there was no public exclusion and no obligation to perform humiliating public penances over a long period, and moreover since the sacrament could be often repeated, then logically it could also apply to small offences. Therefore, from the seventh and eighth centuries onwards, the practice of confessing venial sins developed. Monks from the British Isles brought this system over to the continent from the sixth century onwards, so that by the eighth century repeated confession had spread all over the continent. Penance books (or penitentials) also fixed the amount of satisfaction which sinners had to perform, thus taking this right away from the priest or the bishop. They contained some bizarre elements, and although penance was less severe than in the early Church, it was still rigorous by modern standards.

From the eighth century onwards a greater stress was put on the act of confession, and so the private nature of the sacrament became highlighted. With this increasing private character of confession, there arose the increasing distinction between the external forum of the Church and the internal forum of the conscience. Hence excommunication was used more and more as a punishment inflicted by the Church apart from Penance, especially for public crimes. Increasingly, the bishop delegated the office of hearing confessions to priests, while reserving the absolution of certain sins to himself. Between the ninth and twelfth centuries, discussion took place about the frequency of confession. In the year 1215, the Fourth Lateran Council decreed that the faithful should confess once a year and this injunction was later repeated at the Council of Trent. The general view is that this decree is binding only on those who are in mortal sin.[22]

5.2.3   The Reformation

The ideas of Wyclif in England (died 1384) and Hus in Bohemia (died 1415) and their followers foreshadowed the errors of the Reformers. These precursors of the Reformation had denied that external confession was necessary, only contrition of the heart. They also maintained that confession to a priest was not necessary, and a lay-person could receive confessions with equal efficacy. Of a piece with these ideas was their rejection of the hierarchical structure of the Church associated with the sacrament of Penance.[23] Among the Reformers, Luther fluctuated in his attitude towards the sacrament of Penance. In his early days and at the end of his life, he spoke of it with great praise and received the sacrament often; he believed it to be a sacrament. However, the important aspect for Luther was fiducial and naked faith and so he rejected the idea of an obligatory penance imposed on the penitent as, in his view, this supported the importance of "works". The Lutheran idea was that the sacrament indicated God's forgiveness; sins were merely covered or not imputed. On the other hand, the Catholic position is that the sacrament of Penance brings about real interior forgiveness. Moreover, Luther considered that this sacrament need not be administered exclusively by priests. He also maintained that perfect contrition for sins was necessary, whereas the Catholic position accepted that imperfect contrition (or attrition) is sufficient. A disciple of Luther, Melanchton, also believed in the importance of individual confession, but for him as for Luther the important factor was to be found in the words of absolution, which represented the voice of God. The human responses of penance and satisfaction were undervalued in the Lutheran system.[24] Calvin rejected the sacrament of Penance on the whole, but recommended it to those Christians who suffer anxiety from their sins and so need the help of others. He reduced confession to what would be termed a psychological need in the parlance of today. Another Reformer, Zwingli, totally rejected individual confession. The Council of Trent reacted to the various errors of the Reformation and reaffirmed the institution and necessity of the sacrament of Penance. The Council taught that the parts of Penance are contrition, confession and satisfaction, which form the *quasi matter* of this sacrament. It stated that the priest was the necessary minister.[25] The Anglicans do not generally admit the existence of the sacrament of Penance, but some High Church and Anglo-Catholic groups do propose confession. However, the absolution would not be regarded as valid by the Catholic Church owing to the invalidity of Anglican Orders.[26] The sacramentality of confession is generally accepted by all the Orthodox churches. The sole exception occurred in the seventeenth century when Patriarch Cyrillus Lukaris fell under the influence of Calvin, and denied sacramental confession.

5.2.4   Recent period

The Modernists based their thought on Kantian subjectivism and upon an evolutionary concept of truth. They tended to deny the divine and supernatural aspects of the Church. With their liberal approach to biblical criticism, they attempted to undermine the doctrine of the divine institution of the sacrament of Penance. Instead, since one of the fundamental principles of Modernism was historical development, they regarded it as having developed according to purely human and social factors. This error was among those condemned by Pope St. Pius X in the year 1907.[27]

The New Rite of Penance published after the Second Vatican Council was an occasion for the rediscovery of the ecclesial dimension of the sacrament of Penance, with penitential services for the preparation for individual confessions. Nevertheless, the constant tradition of the Church as regards the individual nature of the sacrament has also been recently stressed by Pope John Paul II: "Although participation by the fraternal community of the faithful in a common penitential celebration is a great help for the act of personal conversion, nevertheless, in the final analysis, it is necessary that in this act there should be a pronouncement by the individual himself with the whole depth of his conscience and with the whole of his sense of guilt and of trust in God."[28] The Pope also indicated that the sacrament of Penance is characterized by both juridical and therapeutic aspects. According to an analogy with human courtrooms, the confessional is a kind of tribunal of divine mercy. However, Penance is also a sacrament of healing in which Christ pours the balm of his healing into the diseased soul of the sinner.[29] The juridical tendency has been more evident in the West and the medicinal approach has been more stressed in the East. It is helpful to see the various aspects of the sacrament of Penance in terms of conversion, penance, confession, forgiveness, reconciliation both with God (vertical dimension) and with man (horizontal dimension). These descriptions summarize the whole history of the sacrament.[30]

5.3   The sacramental sign

5.3.1   The quasi matter

The discernment of what constitutes the matter of this sacrament is not so straightforward because there is no immediately visible element upon which the creative word can confer a salvific meaning. Nevertheless, the tradition of the Church has always indicated two factors in the sacrament: the sorrow and penance of the penitent and the absolution of the Church. During the course of history, a variety of positions were taken by theologians, some giving more importance to the Church's absolution, others to the repentance of the sinner. Under consideration therefore is the relation between an objective element (the Church's absolution) and a subjective element (the sinner's sorrow).

St. Thomas Aquinas regarded the penitential act of the sinner, termed the parts of penance (or contrition, confession and satisfaction), as the matter of the sacrament and the absolution as the form. He envisaged the matter and form working together as a single cause of forgiveness.[31] They combine in blotting out the guilt if the sin has already been remitted through the repentance which preceded the reception of the sacrament. Hence, in a sense the Church's absolution works in advance: the repentance of the sinner is determined by the Church's absolution because the repentance is ordered to it and has the effect of remitting sin. This approach explains why, when no priest is available to receive confessions, the penitent in mortal sin can, in this case of necessity, make a perfect act of contrition which includes a desire for sacramental confession. However, the certainty of obtaining forgiveness of mortal sin only comes through the confessional, precisely because it is difficult for the penitent to know whether his act of contrition has been perfect of not.[32] Blessed John Duns Scotus maintained that the Church's absolution alone is the external sign of the sacrament, and the subjective acts of the penitent are not an essential part of the sacrament but its prerequisite, or basic conditions. Scotus' view is supported by the fact that the Councils of Florence and Trent speak of the acts of the penitent as *quasi matter* (quasi meaning "as it were").[33] The practice of giving at least conditional absolution to unconscious persons also implies some support for the Scotist position.

From the Latin derivation of the word, contrition signifies a desire to crush sin. The Council of Trent defined contrition in the following terms: "The sorrow of the soul and the detestation of the sin committed, together with the resolve not to sin any more."[34] This sorrow must penetrate into the past for sins committed and extend into the future with a firm purpose of amendment. Thus contrition unto salvation must be inward, but shown externally in self-accusation. It must also be supernatural, occurring under the influence of actual grace. A merely natural sorrow has no salutary value; for example, a bank-robber who is sorry only because he fears being sent to prison is under the influence of natural sorrow. Contrition must also be general, extending to all grievous sins committed since the last confession. Contrition is divided into two types, perfect and imperfect, which is also termed attrition. While perfect contrition proceeds from the motive of the perfect love of God, imperfect contrition is based upon the motive of imperfect love of God or other supernatural motivation including fear of hell. However, perfect love does not exclude a desire for one's blessedness in God. Thus, the pitfall of disinterested love is to be avoided. The desire for one's heavenly reward does not make contrition imperfect.[35] Perfect contrition bestows the grace of justification on the mortal sinner even before the actual reception of the sacrament of Penance, for "charity covers a multitude of sins" (I Pt 4:8). This perfect contrition must however include a desire for the sacrament.[36]

The Council of Trent taught that imperfect contrition is sufficient for sacramental confession.[37] Before that Council, theologians such as Peter Lombard, Alexander of Hales and St. Bonaventure held that perfect contrition was necessary. For the Angelic Doctor, attrition denoted an approach to perfect contrition and hence disposed the penitent to the sacrament of Penance.[38] Blessed Duns Scotus went further and held that attrition was sufficient for receiving the sacrament of Penance fruitfully. Since Trent, the common teaching of the Church has been that imperfect contrition is sufficient. Nevertheless, fierce controversy between contritionists and attritionists continued for some time and was only called to a halt by Rome in 1667.[39] Among the condemned errors of the Jansenists was also one which required perfect contrition.[40] Contrition, as the door to the sacrament, includes a purpose of amendment, the resolution not to sin again. This must associated with a desire to avoid the occasions of sin. Contrition and conversion are thus intimately bound together as "a drawing near to the holiness of God, a recovery of one's true identity, which has been upset and disturbed by sin, a liberation in the very depth of self and thus a regaining of lost joy, the joy of being saved, which the majority of people in our time are no longer capable of experiencing."[41]

According to the Scriptures, it is a God-given law that a sinner confess his faults (Gn 3:9–13 ; Jm 5:16). This is more than a fulfilment of a merely psychological need of ridding oneself of the burden of guilt, although this comes as a consolation of the sacrament. Rather, it is a means by which the

sinner may know himself before God, may see and experience God's judgment, His mercy and His healing, "for if the
sick person is too ashamed to show his wound to the doctor,
the medicine cannot heal what it does not know."[42] Thus, all
mortal sins committed after baptism must be confessed
according to kind and number. The circumstances which
alter the gravity of a sin must be confessed. There is no obligation to confess venial sins, though it is "right and profitable
to declare them."[43] The frequent and regular confession of
venial sins "helps us form our conscience, fight against evil
tendencies, let ourselves be healed by Christ and progress in
the life of the Spirit."[44]

Satisfaction takes account of the three negative effects
which sin causes in relation to God, to others and to the sinner. Sacramental satisfaction involves works of penance
imposed on the penitent in atonement for the temporal punishment due to sins which remain after the guilt of the sin
and its eternal punishment have been forgiven. Absolution
removes sins and the eternal punishment due to mortal sin,
but does not remedy all the disorders that sin has caused.[45]
Satisfaction may include restitution or the making up of
damage in the case of serious sins. For instance, if a penitent
has damaged an individual or a group of individuals by steal-
ing a large sum of money, he may be asked to pay back a part
in such a way that his identity would not be revealed.
Extra-sacramental penitential works, such as the performance of voluntary penitential practices and the patient
bearing of trials sent by God, possess satisfactory value.

5.3.2   The form

The form of the sacrament of Penance consists in the words
of absolution. In the Latin Church, the formula of absolution
runs like this: "God, the Father of mercies through the Death
and Resurrection of His Son has sent the Holy Spirit among
us for the forgiveness of sins. Through the ministry of the
Church may God give you pardon and peace and *I absolve you
from your sins in the name of the Father, and + of the Son and of the
Holy Spirit*." In an emergency, the shorter italicized form

suffices for validity. In some of the Byzantine Churches the following form of absolution is used: "The Lord God through Nathan the prophet forgave David his sins, and the prostitute weeping at His feet, and Peter shedding bitter tears for his betrayal, and the publican and the prodigal son. May the same Lord God through me a sinner, forgive you all the sins of your life. And may He make you stand uncondemned at His awesome tribunal for He is blessed for ever and ever." The priest may then add the additional formula: "May Our Lord and God Jesus Christ who gave His holy Apostles the command to retain or forgive the sins of mankind forgive you, from on high, for all your sins. I, His unworthy servant, who have received from these Apostles the mandate to do the same, absolve you from all the sins of your life in the name of the Father and of the Son and of the Holy Spirit."[46]

The words of absolution should be said aloud, and imply an encounter between the penitent and the priest, who acts in the person of Christ. This means that the penitent and priest must be present to one another, and therefore confession by letter is invalid.[47] Confession at a distance by telephone would also be excluded, as also by modern means of communication such as e-mail.

5.4 The minister

Only the bishop and the priest are valid ministers of the sacrament of Penance. In the past, in both East and West, cases occurred in which the faithful confessed to deacons and clerics of lower rank and even to lay-people. This should be understood as non-sacramental confession in the spirit of St. James's injunction: "Confess your sins to one another." (Jm 5:16) The idea was a type of salutary self-accusation, which was been preserved in the chapter of faults in some forms of religious life. Here, the religious publicly accused himself or herself before the community of faults committed during the course of the day.

The remission of sins effects reconciliation with God, and also with the Church. In ecclesial tradition, the Pope as visible head of the universal Church and the bishop, as visible head of a particular Church, principally enjoy the power and ministry of reconciliation: they are moderators of the penitential discipline.[48] Hence, the Pope, cardinals and bishops may hear confessions anywhere. In order to hear confessions validly, a priest must be delegated with the necessary faculties, either from his bishop (or religious superior) or from the Pope.[49] Those who have the faculty to hear confessions habitually in a place where they have a domicile, may use this faculty everywhere unless in a particular case the local ordinary has refused it. In danger of death any priest, even one who has been laicized, may hear confessions and validly absolve.

In keeping with the very special role which the Pope and the bishops enjoy in the ministry of reconciliation, certain very grave sins are linked with censures reserved to the Pope or to the bishop. One censure is excommunication, "the most severe ecclesiastical penalty, which impedes the reception of the sacraments and the exercise of certain ecclesiastical acts, and for which absolution consequently cannot be granted... except by the Pope, the bishop of the place or priests authorized by them."[50] The censures of excommunication specially reserved to the Holy See are first, sacrilege against the Sacred Host; second, an act of physical force against the Roman Pontiff; third, the case of a bishop who consecrates a bishop without an Apostolic mandate, or one who receives such an episcopal consecration. The fourth instance is that of a priest who absolves an accomplice in an external sin against the sixth commandment. Such an absolution is invalid except in case of danger of death. The fifth case incurring such excommunication is that of a confessor who directly violates the seal of confession. The sins which incur censures reserved to the bishop of a diocese vary from region to region, one example being the crime of abortion. In the Eastern Churches, the sin of procured abortion is reserved to the bishop.[51] In some dioceses there are no special reserved censures. When the penitent is in danger of death any priest, even if he is without the necessary faculties for hearing confessions, can absolve from every sin and

excommunication.[52] The distinction between absolution
from sin and lifting of the censure is an important one, also
since it is the removal of the censure that is reserved. Moreover, the conditions for a sinner to incur a censure for his
grave sin are most strictly limited.[53]

The minister of the sacrament of Penance is bound most
strictly to the seal of the confessional. This means that he
cannot reveal, under any circumstances, directly or indirectly any information which is received through the confessional. The Fourth Lateran Council in the year 1215
instructed confessors to take great care not to "betray the
sinner through word or sign". Anyone who committed this
offence was "to be consigned to a closed monastery for perpetual penance."[54] The confessor may not use knowledge
gained in the confessional to the detriment of the penitent,
even if there is no danger of revealing who he is. Similarly a
person in authority may not use information which has come
to him in the course of hearing confessions. Thus a superior
of seminarians, hearing in the confessional for instance that
one of his subjects was unworthy for ordination, could not
use the information to impede or defer the ordination. Even
if information had come to the superior through another
channel the great risk of scandal would preclude the employment of that knowledge. For this reason, directors of religious and rectors of seminarians are not generally permitted
to receive the confessions of their students. If an interpreter
is required to help a penitent and his confessor to carry out a
confession, he or she is also bound by the seal of the confessional. Similarly bound are those who overhear a confession
accidentally. It is a grave sacrilege to listen in to a confession
deliberately, or to attempt to record the sacrament of Penance in any way.[55] In the case of a dumb penitent, when sign
language is employed or else a written confession is
employed, the written confession must be scrupulously
destroyed.

5.5   Reconciliation in the life of the Church

The Church herself is the great Sacrament of reconciliation: "The Church in heaven, the Church on earth and the Church in purgatory are mysteriously united in this cooperation with Christ in reconciling the world to God."[56] The mission of the Church in bringing God's forgiveness to the world is rendered more difficult today because there is a widespread feeling that this forgiveness is not necessary. In other words, the sense of sin, and indeed of the moral order, has often been lost. This phenomenon is clearly connected with *secularism*, which denotes a "humanism totally without God, completely centred upon the cult of action and production and caught up in the heady enthusiasm of consumerism and pleasure-seeking, unconcerned with the danger of 'losing one's soul'."[57] Despite this problem, the Church continues to proclaim and to be Christ's Sacrament of reconciliation which is carried out in various ways, and in a special way in the sacrament of Penance, precisely so as to re-awaken in God's people their need of His forgiveness. This sacrament is not intended to be psychological counselling, nor spiritual direction, nor catechesis.

One way of celebrating the sacrament is through reconciliation of individual penitents. Here the penitent is welcomed by the confessor, who reads a passage of the Word of God. There follows the confession of sins and acceptance of satisfaction, then an act of contrition on the part of the penitent and finally the absolution given by the confessor. The second rite is that of the reconciliation of several penitents with individual confession and absolution; here the faithful gather in a church and several confessors are available. This is also known as the Penitential Service. The service begins with the introductory rites, followed by readings from the Word of God and a short homily. A general examination of conscience is then provided to stimulate reflection by the assembled people. Then each penitent who wishes goes to an individual priest and confesses his sins, receives a penance and gets absolved. The service concludes with a prayer

and a blessing. The third possibility is the rite for reconciliation of several penitents with general absolution. This
option consists of an instruction, in which the celebrant
explains the nature and significance of this form of celebration. General confession ensues using the "I confess" for
instance. The celebrant invites those who wish to receive
general absolution to indicate by bowing their heads or
kneeling, and general absolution follows. This third option
should only be employed in the case of grave necessity,
which would be constituted by imminent danger of death
with insufficient time for the priest or priests to hear each
penitent's confession. "Grave necessity can also exist when,
given the number of penitents, there are not enough confessors to hear individual confessions properly in a reasonable
time, so that the penitents through no fault of their own
would be deprived of sacramental grace or Holy Communion
for a long time."[58] The condition of grave need would not be
fulfilled simply by a large gathering of people for a major feast
or for a pilgrimage. The decision as to whether or not the conditions required for general absolution are satisfied is
reserved to the diocesan bishop.[59] When general absolution
does take place its validity depends on the fact that the faithful must have the intention of individually confessing their
sins within due time, and if possible, at least before the next
time they receive general absolution.[60]

Since the sacrament of Penance is a sacred and liturgical
act, it should be carried out in a sacred place, like a church or
an oratory.[61] The faithful must be free to choose the secrecy
of a fixed grille between the penitent and the confessor.
Some penitents prefer "face-to-face" confession so it is good
to make this available as well if possible. The need for provid-
ing both options has led to the design of reconciliation rooms
within churches which are both practical and welcoming.

5.5.1 The recipient

The basic minimum frequency of confession is now much as
was stipulated at the Fourth Lateran Council in 1215,
namely that "all the faithful who have reached the age of

discretion are bound faithfully to confess their grave sins at least once a year."[62] This provision is ordered so that the People of God can receive Holy Communion around Easter time.[63] It is of course desirable that confession should be more frequent. When it is also regular and well-prepared, it becomes easier.

As regards ecumenical hospitality in the confessional, the usual distinction applies between Churches, which possess the seven valid sacraments, and ecclesial communities which only have baptism and also marriage between their own subjects. Eastern Christians separated from full communion with the Holy See may, in cases of *necessity*, in the absence of confessors of their own Church, seek confession from a Catholic priest. Similarly, a Catholic not finding a priest of his own may, in a case of necessity, approach an Orthodox priest. However, such reciprocity is not possible where non-Catholic ministers have invalid Orders, as in the case of the communities resulting from the Reformation. Where a non-Catholic who may not have faith in the sacrament of Confession asks for the sacrament in a case of urgency, a priest can give conditional absolution.[64]

5.5.2   The effects

The effect of the sacrament of Penance is to restore the sinner to friendship with God in a kind of spiritual resurrection. This sacrament also brings about reconciliation with the Church, and communion within the Church is strengthened by Penance. Reconciliation with God leads to the repair of the other breaches caused by sin. "The forgiven penitent is reconciled with himself in his inmost being, where he regains his innermost truth. He is reconciled with his brethren whom he has in some way offended and wounded. He is reconciled with the Church. He is reconciled with all creation."[65] The sacrament of Penance foreshadows and anticipates the judgment which the penitent will undergo at the end of this earthly life. "In converting to Christ through penance and faith, the sinner passes from death to life and does not come into judgment."[66]

While the sacrament of Penance brings about the forgiveness of all mortal sins confessed as well as venial sins, it also
sometimes infuses a peace of soul and deep sense of spiritual
consolation. Confession also brings about the revival of grace
in the case of an unworthily received sacrament, as mentioned in chapter one.[67] This holds in all the sacraments apart
from the Holy Eucharist and Penance. Furthermore, the
merits due to good works performed in a state of grace which
have then been lost by mortal sins are also revived by the sacrament of Penance. While confession forgives the eternal
punishment due to sin, the temporal punishment is not
always forgiven in its entirety as this depends upon the fervour with which the penitent enters into the sacrament.

5.5.3 Indulgences

The consequences of sin are twofold. Mortal sin destroys
communion with God and thereby makes the sinner incapable of eternal life, which leads to the "eternal punishment"
of sin. Also, every sin, even venial, involves a turning away
from God towards His creatures, or else a disorder induced
among His creatures which must be purified or repaired
either here on earth, or after death in the state called Purgatory. Temporal punishment due to sin is precisely connected
with the undue attachment to or the disorder caused among
God's creatures. "These two punishments must not be conceived of as a kind of vengeance inflicted by God from without, but as following from the very nature of sin."[68] The fact
that the sinner must suffer punishment even after the forgiveness of the guilt can be seen in the case of the sin of
David in the Old Testament (2 S 12:13f). Similarly, the Apostle affirms that "pain and suffering will come to every human
being who employs himself in evil" (Rm 2:9).

. Indulgences can be seen in this context. By an indulgence
is meant the extra-sacramental remission of the temporal
punishment due to sin remaining after the guilt of the sin has
been remitted. Divine mercy forgives the guilt of the sin.
Divine justice requires a further act for the remission of the
temporal penalty due to sin. An indulgence is a sacramental

rather than a sacrament, and thus involves a greater degree of disposition on the part of the recipient. Contrition and confession are the preconditions for receiving an indulgence which is the removal of the last effects of sin. The indulgence can be applied to oneself or to others including the dead. Only the Pope has a universal power of indulgence. Nowadays indulgences are simply divided into partial and plenary.[69]

Having seen the healing which the sacrament of Penance brings about in the sinner it is now time to turn to the healing effect of the Anointing of the Sick.

Notes

1   See my *Mystery of Creation* (Leominster: Gracewing, 1995), pp.117–128.
2   For an exposition of the meaning of the power of the keys, see S.L. Jaki, *The Keys of the Kingdom* (Chicago: Franciscan Herald Press, 1986).
3   See *CCC* 1854–1864. See also Pope John Paul II, Post-Synodal Apostolic Exhortation *Reconciliation and Penance* (1984), 17.
4   See Pope John Paul II, Encyclical Letter *Dominum et Vivificantem* (1986), 46.
5   See Pontifical Theological Commission, *La riconciliazione e la penitenza* (1982) C III.4 in Commissione Teologica Internazionale, *Documenti* (Vatican City: LEV, 1988), p.415. See also St.Thomas, *De Veritate* 27,1, ad.9.
6   See *Didaché*, 4:6,14; 8:1–3; 11:7, 14:1; 15:3 in *Sources Chrétiennes* 248 (Paris: Cerf, 1978) pp. 160–161, 164–165, 172–175, 184–185, 192–193, 194–195.
7   St. Ignatius of Antioch, *Letter to the Philadelphians*, 8 in *PG* 5, 703–704.
8   See *Didascalia Apostolorum*, 6 in *SF* pp.61–62.
9   See *SF* p.59.
10   See Tertullian, *De paenitentia* 4, 2 in *CCL* 1, 326. See also St. Jerome, *Epistola 84 ad Pammachium et Oceanum*, 6 in *PL* 22, 748.
11   See Nicaea I, canons 8 and 13 in ND 1601–1602.
12   St. Cyprian, *Epistle 55*, 20 in *SF* p.52.
13   See St. Cyprian, *On the Lapsed* in *PL* 4, 447–510.
14   Pope Celestine I, *Letter to the bishops of Narbonne and Vienne* in ND 1604.

15 Pope St. Leo I, *Letter to the Bishops of the Roman rural districts* (459) in ND 1606.

16 See Pope St. Leo I, *Letter to Theodore, Bishop of Frejus* (452) in ND 1605.

17 See St. Basil, *Epistle 217 To Amphilochius* in *SF* pp.75–76.

18 See Faustus of Riez, *Sermon 3* in *SF*, p.128.

19 St. Caesarius of Arles, *Sermon 261* in *SF* p.130.

20 See Third Council of Toledo as found in ND 1607.

21 See *SF* pp.147–148 for some extracts from the Penitential of Theodore. From this it can be seen that the period of penance for fornication was one year, for adultery four years, for homosexual acts ten years. Theft and manslaughter were punished with seven years of penance.

22 See Lateran IV in ND 1608. See also *CIC* 989 and *CCC* 1457.

23 See the General Council of Constance, Condemned error of Wyclif in ND [1610] and Pope Martin V, Bull *Inter cunctas* in ND 1611/20, 21, 25.

24 See Pope Leo X, Bull *Exsurge Domine* (1520) in ND [1614/5–14].

25 See Council of Trent, Fourteenth Session, *Doctrine on the Sacrament of Penance* in ND 1615–1634, 1641–1655.

26 Even though this absolution is sacramentally invalid, it may still open the way to God's forgiveness by leading to true contrition. He, who with the help of grace does that which lies in his power, is not denied further grace by God.

27 See Holy Office, Decree *Lamentabili* in ND [1660/46–47].

28 Pope John Paul II, Encyclical *Redemptor Hominis* (1979) 20.6.

29 See Pope John Paul II, Apostolic Exhortation *Reconciliatio et Penitentia*, 31.

30 See *CCC* 1423–4.

31 See St. Thomas Aquinas, *Summa Theologiae* III, q.90, a.3.

32 See *CCC* 1452, 1457; *CIC* 916; *CCEO* 711.

33 See the Council of Florence, *Decree for the Armenians* in ND 1612; Council of Trent, *Doctrine on the sacrament of Penance* in ND 1620.

34 Council of Trent, *Doctrine on the sacrament of Penance* in ND 1622.

35 See Innocent XII, Brief *Cum alias ad apostolatus* which condemned certain semi-quietist errors of Archbishop Fénelon, in particular DS 2356 and 2369.

36 Council of Trent, *Doctrine on the sacrament of Penance* in ND 1623.

37 Council of Trent, *Doctrine on the sacrament of Penance* in ND 1624 and 1645.

38 See St. Thomas Aquinas, *Summa Theologiae* Supplement, q.1, a.2.

39 See Holy Office, Decree of 5th May 1667, in DS 2070.

40   See Holy Office, Condemned Jansenist errors in DS 2315; Pius
      VI, Constitution *Auctorem fidei* in DS 2625.
41   Pope John Paul II, Apostolic Exhortation *Reconciliatio et
      Penitentia*, 31/III.
42   St. Jerome, *Commentarius in Ecclesiasten* 10, 11 in *PL* 23, 1152.
43   Council of Trent, *Doctrine on the sacrament of Penance* in ND 1626.
44   *CCC* 1458. See also *Introduction to the Rite of Confession*, 7(b) which
      states: "Moreover, frequent and careful celebration of this sacra-
      ment is also very useful as a remedy for venial sins. This is not a
      mere ritual repetition or psychological exercise, but a serious
      striving to perfect the grace of baptism so that, as we bear in our
      body the death of Jesus Christ, his life may be seen in us ever
      more clearly. In confession of this kind, penitents should try to
      conform more closely to Christ and follow the voice of the Spirit
      more attentively."
45   See Council of Trent, *Doctrine on the sacrament of Penance* in ND
      1630–1633, 1652–1654.
46   *Byzantine Daily Worship* (Allendale, N.J.: Alleluia Press, 1969),
      p.932.
47   See Holy Office, *Decree of 20 June 1602* in DS 1994.
48   See *CCC* 1462. See also Vatican II, *Lumen gentium* 26.3.
49   See *CIC* 844; 967–969; 972. *CCEO* 722, §§3–4.
50   *CCC* 1463. See also *CIC* 1331, 1354–1357. *CCEO* 1431, 1434,
      1420.
51   See *CCEO* 728 §2.
52   See *CIC* 976. *CCEO* 725.
53   See *CIC* 1323–1324.
54   See Lateran IV in ND 1609.
55   See *CIC* 983–985, 1388.
56   Pope John Paul II, Apostolic Exhortation *Reconciliatio et
      Penitentia*, 12.1.
57   *Ibid.*, 18.5.
58   *CCC* 1483.
59   See *CIC* 961.
60   See *CIC* 962 §2; 963.
61   See *CIC* 964.
62   *CIC* 989.
63   Cf. CIC 920; *CCC* 1457.
64   See *ED* 122–123, 129–132.
65   *CCC* 1469.
66   *CCC* 1470. See Jn 5:24.
67   See chapter 1, section 1.9 above.
68   *CCC* 1472.

69   See Pope Clement VI, Bull *Unigenitus Dei Filius* in ND 1682.
      Council of Trent, Twenty-Fifth Session, *Decree on Indulgences* in
      ND 1686. See especially Pope Paul VI, *Indulgentiarum Doctrina*
      (1967) in ND 1687–1690.

6

Anointing of the Sick

And the resplendent olive bore fruit; in the olive there
is the sign of the sacrament of life, in which Christians
are perfected as priests and kings and prophets; oil
illumines the darkness, anoints the sick, and by its
hidden sacrament leads back the penitent.

Aphraates the Syrian, *Demonstrations*

Sickness is one of the negative consequences of the fallen
human condition which came about in the wake of original
sin. Despite great advances in medical science, human reason finds itself at present somewhat helpless in the face of
the mystery of disease and death as well as of seemingly
incurable illnesses like cancer and AIDS. Sickness presents a
great challenge and reminds man of his fragility. The human
reaction to suffering can be one of self-centredness and even
despair or the temptation to turn away from God. However,
"it can also make a person more mature, helping him discern
in his life what is not essential so that he can turn toward that
which is. Very often illness provokes a search for God and a
return to him."[1] In the light of the Redemption and Revelation wrought by Christ came the possibility of physical healing in certain cases, or at least of shedding a new light upon
sickness and death and giving a new meaning to these twin
enemies of mankind. All the sacraments apply the power of
Christ's Paschal mystery to human suffering and death and

145

one sacrament in particular, the Anointing of the Sick, applies the power of Christ's Redemption to the sick person. In this sacrament, as elsewhere in the Christian economy, the relation between physical and spiritual healing is unfolded.

6.1   Scriptural data

6.1.1   Old Testament

In the Old Covenant, sickness was often regarded as a direct consequence of sin. The origin of suffering and therefore sickness is indicated in original sin (Gn 3:16–19). Sometimes sickness was almost regarded as a punishment for sin: "If a man sins in the eyes of his Maker, may he fall under the care of the doctor"(Si 39:15). Nevertheless healing also comes from God: "My son, when you are ill, do not be depressed, but pray to the Lord and He will heal you" (Si 38:9). Elsewhere, as in the Book of Job, illness has a mysterious origin in a direct affliction by the spirit of evil, which although not willed by God, is permitted by Him for a greater good, namely the manifestation of God's victory over suffering. Tobias' words seemed to imply that both sickness and healing come from God: "For He had scourged me and now has had pity on me" (Tb 11:15). This theme is seen in several places in the Old Testament: "It is I who deal death and life; when I have struck it is I who heal" (Dt 32:39). Man implores healing from God (Ps 6:1–3) and this process is often linked to conversion, as God's forgiveness of sin initiates the physical healing (Ps 37:1–3). The initiative for healing comes from God, especially when the sickness is mysterious in origin: "No herb, no poultice cured them, but it was your word, Lord, which heals all things"(Ws 16:12). In some cases, a miraculous cure such as that of Hezekiah was accompanied by other wondrous external signs, prefiguring a sacramental view of healing (Is 38). In the prophetic literature of the Old Testament, the redemptive meaning of suffering was evident, a meaning which would be fulfilled in the coming of Christ: "By his sufferings shall my servant justify

many, taking their faults on himself" (Is 53:11). The prophetic vision also hoped for a messianic era when sin would
be overcome and illness would be vanquished (Is 57:18;
58:11).

6.1.2 New Testament

In the New Testament, sickness is also seen to be closely
bound up with man's sinful state, but Christian revelation
does not make a hasty identification between sickness and
punishment for sin. In regard to the man born blind, Jesus
affirmed: "Neither he nor his parents sinned, he was born
blind so that the works of God might be displayed in him" (Jn
9:3). Christ came to heal and redeem the whole person, body
and soul. In His ministry He very often took compassion on
the sick and cured them. In these healing episodes, Christ
frequently adopted external signs to manifest the action of
bringing relief to the sick. These signs included spittle and
the laying-on of hands (Mk 7:32–36), mud and washing (Jn
9:6–7). Physical contact with Jesus was an important factor in
the healing of the sick, for "power came out of Him that cured
them all" (Lk 6:19). Thus, the imposition of hands, a privileged sacramental sign, derives its meaning from Christ's
ministry. The healing of sickness, connected with Christ's
Resurrection, is an occasion for the showing forth of God's
glory; it is a special and theophanic moment (See Jn 11:4).

In His turn, Christ the Divine Physician sent out His
Apostles to heal people: the Twelve "anointed many sick
people with oil and cured them" (Mk 6:13; see Mt 10:1,8; Lk
9:2). This can be seen as the pre-Paschal institution of the
sacrament of Anointing of the Sick. The Redemption
brought about by Christ is an all-encompassing victory over
evil, sin and death, of which illness is but one aspect. As the
sacraments derive their power from the Paschal Mystery, the
post-Paschal actualization is made explicit by Christ before
His Ascension: "they will lay their hands on the sick who will
recover" (Mk 16:18).

The Anointing of the Sick was made yet more explicit in
the life of the Apostolic period of the Church as described by

St. James: "If one of you is ill, he should send for the elders of the Church, and they must anoint him with oil in the name of the Lord and pray over him. The prayer of faith will *save* the sick man and the Lord will *raise him up* again; and if he has committed any sins, he will be forgiven" (Jm 5:14–15). This passage indicates that the true elements of a sacrament are present, namely an outward sign of inward grace consisting of anointing with oil (the matter) and the prayer of the priest over the sick person (the form). The outward sign is accompanied by an inner operation of grace implied by the saving and raising up of the sick man. This denotes a curative process which is not exclusively the healing of the body, but above all the saving of the soul and the raising up of the soul by divine grace, and its preservation from despondency and despair. The institution by Christ of the sacrament is not explicit, but is implicit in the words "in the name of the Lord", that is according to the mandate and authority of Our Lord Jesus Christ, with which He had sent out the Apostles. Many Eastern Churches focus particularly on the anointing of the dying as prefigured in St. John's Gospel, where Mary anointed Christ six days before His Passion (Jn 12:3–8). While this episode clearly does not involve impending death through sickness, it can be seen in terms of the sickness of sin, which Jesus heals through His death. The relationship between a sacrament of the sick and one of the dying (Extreme Unction) recurs within the history of this sacrament, as will now be examined.

6.2   *Historical and theological development*

In the early centuries, there was not much written concerning the Anointing of the Sick. One reason for this may be that while the sacrament of Penance was carried out publicly, Anointing was administered privately. Therefore the latter rite attracted less attention and required less explanation than the sacraments of Christian initiation and of Penance. Nevertheless, even in the very early centuries, there is evidence that the sacrament of the Anointing of the Sick took place.

In the *Apostolic Tradition*, dating from around the year 215 and attributed to Hippolytus, a rite for the blessing of the oil of the sick by the bishop was indicated at the end of the Eucharistic prayer.[2] Tertullian, during his Montanist phase, in the early part of the third century referred in an obscure passage to the fact that the Christian Proculus had healed Severus "with oil."[3] A letter written in the year 416 by Pope Innocent I to the Bishop of Gubbio indicated the understanding of Anointing of the Sick at that time. The Pope affirmed the continuity of this sacrament with the rite mentioned by the Apostle St. James, and stated that the oil had to be blessed by the bishop; however, priests could also perform the anointing. Moreover, Innocent spoke of anointing carried out by lay people, but this must be considered as a sacramental rather than a sacrament, even though the distinction was not clear at that time. Nevertheless, Anointing of the Sick was regarded as "of the nature of a sacrament" since it could not be administered to someone undergoing Penance, and who was therefore excluded from the Eucharist.[4] Also in the fifth century, but in the East, St. Cyril of Alexandria insisted on "calling in the presbyters" after the manner of the Letter of St. James in the case of sickness.[5] Victor of Antioch described the significance of oil in the sacrament of Anointing: "Now oil is both a remedy against fatigue and a source of light and gladness. And so the anointing with oil signifies the mercy of God, a remedy for sickness and enlightenment of the heart."[6]

In the sixth century, St. Caesarius of Arles exhorted the faithful, in time of illness, to rely on the Eucharist and on the Anointing of the Sick, rather than be tempted to invoke pagan rites: "How much more correct and salutary it would be to hurry to the church, to receive the Body and Blood of Christ, and with oil that is blessed to anoint in all faith themselves and their dear ones; for according to what James the Apostle says, not only would they receive health of body, but also remission of sins."[7] It is notable that Caesarius encourages lay anointing, and also that Anointing was not restricted to those in danger of death. In the eighth century, the

Venerable Bede wrote the first extant commentary on the
Letter of St. James. St. Bede's references to the Sacrament
of the Sick indicate that anointing was carried out by the
presbyters, but also that lay people could make use of the oil
blessed by the bishop. He also seems to regard forgiveness of
sins as exclusively caused by the sacrament of Penance.[8] In
the early centuries, the oil which had been blessed by the
bishop was also employed by lay persons to anoint the sick
and the sick person could even anoint himself or herself with
the oil. As time went on, the distinction between this application of blessed oil as a sacramental and its employment as
the sacrament became progressively clearer. By the Middle
Ages, the oil was always exclusively reserved to the priest or
bishop in the context of the sacrament of Anointing of the
Sick.

During the Carolingian era, discipline had reached a low
ebb on the European Continent, and priests had become lax
in their obligations to anoint the sick. The reform of Charles
the Great insisted on the obligations of the clergy in administering the last rites of the Church, namely Penance, Extreme
Unction and Viaticum. These duties were inspired by Celtic
practice brought over by Irish monks and English missionary
scholars. Charles the Great decreed at Aachen in the year 801
"that all priests mercifully bestow on all who are sick before
the close of life Viaticum and Communion of the Body of
Christ. That, in accordance with the decisions of the holy
Fathers, if anyone is sick, let him be carefully anointed by
priests with oil to the accompaniment of prayers."[9] In this
manner, the Sacrament of the Sick gradually came to be
regarded as a sacrament of the dying. Actual texts exist, dating from the Carolingian period, which indicate the way the
rite of anointing was carried out. The rite is said to have been
developed from Roman, Gallican and Mozarabic sources in
the early part of the ninth century. After introductory
prayers, the sick person was anointed with sanctified oil,
making the sign of the cross on the back of the neck and on
the throat, and between the shoulders and on the breast.

The place where the pain was greatest was also anointed. The prayer which accompanied the anointing ran as follows:

> I anoint thee with holy oil in the name of the Father and of the Son and of the Holy Spirit, that the unclean spirit may not remain hidden in thee, nor in thy members, nor in thy organs, nor in any joint of thy members; rather, through the working of this mystery, may there dwell in thee the power of Christ, all-high, and of the Holy Spirit. And through this ointment of consecrated oil and our prayer, cured and warmed by the Holy Spirit mayest thou merit to receive thy former and even better health. Through Christ our Lord.[10]

It is notable that this prayer involved a triple invocation of the Holy Spirit, the Giver of both bodily and spiritual health. Also the sacrament was often administered by more than one priest. A final rubric in this rite also mentions additional anointing on the five senses, which had its influence on medieval practice.

In the Middle Ages, the idea developed that the sacrament of Anointing was not so much a healing of the body but more a preparation of the body and soul for the glory of the beatific vision. However, two schools of thought can be discerned among the writers of the twelfth and early thirteenth centuries. The first school regarded Anointing as essentially the Sacrament of the Sick, although it admitted that bodily healing does not always take place. An exponent of this first view was Hugh of St. Victor (died in 1141) who stated: "This sacrament was instituted for a twofold reason, namely both for the remission of sins and for the alleviation of bodily sickness.... But if perchance it is not expedient for him to have soundness of health and body, he unquestionably acquires by the reception of this anointing that health and alleviation which is of the soul."[11]

The other school of thought regarded the Anointing of the Sick as the sacrament of the departing, as can be seen in the writing of William of Auvergne, bishop of Paris, who died in 1248 and who prepared the way for the great scholastic doctors of the thirteenth century: "Now since those who are departing this world are soon to be presented to God, it is not

proper to doubt that they are to be sanctified from those
faults which have clung to them while in this world, just as
dust clings to the feet of the wayfarer, and from those slight
and daily blemishes which are usually called venial sins; for a
bride never approaches the bridegroom without some prepa-
ratory ablutions and fitting attire."[12] The great doctors who
followed, namely St. Albert the Great, St. Thomas Aquinas,
St. Bonaventure and Blessed John Duns Scotus all agreed
that the fundamental purpose of this sacrament was the
preparation of the soul for glory, and indicated that
Anointing should be conferred when the recipient was close
to death; hence the expression Extreme Unction was formulated. Nevertheless, there were differences among these
great Scholastics as to the principal effect of the sacrament.
For Bonaventure and Scotus, the main effect was seen to be
the final remission of venial sins: "But if we talk about venial
sin in the soul of one who is about to depart, then it can be
cured without danger of recurrence; and so, because the soul
can bear along with it such sins that must be purged by fire,
and which would hold it back from glory, God's mercy has
instituted a remedy by which the soul might be healed with
respect to the remission of guilt, as well as the remission in
part of punishment; and this is the sacrament of Extreme
Unction."[13] Blessed John Duns Scotus expressed the common later Scholastic view that Anointing was the sacrament
of the dying and was better administered at the point when
the person could no longer sin.

On the other hand, for St. Albert the Great and St.
Thomas Aquinas the principal effect was seen in terms of the
removal of the remnants of sin. By the expression "remains of
sin" (*reliquiae peccati*) is meant the consequences which weigh
upon the souls as a result of original and actual sin, and
includes the temporal punishment due to sin. St. Thomas
admitted that the sacrament does remit mortal and venial
sin, provided that the recipient places no obstacle to this forgiveness. However, the Angelic Doctor disagreed with the
view that it was instituted chiefly as a remedy for venial sin
which cannot be cured in this life, and concluded that "the

principal effect of this sacrament is the remission of sin, as to its remnants, and, consequently, even as to its guilt, if it is to be found."[14] The medieval vision then developed the concept that just as there are three sacraments of initiation (Baptism, Confirmation, Eucharist) which open the way to the Church on earth, so also there are three sacraments of the dying (Penance, Anointing, Eucharist), which open the way to the Church in Heaven.[15] Thus, Penance, Anointing, and the Eucharist are joined together as the three sacraments of Christian completion. Penance is administered for the remission of sins, Anointing for the remission of sin and its remnants and the Eucharist for the Communion of peace with God.

In 1439, the Council of Florence further encapsulated the preceding theological reflection and stated that Extreme Unction was to be administered to a sick person "whose life is feared for." The Council also explained that the recipient was to be anointed "on the eyes on account of sight, on the ears on account of hearing, on the nostrils on account of smelling, on the mouth on account of taste and speech, on the hands on account of touch, on the feet on account of movement, on the loins on account of the lust seated there."[16] This ritual sequence remained in place until after the Second Vatican Council. The Council of Trent taught that the Sacrament of the Sick is insinuated in the practice of the disciples of healing the sick, since they anointed many with oil and they recovered. Trent expounded, against the errors of the Reformers, the doctrine that the sacrament was "truly and properly" a sacrament instituted by Christ and promulgated by St. James.[17] The Council also rejected the error of Calvin that the text of St. James' Letter only refers to a charism of healing which no longer exists.[18] Trent also indicated that the sacrament forgives any sins which are still to be expiated and also removes the remains of sin, and by employing this formulation did not decide between the Thomistic and Scotistic positions as to the precedence given to the forgiveness of sin or to the remission of the remnants of sin. The Council of Trent also taught that Anointing "comforts and strengthens" the sick person in this hour of need, and furthermore restores physical health when this "is expedient for the salvation of the soul."[19] It is significant also that Trent did not only use the term Extreme Unction, but also the older expression Anointing of the Sick. Moreover, it taught that the sacrament could be administered to the seriously sick and not exclusively to those close to death.[20]

Further developments in the Church's teaching concerning Anointing of the Sick took place in the twentieth century. In the year 1907, the Holy Office condemned some of the errors of Modernism, among which was a denial that James intended to promulgate a sacrament of Christ. The Modernist idea proposed that the rite was simply a pious custom.[21] Later, in 1921, Pope Benedict XV gave a clearer idea of when the sacrament should be administered, and encouraged a broader interpretation of what constituted a danger of death. He instructed that those who were in their last crisis should not delay the reception of Anointing and Viaticum until they were about to lose consciousness, but rather "according to the teaching and precepts of the Church, they should be strengthened by these sacraments as soon as their condition worsens and one may prudently judge that there is danger of death."[22]

Along with the Second Vatican Council came the impetus to renew the rite of Anointing along the lines of a sacrament of healing rather than simply as a preparation for death. This was indicated by a return to the more ancient name for the sacrament: " 'Extreme Unction,' which may also and more fittingly be called 'Anointing of the Sick,' is not a sacrament for those only who are at the point of death. Hence, as soon as anyone of the faithful begins to be in danger of death from sickness or old age, the fitting time for him to receive the sacrament has certainly already arrived."[23] In 1972, Pope Paul VI, invoking his apostolic authority, modified the rite of Anointing so as to express more clearly the effects of the sacrament.[24] The community aspect of Anointing of the Sick was also rediscovered: "By the sacred Anointing of the Sick and the prayer of the priests the whole Church commends those who are ill to the suffering and glorified Lord that He may raise them up and save them. And indeed she exhorts them to contribute to the good of the People of God by freely uniting themselves to the passion and death of Christ."[25] The attitude of recent theology is clear on the one hand, that illness is an evil which should be strenuously resisted. On the other hand, sickness has a positive meaning as an opportunity to complete what is lacking in the sufferings of Christ for the salvation of the world, at the same time looking forward to the liberation of all creation to enjoy the glory of the children of God.[26]

6.3   The external sign

6.3.1   The matter

The remote matter of Anointing is oil which is generally blessed on Holy Thursday at the Chrism Mass by the bishop, according to the formula:

> Lord God, loving Father, you bring healing to the sick through Your Son Jesus Christ. Hear us as we pray to You in faith, and send the Holy Spirit, Man's Helper and Friend, upon this oil which nature has provided to serve the needs of men. May Your blessing + come upon all who are anointed with this oil, that they may be freed from pain and illness and made well again in body, mind, and soul. Father, may this oil be blessed for our use in the name of our Lord Jesus Christ who lives and reigns with You for ever and ever. Amen.

The oil is to be derived from the olive or substituted "as circumstances suggest, with another oil extracted from plants."[27] Animal or mineral oil cannot therefore be employed. Under special circumstances, when there is necessity to anoint a sick person and no oil consecrated by the bishop is available, a priest may bless the oil. In this case, any remaining oil is to be destroyed after use.[28] The proximate matter of the sacrament is the anointing of the particular parts of the body of the sick person with the oil. In the present rite of anointing, renewed by Pope Paul VI in 1972, the sick person is anointed on the forehead and on the palms of the hands. By custom, a priest is anointed on the backs rather than on the palms of the hands because of the previous anointing at ordination. In a case of necessity it is sufficient that one anointing only be given which should be on the forehead if this is possible, or if not, elsewhere. The minister is to anoint the sick person with his own hand, unless a grave reason indicates the use of an instrument.[29] Circumstances which would warrant the adoption of an instrument would include the risk of infecting, or being infected by, the sick person.

6.3.2   The form

The current form in the Latin Rite is based on the words from the Letter of St. James, and consists of a prayer with two parts: "Through this holy anointing may the Lord in His love and mercy help you with the grace of the Holy Spirit. May the Lord who frees you from your sin save you and raise you up." These words accompany the action of anointing. The rite of Anointing of the Sick can be either individual or for a group, and can occur either outside or within the celebration of Mass.

6.4   The minister

The bishop and priest are the only proper ministers of the sacrament of the sick.[30] Anointing the sick is a right and obligation for all pastors toward the faithful committed to their pastoral care. In the first place, the right and duty belongs to the bishop and this is reflected in the fact that he normally blesses the oil of the sick. The sacramental care of the sick is also entrusted to the parish priest and his assistants, to chaplains of hospitals and old-people's homes, and to superiors of major religious institutes. In the Latin Church anointing is generally celebrated by one priest; however, more than one priest may concelebrate the rite of anointing. In this case one priest should administer the matter and form of anointing, while the others may carry out other parts of the rite. All the priests may impose hands, which is a component of the rite though not part of the essential matter of the sacrament. In the Christian East, on the other hand, the tradition has been to interpret the injunction in the Letter of St. James literally when it states: "send for the elders" (Jm 5:14). The passage can also be interpreted in a general sense meaning "one of the elders", according to the Western practice. To this day in the East it is recommended that where this is the custom, the rite be administered by many priests if possible.[31] In some Eastern Churches, the ideal would be a concelebration with the mystical number of seven priests. For practical reasons, especially in rural areas, this presents some practical difficulties in emergencies.

In the history of the Church, as has been mentioned above, there have been cases of anointing by lay-people but this was not a sacrament. At present, in charismatic circles this still exists and should be regarded with the esteem of a sacramental. However, care should be taken to explain the difference between Anointing as a sacrament, and an anointing given in the manner of a blessing.

6.5   The recipient

6.5.1   Serious illness

The general condition for anointing is that any member of the faithful whose health is seriously impaired by sickness or old age can receive this sacrament. In many Orthodox Churches, this sacrament is not used exclusively for the sick, and sometimes the expression *euchelaion* (anointing with a prayer) is used instead of Anointing of the Sick. Nowadays, the condition of anointing is no longer that the recipient should to be close to death to be anointed. A sick person can be anointed before surgery whenever a serious illness is the reason for the surgery. The estimation of what constitutes serious illness has undergone considerable evolution in recent times. A sickness which was serious fifty years ago may no longer be so considered because of advances in medical science. For instance, pneumonia may often have been fatal in the past before the discovery of antibiotics. Nevertheless, judgment should generally be in favour of administering the sacrament when doubt arises concerning the gravity of the sickness. Elderly people may be anointed if they have become notably weakened even though no serious illness is present; the care of the elderly must take pride of place in the life of the Church. Since, for the legitimate administration of this sacrament, the danger of death must be intrinsically connected with sickness, causes such as shipwreck, an impending death sentence or threat of war would not justify the administration of Anointing of the Sick. In these latter cases, the sacrament to be offered is Penance. Sick children may be anointed if they have sufficient use of reason to be strengthened by the sacrament. The theological foundation for this condition is that because Anointing is orientated towards the forgiveness of sins, the recipient must have had the capacity for committing sin. As a rule of thumb, the age of reason is said to be around seven years. Below this age a sick child is to be confirmed, if that sacrament has not already been received. In cases of doubt as to whether or not a sick person has reached the age of reason, as can happen in the case of sub-normal young people, the sacrament of Anointing may be administered.[32] The unconscious may be anointed: it seems more appropriate that in the case of an unconscious sick person the Anointing of the Sick be administered rather than Penance. In other cases of unconsciousness, absolution would be indicated. Canon law discourages the administration of Anointing upon those who "obstinately persist in a manifestly grave sin."[33] The dead cannot be anointed, but if there is doubt, conditional anointing may be used. The issue also depends on theories about how long the soul takes to leave the body after death: some authors accept that anointing may be legitimately carried out until three hours after apparent death has taken place, but not after *rigor mortis* has set in.

6.5.2   Care of the dying

The care of the dying involves a continuous rite in which the sacrament of Penance is first administered, then Anointing and finally Viaticum. The basis for this order is that the recipient must be in a state of grace to receive Anointing if he or she is conscious. The Apostolic Indulgence at the moment of death is conferred after absolution according to the formula: "By the authority which the Apostolic See has given me, I grant you a full pardon and remission of all your sins in the name of the Father and of the Son + and of the Holy Spirit." This bestows the remission of all temporal punishment due to sin. Viaticum rather than Anointing is the sacrament for the dying; a distinctive feature of Viaticum is the renewal of baptismal promises if the recipient is still capable.

In the case of deathbed conversions, another sequence of sacraments may be involved in the pastoral care of the dying. For a non-Christian, this would consist of Christian Initiation for the dying, comprising Baptism, Confirmation and Viaticum. For the reception into full communion with the Catholic Church of a member of an ecclesial community deriving from the Reformation, the required sequence would comprise Penance, reception into full communion with the Catholic Church, Confirmation, and Viaticum. For a member of the separated Eastern Churches, the process would involve Penance, reception into full communion with the Catholic Church and Viaticum.

6.5.3   *Frequency of anointing*

During the Middle Ages when the Sacrament of the Sick was seen in the West as a sacrament of the dying, some theologians like Ivo of Chartres thought that the sick person could be anointed only once. However, this view was generally rejected. The sacrament of anointing may and should be repeated if a sick person suffers a relapse or in the same illness if the condition gets more critical. If a sick person who received the sacrament of Anointing recovers his or her health, he or she can receive this sacrament again in the case of another grave illness. An elderly person whose "frailty becomes more pronounced" may also receive the Anointing of the Sick on several occasions.[34]

6.5.4   Ecumenical questions

Eastern Christians (namely the Ancient Eastern Churches and the Orthodox Churches) separated from full communion with the Catholic Church can request the Sacrament of the Sick from a Catholic priest, when they have no possibility to receive this sacrament from their own priest. These recipients must ask for the sacrament of their own free will, and be properly disposed.[35] Similarly, Catholics may request Anointing from non-Catholic ministers who have valid orders, for example from Ancient Eastern, Orthodox, and Old Catholic priests.[36]

The possibility of conferring Anointing on members of those Christian denominations which have not maintained Apostolic Succession is more limited, because their degree of communion with the Catholic Church is more distant. As an exception the sacrament of Anointing may be given to a member of an ecclesial community. A precondition which must be met in this case is danger of death or other grave and pressing need, of which the local Ordinary is the judge. Also, the person must be unable to have recourse to his or her own minister. Furthermore, the Christian of an another denomination must freely ask for Anointing and be properly disposed.[37] When separated Christians do not have faith in this sacrament, then it is not permissible to give it. Moreover, Catholics may not receive Anointing of the Sick from those ministers belonging to Christian confessions whose Orders are not recognized as valid by the Catholic Church.

6.6   The effects

The ecclesial effect of Anointing is "the uniting of the sick person to the passion of Christ, for his own good and that of the whole Church."[38] The sacrament of Anointing brings about spiritual healing including the forgiveness of sins, if this has not already occurred through Penance. As regards this remission of sins, if a person is conscious, he should receive the remission of sins through confession. However, if he is unconscious, Anointing will eradicate mortal sins. A necessary condition for the forgiveness of sins is that the sinner has turned away from sin at least by a habitually continuing imperfect contrition. By Anointing of the Sick, venial sins and also temporal punishments due to sin are remitted. Therefore, the recipient with due disposition to whom this sacrament is administered will go straight to heaven after death, according to the theology of St. Thomas Aquinas and Blessed Duns Scotus. A further effect is that if it is God's will, physical healing can ensue, be it partial or total. Whether or not physical healing occurs is a mystery, but is surely connected with how, in God's providence, this gift would lead to the salvation of the healed person, and also to the spiritual benefit of those around him. A final effect of Anointing is the conferral upon the recipient of spiritual aid to face illness and eventually to prepare for his passing over to eternal life. The sacrament gives the person an awakened confidence in God's mercy and infuses strength to bear the hardships of sickness and of mortal agony, and to resist the temptations of the devil.

Notes

1   *CCC* 1501.
2   See Hippolytus, *Apostolic Tradition* V, 2 in *SF* p.277.
3   Tertullian, *Ad Scapulam* 4, 5 in *CCL* 2, 1130.
4   See Pope Innocent I, *Letter to Decentius, Bishop of Gubbio* (416) in ND 1603.
5   See St. Cyril of Alexandria, *On Adoration in Spirit and in Truth*, 6 in *SF* pp.281–282.
6   Victor of Antioch, *Commentary on Mark 6:13* in *SF* p.282.
7   St. Caesarius of Arles, *Sermon 279*, 5 in *SF* p.285.
8   See St. Bede the Venerable, *On the Epistle of James*, 5 in *SF* pp.286–287.
9   Charles the Great, *Capitulary of Aachen* (801), 21 in *SF* p.290.
10   *A Carolingian Rite of Anointing the Sick* in *SF* pp.293–295.
11   Hugh of St. Victor, *On the Sacraments* 2, 15, 3 in *SF* p.297.
12   William of Auvergne, *Opera Omnia*, 1,2,3 in *SF* p.298.
13   St. Bonaventure, *On the Sentences*, 4, dist. 23, a.1, q.1, in *SF* p.300.
14   St. Thomas Aquinas, *Summa Theologiae* Supplement, q.30, a.1.

15   See *CCC* 1525.
16   Council of Florence, *Decree for the Armenians* in ND 1613.
17   Council of Trent, Fourteenth Session, *Doctrine on Extreme Unction* in ND 1636, 1656.
18   Council of Trent, Fourteenth Session, *Doctrine on Extreme Unction*, canon 2 in ND 1657.
19   Council of Trent, Fourteenth Session, *Doctrine on Extreme Unction*, in ND 1637.
20   Council of Trent, Fourteenth Session, *Doctrine on Extreme Unction*, in ND 1638: "This anointing is to be administered to the sick, especially to those who are so seriously ill that they seem near to death."
21   See Holy Office, Decree *Lamentabili* in ND[1660/48].
22   Pope Benedict XV, Apostolic Letter *Sodalitatem Nostrae Dominae* in ND1661.
23   Vatican II, *Sacrosanctum concilium*, 73.
24   Pope Paul VI, Apostolic Constitution *Sacram unctionem infirmorum* (1972).
25   Vatican II, *Lumen gentium*, 11.3. See also Sacred Congregation for Divine Worship *Hominum dolores* (1972), 33.
26   See Sacred Congregation for Divine Worship *Hominum dolores* (1972), 3. See also Col 1:24; Rm 8:19–21.
27   Pope Paul VI, Apostolic Constitution *Sacram unctionem infirmorum* (1972).
28   See *CIC* 999 and also Sacred Congregation for Divine Worship, *Hominum dolores* (1972), 22.
29   See *CIC* 1000, §1.
30   Council of Trent, Fourteenth Session, *Doctrine on Extreme Unction*, in ND 1638, 1659.
31   See *CCEO* 737 §2.
32   See *CIC* 1005.
33   *CIC* 1007.
34   *CCC* 1515.
35   See *ED* 124.
36   See *ED* 132.
37   See *ED* 130–131.
38   *CCC* 1532.

7
Sacred Orders

Christ is at once Priest and Sacrifice, God and Temple: the Priest through Whom we are reconciled, the Sacrifice by which we are reconciled, the Temple in which we are reconciled, the God to Whom we are reconciled.

St. Fulgentius of Ruspe, *To Peter on faith*

In nearly all religions, there is a figure who presides, officiates, and most especially offers worship on behalf of the people, one who is set apart in order to be a mediator between God and people. These cult figures foreshadow, even in a primitive way, the priesthood of the Eternal Priest Jesus Christ. The Lord wished that His priesthood, by which He offered the sacrifice for the Redemption of the human race, be continued after He rose again and ascended to His Father. He shared this priesthood with His closest followers, His Apostles, to whom He gave the command to hand on this priestly dignity within the Church.

7.1 Institution

7.1.1 Old Testament prefiguration and preparation

In the Old Testament which charts the life of God's chosen race, this entire people was set apart by God to be "a kingdom of priests and a holy nation." (Ex 19:6; see Is 61:6). The priestly people of Israel were set apart and called by God from among the nations, and they entered into communion with the Lord through the Covenant. However, within the people of Israel, God chose one of the twelve tribes, that of Levi, and set it apart for liturgical service; the Lord Himself was its inheritance (Nb 1:48–53). The Church sees in the ministry of the Levites a prefiguration of the diaconate, reflected in the consecratory prayer for their ordination:

> Almighty God. . . You make the Church, Christ's body, grow to its full stature as a new and greater temple. You enrich it with every kind of grace and perfect it with a diversity of members to serve the whole body in a wonderful pattern of unity. You established a threefold ministry of worship and service, for the glory of Your name. As ministers of Your tabernacle You chose the sons of Levi and gave them Your blessing as their everlasting inheritance.[1]

Among the chosen people of God, particular men were called to exercise priesthood in a special way and were a type of Christ the Eternal High Priest. Melchizedek was a priestly figure who foreshadowed Christ, the High Priest: "Melchizedek king of Salem brought bread and wine; he was a priest of God Most High" (Gn 14:18; cf. Heb 7:1–10). The sacerdotal office involved offering sacrifices and governing the people of God. The high priests of the Old Covenant foreshadow the bishops of the New Law, as expressed in the consecratory prayer for episcopal ordination: "God the Father of our Lord Jesus Christ, . . . by Your gracious word You have established the plan of Your Church. From the beginning, You chose the descendants of Abraham to be Your holy nation. You established rulers and priests and did not leave Your sanctuary without ministers to serve You."[2]

Moses consecrated Aaron and his sons as priests of the Old Law, with a special rite (see Ex 29:1–30; Lv 8–10). He also set apart seventy elders with whom he shared the spirit of wisdom, and they helped him to rule the people (Nm 11:24–25). The Church understands that these assistants prefigure the presbyteral rank of the priesthood, as is expressed in the consecratory prayer from the rite of ordination: "Lord, holy Father,... when you had appointed high priests to rule your people, you chose other men next to them in rank and dignity to be with them and to help them in their task.... You extended the spirit of Moses to seventy wise men.... You shared among the sons of Aaron the fullness of their father's power."[3]

The Messianic psalm can be applied to the royal aspect of the priesthood of Christ:

> The Lord will wield from Sion
> your sceptre of power:
> rule in the midst of all your foes.
>
> A prince from the day of your birth
> on the holy mountains;
> from the womb before the dawn I begot you.
>
> The Lord has sworn an oath He will not change.
> 'You are a priest for ever,
> a priest like Melchizedek of old' (Ps 109:2–4).

The psalm is a prophetic reminder of the divinity of Christ, expressed in His co-eternity with the Father: "from the womb before the dawn I begot you." It is this divinity united with His human nature, which makes Christ's priesthood possible. At the same time, the kingly aspect of the priesthood builds on the kingly element in man's nature, given to him in creation: "You formed man in Your own likeness and set him over the whole world to serve You his Creator, and to rule over all creatures."[4]

Some of the prophets were priests of the Old Dispensation. It seems that Isaiah received his vision of the Lord within the Temple (Is 6:1–9). Ezekiel was also a priest (Ez 1:3). Jeremiah, as a member of a priestly family (Jr 1:1), looked forward to an increasing interiorization of God's covenant among His people, and this was fulfilled in the New and Eternal Covenant which God made in Christ (Jr 31:33). In the Old Testament, the glories of the priesthood were prefigured in the offerings of Melchizedech, and the Sacrifice of

Abraham "our father in faith". These glories are described, among other places, in the book of Ecclesiasticus:

> How splendid he was with the people thronging
>   around him,
> when he emerged from the curtained shrine,
> like the morning star among the clouds,
> like the moon at the full,
> like the sun shining on the Temple of the Most High,
> like the rainbow gleaming against brilliant clouds,
> like roses in the days of spring,
> like lilies by a freshet of water,
> like a sprig of frankincense in summer time,
> like fire and incense in the censer,
> like a vessel of beaten gold
> encrusted with every kind of precious stone,
> like an olive tree loaded with fruit,
> like a cypress soaring to the clouds;
> when he put on his splendid vestments,
> and clothed himself in glorious perfection,
> when he went up to the holy altar,
> and filled the sanctuary precincts with his grandeur.
>   (Si 50:5–11)

The permanence of the priesthood, deriving from the eternity of the union between Christ and His Mystical Bride, the Church, is prefigured already in the Old Testament Song of Songs: "Set me like a seal on your heart" (Sg 8:6). However, in comparison with the reality, the Old Testament is like a shadow: "Types and shadows have their ending, for the newer rite is here."[5] The priesthood of the Old Law, while it was "instituted to proclaim the Word of God and to restore communion with God by sacrifices and prayer," nevertheless remained "powerless to bring about salvation, needing to repeat its sacrifices ceaselessly and being unable to achieve a definitive sanctification, which only the sacrifice of Christ would accomplish."[6]

7.1.2   Institution of Orders by Christ

The priesthood of Christ is based upon the mystery of the Incarnation. In His own Person, Christ unites God and Man, which is the essence of the sacerdotal office. Christ is at one and the same time a transcendent and a compassionate High Priest (see Heb 4: 15–16; 5:1–10; 7:20–28; 8; 9). The power to save belongs to God alone and comes from Him and yet "it is not as if we had a high priest who was incapable of feeling our weaknesses with us; but we have One who has been tempted in every way that we are, though He is without sin" (Heb 4:15). Therefore, in Christ, the power to save comes from His Godhead, and the ability to save mankind in particular derives from His Manhood. In the words of Pope St. Gregory the Great: "Unless He were true God, He could bring us no aid; unless He were true Man, He could offer us no example."[7] Christ is the Mediator of the New Covenant (Heb 8:6) and "there is only one mediator between God and man, Himself a Man, Christ Jesus" (I Tm 2:5). Christ's central priestly action was accomplished through His single sacrifice on the Altar of the Cross, where He "achieved the eternal perfection of all whom He is sanctifying" (Heb 10:14).

The entire ministry of Christ upon this earth was prophetic. Christ is "the Way, the Truth and the Life" and no one can approach the Father except through Him (Jn 14:6). Christ is the Truth who has come to reveal all truth to mankind, the truth about the relation between God and man. Christ shares the very life of the Holy Trinity, by the power of the Holy Spirit, Who continues the prophetic action of Christ in His Church: "The Holy Spirit Whom the Father will send in My name will teach you everything and remind you of all I have said to you" (Jn 14:26).

The kingly aspect of Christ's priesthood consists in various aspects. First, He is God, the Lord of creation Who "sustains the universe by His powerful command" (Heb 1:3), and all things were created through Him (cf. Jn 1:3). Second, His human nature is royally anointed with the Holy Spirit: "Therefore God, your God, has anointed you with the oil of gladness above other kings: your robes are fragrant with aloes and myrrh" (Ps 44:7–8). Third, in His victory over sin and

death, Christ is King. But in the battle against the powers of
death, Christ's kingly Head was crowned with thorns:

> Death with life contended:
> combat strangely ended!
> Life's own Champion, slain,
> yet lives to reign.[8]

The aim of the sacerdotal action of Christ, Priest, Prophet
and King lies in accomplishing the Father's plan for the
fulness of time to "bring everything together under Christ, as
Head, everything in the heavens and everything on earth"
(Ep 1:10).

Between the perpetuation of the redemptive sacrifice and
that of the priesthood of Christ, there exists a close analogy.
Both are unique and irrepeatable. Yet, as has been seen, the
Eucharistic Sacrifice of the Church renders present the Sacrifice of Christ upon Calvary. "The same is true of the one
priesthood of Christ; it is made present through the ministerial priesthood without diminishing the uniqueness of
Christ's priesthood."[9] Various steps in the New Testament
indicate Christ's foundation of a permanent sacrament of
Order, allowing chosen men to share His priesthood within
His Church. These steps run side by side with the very foundation of the Church, and are intimately connected with it.
The institution of the Petrine office is promised before
Easter and realized after Christ's Resurrection (Mt
16:13–19; Jn 21:15–17). The Pope as St. Peter's successor
enjoys a special power over the sacraments and their ministers, as implied by the conferral upon him of the ministry of
"binding and loosing". During His earthly ministry, Jesus
Christ chose twelve Apostles, who were prefigured in the
twelve tribes of the people of the Old Covenant (Mk
3:13–19; Lk 6:12–16). Christ endowed them with His own
mission and intended that the apostolic office continue permanently in the Church. (Mt 10:1–16). After His Resurrection, Christ instructed the Apostles to preach the Good
News of salvation to all the world (Mt 28:16–20; Mk
16:14–18). The apostolic office is part of the very nature of
the Church as indicated in the Book of the Apocalypse,

where in the New Heavens and New Earth, the New Jerusalem, "the city walls stood on twelve foundation stones, each
one of which bore the name of one of the twelve Apostles of
the Lamb" (Rv 21:14). The apostolic office cannot therefore
be considered as merely a role or a function but a reality eternally inscribed upon the very nature of the Church. It would
seem that the Apostles received their consecration as
high-priests of the New Law, from Christ at the Last Supper.
In His priestly prayer, Christ ordained His Apostles with
these words: "Consecrate them in the truth; Your word is
truth. As You sent Me into the world, I have sent them into
the world, and for their sake I consecrate Myself so that they
too may be consecrated in truth. I pray not only for these, but
for those also who through their words will believe in Me" (Jn
17:17–20). This prayer implies an apostolic succession in
which the power of the priesthood would be handed on in
such a way that all ages would hear God's word and celebrate
Christ's sacraments. When Christ instituted the Holy
Eucharist, He offered a true Sacrifice and instructed His
Apostles in the following terms: "Do this as a memorial of
Me" (Lk 22:19). In order that the Eucharistic Sacrifice be
renewed continually, Christ gave his Apostles power to bring
this about, by conferring the fulness of His priesthood upon
them. After His Resurrection, Christ imparted to His consecrated Apostles the power to remit sins, a power which
derived from His newly-accomplished Paschal Mystery (cf.
Jn 20:22–23).

Alongside the Apostles, Christ chose seventy-two co-
workers, who would collaborate with His Apostles at a lower
level (Lk 10:1–20). The Church sees in these co-workers the
origin of the presbyteral order, who are fellow workers with
the bishops. Despite the fact that Christ does not explicitly
mention deacons, they are implicitly part of His economy in
the sacrament of Order, and He willed their institution. The
whole exercise of Christ's priestly ministry was diaconal, for
He "came not to be served but to serve, and to give His life as
a ransom for many" (Mt 20:28). This passage illustrates both
the diaconal aspect of Christ's service and the sacerdotal

aspect of offering His life as a ransom. It will be seen that in the development of the sacrament of Order, both the sacerdotal and diaconal aspects are present both in being and in action.

The sacrament of Order is of divine institution, which means that Christ willed to set up this sacrament and actually instituted it. Divine institution should be distinguished from, but not set up in opposition to, ecclesiastical institution. Ecclesiastical institution is applied to structures and offices which the Church has erected in the course of time, and which, in themselves, are not contained in the deposit of revelation. Thus we hold that the Papacy, the episcopate, presbyterate, and diaconate are of divine institution while cardinals, monsignors, canons and minor orders are of ecclesiastical institution. Because an office is of ecclesiastical institution means that it can be changed, but it does not imply that it is unnecessary or that it is of merely human invention. Certain structures of ecclesiastical institution are, in fact, often intimately connected with other features which are themselves of divine institution. For instance, the cardinalate is a structure tightly connected with the election of the Pope, whose office is divinely willed and instituted. A further example is that the religious life in general is of divine institution (Mt 19:20–22; cf. 13:44–46), but a particular religious order is, under divine inspiration, erected by the Church. Thus religious life will never die out in the Church, even though the continuation of each concrete religious order is not guaranteed.

7.2 Historical and theological development

7.2.1 Orders in the primitive Church

The title of apostle was gradually extended beyond those who constituted the group of the Twelve. Matthias was elected to fill the place left by Judas, and so was listed as one of the twelve Apostles (Ac 1:15–26). James, mentioned in the Letter to the Galatians, is no longer considered to be James the son of Alphaeus, but rather one who had known

Jesus and who had a certain prominence in the primitive
Church. He is regarded as enjoying apostolic power (Gal
1:19; 2:9). The title of Apostle was also assigned to Paul and
Barnabas (Ac 14:4, 14). The progression in the use of this
title is seen in St. Paul's description of the appearances of
the risen Christ: "First He appeared to Cephas and secondly
to the Twelve. Next He appeared to more than five hundred
of the brothers at the same time, most of whom are still alive,
though some have died; then He appeared to James, and
then to all the apostles; and last of all He appeared to me too"
(I Co 15:5–8). The office of being an Apostle involved an
investiture which consisted of the laying-on of hands and a
prayer, as can be seen in the case of Paul and Barnabas (Ac
13:3). Those who were Apostles, but not numbered among
the Twelve shared in common with the Twelve an episcopal
power and also the privilege of having seen the risen Christ,
and sharing the foundational quality of the experience of the
early Church. However, being part of the Twelve involves
more: it means having been present the whole time the Lord
Jesus was exercising His ministry, and sharing the experience of the Paschal Mystery (Ac 1:22). St. Paul, in particular,
was conscious of a priestly role, which he had received and
which he was to transmit: "He has appointed me as a priest of
Jesus Christ, and I am to carry out my priestly duty by bringing the Good News from God to the pagans, and so make
them acceptable as an offering, made holy by the Holy
Spirit" (Rm 15:16).

It is evident that the Apostles shared with others the sacrament of Order which they possessed in its fulness. What
remains less clear is the concrete way in which they handed
on their power of Orders in the primitive Church. Not all
scholars agree that those who were designated with the title
of overseer (*episcopos*) in the apostolic era were in fact
endowed with the fulness of the priesthood.[10] Nevertheless,
it is commonly held that at least Timothy and Titus, whom
St. Paul set over the churches of Ephesus and Crete, enjoyed
episcopal orders. Titus was given the power of organizing the
church in Crete and of appointing elders (*presbyteroi*) in the

various towns (Tt 1:5). Timothy was reminded about the gift which he received in episcopal ordination: "You have in you a spiritual gift which was given to you when the prophets spoke and when the body of elders laid their hands on you; do not let it lie unused" (I Tm 4:14). This text can be taken to indicate the laying-on of hands as a central rite in ordination, its collegial quality and also the sacramental character imparted thereby.

As regards the delineation of a second rank of the sacrament of order, there is a problem, namely that the Greek New Testament expressions elder (*presbyteros*) and overseer or presiding elder (*episcopos*), in the earliest times did not univocally correspond to the later terms priest and bishop.[11] Indeed in some passages, the overseers seem to be identified with the elders (Tt 1:5, 7; Ac 20:17, 28). What seems clear however, is that both in the Jewish-Christian communities and among the Gentiles, the primitive Christian communities were governed by a body of elders. It is probable that these elders were endowed with the fullness of the priesthood, so as to be able to confer the power of orders to other elders. In this primitive era, a high concentration of men of episcopal rank would have been necessary to ensure a rapid expansion of the Church. The spread of the Church would have required the convenient ordination of men to celebrate the Eucharist. This rapidity of expansion and corresponding ordination is borne out by St. Paul's prudent injunction to Timothy: "Do not be too quick to lay hands on any man" (I Tm 5:22). The overseers and elders were appointed by the apostles (Ac 14:23) or their representatives (Tt 1:5) by the laying-on of hands (I Tm 5:22), and their powers were of divine institution (Ac 20:28). The body of elders gradually developed into communities ruled by one bishop and a college of priests; a system involving a monarchical episcopate would have been in place by about 100 AD. There may have also been some intermediate development but this is subject to a certain amount of speculation. In other words, within a relatively short period, those with episcopal powers were regularly ordaining men of the second rank, who enjoyed sacramental orders corresponding to the priesthood which we know today.

A further question regards the diaconate. The ordination of the Seven described in the Acts of the Apostles (Ac 6:1–6), the earliest existing account of an ordination, is accepted by many theologians, right from the time of St. Irenaeus, to refer to that of deacons.[12] Nevertheless, there is another school of thought, dating back to St. John Chrysostom, which does not make this rapid identification.[13] More recently some scholars consider that the Seven were ordained presbyters.[14] However, the presence of a diaconal office elsewhere in the New Testament (I Tm 3:8–13) indicates that a lower rank of orders existed which was associated with service (they should "carry out their duties well") and preaching ("conscientious believers in the mystery of faith"). It is possible that the *diaconos* mentioned in the New Testament is also not yet the deacon known by the later Church, but a figure endowed with a higher power of orders; however he was entrusted with a specific role of service.

In conclusion, it can be proposed that the Apostles had all the power of orders which they shared in different ways with those whom they subsequently ordained. It is also accepted that in the generation succeeding the Apostles a hierarchy of bishops, priests and deacons was established everywhere in the early rapidly-growing Church of Christ.

7.2.2   *Patristic period*

At the beginning of the second century, around 100 AD, St. Ignatius of Antioch wrote about the threefold sacrament of order: "Let everyone revere the deacons as Jesus Christ, the bishop as image of the Father, and the presbyters as the senate of God and the assembly of the apostles. For without them, one cannot speak of the Church."[15] St. Ignatius bore witness to the monarchical episcopate at Antioch, in his letter to the Ephesians: "Your justly respected clergy, who are a credit to God, are attuned to their bishop like the strings of a harp, and the result is a hymn of praise to Jesus Christ from minds that are in unison, and affections that are in harmony."[16] Around the middle of the second century, St. Irenaeus drew up a list of the bishops of Rome, and documented the monarchical succession of the bishops of Smirne and also of all the other local churches in the world at that time.[17]

St. Gregory of Nyssa outlined an analogy between the other sacraments, in particular the Holy Eucharist, and the priesthood:

> Also, the bread at the beginning is only common bread, but when it is consecrated during the Mysteries it becomes the Body of Christ.... The same power of the word makes the priest venerable and worthy of respect.... Recently, only yesterday, he was one of many, one of the people. Then at once he becomes the guide, the head, the master of piety, the initiator into the hidden mysteries. And this is without a change in his bodily shape. Externally he remains the same as he was, but his soul has been transformed for the better by an invisible force and grace.[18]

In the Gospel of Saint John and in the letter to the Hebrews, the essential unity between the priesthood of Christ and the Holy Sacrifice of the Mass, identical with the Sacrifice of Calvary is clearly shown. The Church Fathers further elaborated this doctrine. For instance, St. John Chrysostom, in one of the earliest and greatest monographs on the priesthood, stated: "Since no one can enter the kingdom of heaven if he be not regenerated by water and the Holy Spirit, and since whoever does not eat of the flesh of the Lord is deprived of eternal life; moreover since these things can only be carried out through the hands of priests, who without their help can flee from the fires of hell or obtain the crown set aside for the elect?"[19] Testimonies to the existence of the diaconate are ancient. St. Hippolytus described the ceremony of the ordination of deacons which involved the laying-on of hands and by a prayer.[20] St. Ignatius of Antioch regarded deacons as "ministers of the mysteries of Jesus Christ... and not simply distributors of food and drink, but servants of the Church of God."[21]

From the third century, alongside the divinely instituted diaconate, presbyterate and episcopate, there emerged in the West five other levels according to the Church's institution: subdeacon, acolyte, exorcist, lector, porter (doorkeeper). A letter of Pope Cornelius to Bishop Fabius dating from around 250 AD listed seven ranks in the Church of Rome: priest, deacon, subdeacon, acolyte, exorcist, lector and porter.[22] The subdiaconate and the four minor orders developed because of liturgical needs for auxiliary ministers in divine worship. The four levels preceding the subdiaconate became known as minor orders, and priesthood diaconate and subdiaconate were known as major orders. This structure remained in place in the West until the reforms which took place in the wake of the Second Vatican Council. In Eastern Christendom on the other hand, the hierarchy was structured according to the following scheme: bishop, priest, deacon, subdeacon, lector.

The question of the relation between the presbyterate and the episcopate became the subject of discussion in the West under the influence of Ambrosiaster and St. Jerome. The latter maintained that the difference between bishops and priests was merely a matter of jurisdiction and not of sacramental grace or power. Blessed Rabanus Maurus divided the episcopate in a three-fold hierarchy, listing the dignity of patriarch, metropolitan and bishop.[23] The issue of the nature of the episcopal office developed further in the Middle Ages.

7.2.3   Later development

Among the Scholastic theologians of the West, the sevenfold structure of the sacrament of Order was taught in the Middle Ages. Many theologians during that epoch held that all seven Orders had sacramental value and impressed a character. The highest order was the priesthood, which was considered by Hugh of St. Victor and Peter Lombard to be divided into two dignities, the presbyterate and the episcopate. However, the episcopate was not regarded as an order, since it does not confer any extra power with respect to the Eucharist. St. Albert the Great held that the episcopal office

merely involved an increased power of jurisdiction. St.
Thomas Aquinas and St. Bonaventure took a more nuanced
position. For Bonaventure, while the episcopate was not
regarded as a separate order, nevertheless he thought that
there was a dignity which was not taken away when the jurisdiction was removed. St. Thomas indicated that the episcopate is an order in a certain sense, since the Bishop has a
greater power over the Mystical Body of Christ than does the
priest; however, with respect to the Eucharistic Body of
Christ, the bishop has no more power than the priest.[24]
There were, however, other medieval positions. William of
Auxerre followed the Decree of Gratian and proposed nine
ranks in the sacrament of order: doorkeeper, lector, exorcist,
acolyte, subdeacon, deacon, priest, bishop, archbishop.[25]
Peter Olivi maintained that only the priesthood and the
episcopate conferred a sacramental character. Blessed John
Duns Scotus clearly taught that the episcopate was a distinct
order; the bishop had the power of conferring all the orders
and thus possessed a supreme value.[26]

The Reformation provided a need to reaffirm the existence and the nature of Christ's priesthood as it is shared by
His ministers in the Church. The Reformers insisted on a
one-sided and exclusive interpretation of the unicity of
Christ as the Mediator. Therefore they rejected the existence of a ministerial priesthood within the Church, so that
they accepted only the universal priesthood of all the faithful. The denial of the existence of the sacrament of Order
was of a piece with the Reformers' rejection of the sacrificial
nature of the Mass. In response to these errors, the Council
of Trent affirmed: "Sacrifice and priesthood are by the ordi-
nance of God so united that both have existed under every
law. Since, therefore, in the New Testament the Catholic
Church has received from the institution of Christ the holy,
visible sacrifice of the Eucharist, it must be acknowledged
that there exists in the Church a new, visible and external
priesthood."[27] The Council also taught that bishops were
superior to priests, but did not enter into the precise nature
of the superiority, be it juridical or sacramental. Nevertheless

the Council did take a step in the direction of the sacramental superiority of the episcopate by stating that "the bishops who have succeeded the apostles, principally belong to this hierarchical Order."[28] Thereafter, the majority of post-Tridentine theologians affirmed the sacramentality of the episcopate. Similarly, the Council did not decide the question whether the superiority of the bishop over the priest with regard to the power of jurisdiction and the power of consecration was of divine or simply of ecclesiastical institution.

The Modernist tendency towards a subjectivist and an evolutionary concept of truth coupled with a liberal approach to biblical criticism, led to an attempt to undermine the doctrine of the divine institution of the sacrament of Order. Instead, since one of the fundamental principles of Modernism was historical development, this system proposed that bishops and priests developed according to purely human and social factors. Thus the Modernists asserted that those presiding over the Eucharist gradually acquired power as it became a liturgical action. They also denied the bishops perpetuated the office and mission of the Apostles. These errors were among those condemned by Pope St. Pius X in the year 1907.[29]

Pius XII reinforced, in his teaching on the matter of the sacrament of Ordination, the theological development towards an acceptance that only episcopate, presbyterate and diaconate are of divine institution, while the lower orders are of ecclesiastical institution. He considered under the heading of the sacrament of Order only the diaconate, presbyterate, and episcopate.[30] The Second Vatican Council took this development further by specifying that the episcopate is a sacramental step above the presbyterate:

> The holy synod teaches, moreover, that the fullness of the sacrament of Orders is conferred by episcopal consecration, that fullness, namely, which both in the liturgical tradition of the Church and in the language of the Fathers of the Church is called the high priesthood, the acme of the sacred ministry.... In fact, from tradition, which is expressed especially in

the liturgical rites and in the customs of both the Eastern and
Western Church, it is abundantly clear that by the imposition of hands and through the words of the consecration, the
grace of the Holy Spirit is given, and a sacred character is impressed.[31]

The Catechism of the Catholic Church further crystallized
doctrinal teaching on the nature of the sacrament of Order,
and in particular upon the relationship which holds between
the sacerdotal order at episcopal and presbyteral levels and
the diaconal order:

> Catholic doctrine, expressed in the liturgy, the Magisterium,
> and the constant practice of the Church, recognizes that
> there are two degrees of ministerial participation in the
> priesthood of Christ: the episcopate and the presbyterate.
> The diaconate is intended to help and serve them. For this
> reason the term *sacerdos* in current usage denotes bishops and
> priests but not deacons. Yet Catholic doctrine teaches that
> the degrees of priestly participation (episcopate and pres-
> byterate) and the degree of service (diaconate) are all three
> conferred by a sacramental act called "ordination," that is, by
> the sacrament of Holy Orders.[32]

While the Council of Trent referred to the divine institution of a hierarchy of bishops, priest and ministers, it did not
specify whether diaconate was part of the sacrament of
Order.[33] Although the Second Vatican Council favoured the
idea that diaconate is part of the sacrament of Order, it did
not state clearly that a sacramental character is imparted in
diaconate ordination: "At a lower level of the hierarchy are to
be found deacons, who receive the imposition of hands not
unto the priesthood, but unto the ministry. For, strengthened by sacramental grace they are dedicated to the People
of God, in conjunction with the bishop and his body of
priests, in the service of the liturgy, of the Gospel and of
works of charity."[34] The Catechism went further and is a clear
statement that diaconate is fully part of the sacrament of
Order: "Deacons share in Christ's mission and grace in a special way. The sacrament of Holy Orders marks them with an
imprint ('character') which cannot be removed and which

configures them to Christ, who made Himself the 'deacon' or servant of all."[35] In the West, entrance to the clerical state, incardination into a diocese or religious institute and the promise of celibacy are associated with diaconate. The permanent diaconate was restored by the Second Vatican Council, which allows the possibility of married men being ordained deacons.

The Second Vatican Council reiterated the doctrine concerning the relation between ministerial, hierarchical priesthood and the priesthood of the faithful: "Though they differ essentially and not only in degree, the common priesthood of the faithful and the ministerial or hierarchical priesthood are none the less ordered one to another; each in its own proper way shares in the one priesthood of Christ. The ministerial priest, by the sacred power that he has, forms and rules the priestly people; in the person of Christ he effects the Eucharistic Sacrifice and offers it to God in the name of all the people."[36] The Church has also reaffirmed that the priestly ministry originates in the apostolic succession. Furthermore, in order to counteract certain present day errors, it has been necessary to reiterate the doctrine that only a priest can consecrate the Holy Eucharist, and that this priesthood is conferred by sacred ordination. A restatement of this doctrine was necessary because of the mistaken notion that the priesthood evolves or emerges in some way from the Christian community.[37]

The Church holds that while the episcopate, presbyterate and diaconate are part of the sacrament of Order, those elements known as minor orders are sacramentals. These lower orders were revised in 1972 by Pope Paul VI. At one time, the tonsure received before minor orders marked the beginning of the clerical state; now diaconate is the introduction to the clerical state in the West. In East Christendom, subdiaconate is the point of entry into the clerical state. In the present Western discipline, the first step towards ordination is admission to candidacy, then the ministries of lector and acolyte follow and are given by installation, not by ordination. The ministries of lector and acolyte are lay ministries and can be given to lay-people: they are permanent and, with the permission of the local pastor can be exercised anywhere in the world. This distinguishes them from the commissioned reader or extraordinary minister of communion who exercise their office for a period of time and require renewal. Other lay ministries, such as that of catechist, can be introduced and the episcopal conference must ask the Holy See for permission to introduce these functions.

The relation between the levels of the sacrament of Order can be summarized as follows. The sacerdotal part of Order which consists of presbyterate and episcopate is essentially a participation in Christ's priesthood as mediator between God and men. This mediation proceeds from God to man, and also returns from man to God, as is especially exemplified in the Holy Eucharist. The diaconal level of order is distinct and different from mediation, and rather involves service as its keynote. However, since the presbyterate and episcopate "contain" the diaconate, they are also ministries of service as well as of mediation. This truth was expressed liturgically in the fact that the bishop used to wear a light-weight deacon's dalmatic under the chasuble. In this way, Christ Priest and Servant, shares at different levels with different Orders His sacerdotal and diaconal power. In another formulation, the deacon mediates the Word of God, the priest the Word and the Eucharist; the bishop mediates the Word, the Eucharist and the Church.

7.3   The sacramental sign

7.3.1   The matter

Already in the Old Testament, the laying-on of hands was a significant gesture as regards the constitution of blessing and power within the Old Law. God commanded Moses to set Joshua apart in the following way: "Take Joshua son of Nun, a man in whom the spirit dwells. Lay your hands on him. Then bring him before Eleazar the priest and the whole community, to give him your orders in their presence" (Nb 27: 18–19). In the New Testament a share in the apostolic power was conferred by the laying-on of hands. This was imparted by the apostle himself or by the college of presbyters (II Tm 1:6; I Tm 4:14). Prescinding from the discussion concerning what the rank of deacon meant in the New Testament times, nevertheless it was conferred through the imposition of hands: "They presented these to the apostles, who prayed and laid their hands on them" (Ac 6:6). In Christian antiquity, the *Apostolic Tradition* of Hippolytus, dating from the beginning of the third century indicated that the imposition of hands was the external sign for the ordination of priests which was accompanied by a consecratory prayer. St. Augustine wrote that the practice of the laying-on of hands for ordination was a usage transmitted from the Apostles.[38] In the Christian East, St. John Chrysostom attests the same external sign as the cause of a divine effect: "This is in fact ordination: the hand of a man is imposed, but it is God who effects everything, and it is His hand which touches the head of the ordinand."[39]

Until about the tenth century, all the liturgies of East and West used the imposition of hands as the chief (and often only) external sign of ordination. Gradually, in the Roman rite, there developed a tendency to designate more clearly the specific power of the priesthood. Using the practice in contemporary society, where each rank was invested with the tools of his trade, the soldier with his sword, the king or queen with their orb and sceptre, the Church adopted the giving of the chalice and the paten as a vivid way of expressing the priestly power of consecrating the Body and Blood of the Lord. This ceremony of handing on the instruments was regarded by the Council of Florence as the matter of ordination: "The sixth sacrament is that of Order. Its matter is that by the handing over of which the Order is conferred: thus the presbyterate is conferred by handing over the chalice with wine and the paten with bread; the diaconate by giving the book of the gospels."[40] This declaration is not considered to be irrevocable, nor did it exclude the constant tradition in East and West, whereby the laying-on of hands took place in every ordination. A renewed awareness concerning the

ancient and traditional practice of the Church was expressed
by Pope Pius XII in 1947, who wished to settle the issue
about the matter of ordination in a definitive way: "By virtue
of our supreme apostolic authority we declare with sure
knowledge and, as far as it may be necessary, we determine
and ordain: the matter of the holy Orders of diaconate, presbyterate and episcopate is the laying-on of hands alone, and
the sole form is the words determining the application of the
matter, words by which the effects of the sacrament — that
is, the power of Order and the grace of the Holy Spirit — are
unequivocally signified."[41] Pope Pius XII did not pronounce
on the past and actual status of the handing-on of the instruments, but simply made a pronouncement for the future.

7.3.2   The form

The form of the sacrament of Order is the consecratory
prayer which follows the imposition of hands and gives
meaning to this matter. Within the prayer of consecration, a
central portion is essential for the validity of the sacrament.[42]
In the case of the episcopate, this essential nucleus is:

> So now pour out upon this chosen one
> that power which is from You,
> the governing Spirit
> Whom You gave to Your beloved Son, Jesus Christ,
> the Spirit given by Him to the holy Apostles,
> who founded the Church in every place
> to be Your temple
> for the unceasing glory and praise of Your name.

In the ordination of the priest, the essential part of the form
runs as follows:

> Almighty Father,
> grant to this servant of Yours
> the dignity of the priesthood.
> Renew within him the Spirit of holiness.
> As a co-worker with the order of bishops
> may he be faithful to the ministry
> that he receives from You, Lord God,
> and be to others a model of right conduct.

The formula for diaconate ordination contains the following words which are essential for validity:

> Lord,
> send forth upon him the Holy Spirit,
> that he may be strengthened
> by the gift of Your sevenfold grace
> to carry out faithfully the work of the ministry.

In each case, the role of the Holy Spirit in bringing about the change in the ordinand is clearly stressed.

The form must, along with the other rites of ordination express the content and meaning of what the Order is about. This constitutes the reason why among the reformed ecclesial communities, the Apostolic Succession and the priesthood were lost. The Reformers were clearly contrary to the doctrine of a priesthood which consecrates the Holy Sacrifice of the Mass. Therefore the books of ordination were re-written in order to expunge all reference to the priesthood as understood in a Catholic sense. In particular, the Edwardine Ordinal of 1552 was defective in its form. However, the intention was also defective, because it did not express the desire to do what the Church does, but rather to constitute ministers of the Word and of the Lord's Supper, but not to ordain sacrificing priests. Because of this double defect of form and intention, the Catholic Church regards Anglican ordinations as invalid. Even though the ordination rite has evolved among the Anglicans, nevertheless the defect of intention still remains. Even if, as sometimes happens, an Orthodox or Old Catholic bishop is present at the ordination of an Anglican bishop, this would not necessarily bring about validity, since the intention is still to ordain for the Anglican communion, and therefore not for Orders in the sense that the Catholic Church understands them.[43] Nevertheless, the ministry with which the Anglicans are entrusted in ordination has some value for the community which they serve. The recognition of this ministry has been evident in recent years, when after Anglican ministers have been received into full communion with the Catholic Church and been accepted as candidates for the Catholic priesthood, the pastoral work carried out as an Anglican has been regarded as going towards preparation for the priesthood.

7.4   The minister

In New Testament times, only the Apostles conferred the power of Order on those who were called deacons (Ac 6:6), presbyters (Ac 14:22; 13:3; I Tm 5:22; Tit 1:5) and bishops (I Tm 4:14; II Tm 1:6). At the beginning of the third century, St. Hippolytus asserted that a simple priest could not constitute others in the clerical state.[44] During the same period, a liturgical document from the East stated that: "a bishop must be ordained by three bishops, the presbyter and the deacon by one bishop with the assistance of the clergy; but neither the presbyter nor the deacon can raise the laity to the clerical state."[45] In the fourth century, St. Epiphanius rejected the error of Aerius of Sabaste who suggested that the priest enjoyed the same dignity as the bishop. Epiphanius' argument for asserting the superiority of the episcopate included the fact that the bishop alone possesses the power of conferring orders.[46] In the Middle Ages, St. Thomas Aquinas taught that only a bishop could confer the sacrament of Order. At the same time, the Angelic Doctor opened up the possibility of a priest conferring at least minor orders: "The Pope, who has the fulness of episcopal power, can entrust one who is not a bishop with things pertaining to the episcopal dignity.... Hence, by virtue of his commission a simple priest can confer the minor orders and confirm."[47] While the bishop is the ordinary minister of the sacrament of Order, in the past there have been a few cases of valid and legitimate ordinations conferred by priests. In the year 1400, Pope Boniface IX gave to the abbot of St. Osith in Essex, who was not a bishop, the privilege of conferring both minor and major Orders, including the priesthood, upon his subjects in the monastic community. This concession of the power to be an extraordinary minister of ordination was revoked three years later by the same Pope, because the bishop of London regarded the concession as an infringement of his own rights. There was no doubt, however, that the Pope had the right to confer the privilege validly and licitly.[48] Later, in the year 1427, Pope Martin V extended a similar privilege upon the abbot of the Cistercian Monastery of Altzelle in Saxony, for a period of five years. This concession allowed the abbot to confer all the sacred orders on his subjects.[49] Then, in the year 1489, Pope Innocent VIII gave to the Cistercian abbots of the Monastery of Cîteaux in France and its four daughter foundations of La Ferté, Pontigny, Clairvaux and Morimond, the power to confer the subdiaconate and the diaconate upon his subjects. This privilege extended to the successors of the aforementioned abbot.[50] These powers were used until the end of the eighteenth century. The question is how this historical phenomenon squares with the doctrine of the Council of Trent that the "bishops are superior to priests" and "can perform most of the functions over which those of a lower Order have no power."[51]

A solution may be derived from the concept of Apostolic Succession indicated in the Second Vatican Council: "Christ, whom the Father hallowed and sent into the world, has, through His Apostles, made their successors, the bishops namely, sharers in His consecration and mission; and these, in their turn, duly entrusted in varying degrees various members of the Church with the office of their ministry."[52] Therefore, at the beginnings of the Church, the Apostles ordained bishops who, in turn, shared their power at a lower level with the priest, restricting the use of the power that the priest intrinsically possesses. The power to confirm is present in the priest and under certain circumstances, priests do confirm; could this not also be true of the power to ordain? This power just needs to be "unlocked". Therefore, the status of the Papal indults of the past was to "untie" within the priest a power to ordain, which he would otherwise have obtained only through episcopal consecration.

Clearly to be a valid minister of the sacrament of Orders, a bishop must himself be validly ordained. For liceity, a bishop in performing the ordination of a Catholic cleric, must be in communion with the See of Peter. For the orders of priest and deacon, the ordaining prelate must possess dimissorial

letters if the deacon or priest concerned is not his own subject. These dimissorial letters come from the ordinand's
bishop if he belongs to the diocesan clergy, or from the major
superior of a clerical religious institute of pontifical right if he
is a religious. The bishop should also be of the same rite as
the ordinand.[53] In the case of an episcopal ordination, the
prelate who is the principal consecrator must be in posses-
sion of the apostolic mandate from the Holy See. At least two
other bishops should also assist at the episcopal consecration, unless the Holy See has disposed otherwise.[54]

7.5   The recipient

The ordinand must be a validly baptised and confirmed
male. The requirement of baptism is necessary for the validity of ordination as it is the basis for receiving all the other
sacraments. Confirmation as a prerequisite is required for
the liceity of the sacrament of Orders. Also necessary for lawful reception of Orders is the reception of the preceding
Order. While there have been cases in the past of men, like
St. Ambrose, being raised to the episcopate without any
intervening Order, generally this would be gravely illicit
without the permission of the Holy See. Similarly, for liceity,
the candidate for Orders must be free from legal impediments. For example, the ordination of a married man, in the
Latin rite, to the transitional diaconate or to the priesthood
without the permission of the Holy See would be gravely
illicit. The minimum age in a candidate for transitional
diaconate is the completed twenty-third year, and for the
priesthood the completed twenty-fifth year. As regards the
permanent diaconate, the minimum age-limit is twenty-five
years for a single man and thirty-five years for a married
man.[55] The minimum age requirement for the episcopate is
thirty-five years.[56]

A condition required in the ordinand is that of the male
gender. Where the concept of priesthood has been reduced
simply to a social function, forgetting the vertical divine
choice and the change in being of the recipient, it has been
easier for the idea of the admission of women to the

ministerial priesthood to gain ground. The pretext is then the equality of opportunity for women. While in the New Testament there is a clear reference to a certain Phoebe, deaconess of the Church at Cenchreae (Ro 16:1), those women deacons referred to in St. Paul's First Letter to Timothy (I Tm 3:11) are often identified with the widows mentioned in the same letter (I Tm 5:3–16). As a matter of fact, the office of widow and that of deaconess which had both emerged into Church life by the third century were often one and the same. However, sometimes also virgins or married women living a life of continence were also admitted to the order of deaconess. During the same period, the duties of the deaconess became fixed and included the rite of anointing women during the administration of baptism, service at the door of the church, distributing Holy Communion to sick women. In the Eucharistic celebration, the place of the deaconess was at the left hand of the bishop, while the deacon took the right. Until the middle of the fourth century, deaconesses were not considered to be clerics. Thereafter, they were considered an Order. According to the *Didascalia apostolica*, the bishops had to set up helpers, deacons who would help with the men and deaconesses with the women. While the deacon was meant to be the image of Christ, the deaconess was to be the image of the Holy Spirit.[57] In the ancient texts for the ordination of deaconesses, the rite was listed after the ordination of deacons, but before that of subdeacons. This sequence has encouraged the conclusion that the order of deaconess enjoyed the status of a sacramental rather than a sacrament. Some scholars also regard the deaconesses of Christian antiquity as an early expression of religious life. In any case, when the Church ceased to administer adult baptism, the office of deaconess gradually fell into disuse, and had disappeared by the eleventh century. It was very evident that the deaconess was not a participation in the ministerial priesthood. St. Epiphanius opposed a strange Marian cult offered by the Collyridian sect, where a liturgical rite, bearing some resemblance to the Eucharistic sacrifice was offered by women. Epiphanius wrote that in the Old

Covenant, "no woman ever exercised the priesthood." He then stated that in the Christian era, "if women had received that mandate to offer to God a priestly worship or to attend to the performance of a regulatory function in the Church, Mary herself would have deserved to carry out the priestly ministry in the New Covenant."[58]

Later, in the Middle Ages, some women enjoyed ecclesiastical jurisdiction; in particular some abbesses performed acts normally reserved to bishops, such as the appointment of parish priests or confessors. At that time, however, feudal lords held similar rights, and moreover a certain separation between jurisdiction and order was considered legitimate. Much more recently, in the light of the fact that many Protestant communities were beginning to appoint women ministers, it has become necessary for the Church to reaffirm the traditional doctrine in this matter. The first reproposal took place in 1976 and six arguments in favour of the male subject for ordination were employed. First, the constant tradition of the Church has been to ordain only men to the priestly ministry. Second, Jesus did not invite any women to be members of the Twelve, despite His radical and novel approach towards women. Third, the Apostles did not invite any women to form part of the apostolic college. Fourth, the practice of Christ and the Apostles is permanently normative. Fifth, the priest must bear a "natural resemblance" to Christ, and the male sex is constitutive of this resemblance. Sixth, the issue of equality in the Church and of human rights is a separate issue from that of women's ordinations.[59] The second reaffirmation of the requirement of the male sex in the recipient of ordination occurred in 1994, and on that occasion Pope John Paul II declared: "Wherefore, in order that all doubt may be removed regarding a matter of great importance, a matter which pertains to the Church's divine constitution itself, in virtue of my ministry of confirming the brethren, I declare that the Church has no authority whatever to confer priestly ordination on women and that this judgment is to be definitively held by all Christ's faithful."[60] In the following year, the Congregation for the Doctrine of the Faith replied affirmatively to the question whether this teaching belongs to the deposit of the faith, and in the subsequent explanation made clear that the doctrine has been proposed infallibly by the ordinary and universal Magisterium.[61] Maybe one of the most illustrative points regarding the question is the bridal imagery of the Church. If the Church is to be the bride of Christ, then the priest within the Church represents Christ the bridegroom and in order to complete the symbolism in this respect, the priest must be a man. This statement does not indicate that woman is inferior to man. The Mother of God did not exercise the ministerial priesthood, yet her role is at the highest possible level of participation in the salvific act. Her maternal mediation can be considered as a parallel to the priesthood and complementary to it: "No creature could ever be counted along with the Incarnate Word and Redeemer; but just as the priesthood of Christ is shared in various ways both by His ministers and the faithful, and as the one goodness of God is radiated in different ways among His creatures, so also the unique mediation of the Redeemer does not exclude but rather gives rise to a manifold cooperation which is but a sharing in this one source."[62]

The bridal imagery is also helpful when illustrating the charism of celibacy. In the West, all sacred ministers are celibate with the exception of permanent deacons and those married men who have been received into the Church from Reformed communities and then ordained with a special dispensation from the Holy See. "In the Eastern Churches a different discipline has been in force for many centuries: while bishops are chosen solely from among celibates, married men can be ordained as deacons and priests. This practice has long been considered legitimate; these priests exercise a fruitful ministry within their communities. Moreover, priestly celibacy is held in great honour in the Eastern Churches and many priests have freely chosen it for the sake of the Kingdom of God. In the East as in the West a man who has already received the sacrament of Holy Orders can no longer marry."[63] The bridal imagery of the celibate priest indicates that, representing Christ, he is "wedded" to the Church, and this is expressed in the symbolism of the episcopal ring.

The existence of priestly celibacy is of divine institution, and has apostolic origins.[64] Its application is according to the disposition of the Church. The value of priestly celibacy can be summarized according to a Christological dimension, for Christ the eternal High Priest was celibate. The ecclesiological dimension of this mystery is that celibacy enables the man endowed with the sacerdotal dignity to symbolize a bridegroom totally entrusted to the Church which is the eternally dedicated bride of Christ. Priestly celibacy also reflects an eschatological dimension prefiguring the state of the kingdom of heaven, where "at the resurrection men and women do not marry" (Mt 23:30).[65]

7.6   The effects

7.6.1   Being of the recipient

The recipient of the sacrament of Order is endowed with a sacramental character and grace is bestowed upon him. As regards the character, this is a permanent spiritual power imprinted in the soul of the recipient. As St. Thomas remarked, "to have a sacramental character belongs to God's ministers" and so "in this way those who are deputed to the Christian worship, of which Christ is the author, receive a character by which they are likened to Christ."[66] This character is permanent and at the very least lasts all through this life; however many theologians including the Angelic Doctor teach that it endures through all eternity.[67] The Council of Trent solemnly taught that a character is imparted in ordination.[68] This teaching about the permanent character imprinted by sacred Orders has been reiterated in more recent times, in contrast to certain modern theories about a temporary ministry which some theologians wanted to substitute for the priesthood.[69] The Church teaches that with each order, episcopate, presbyterate and diaconate is imparted a corresponding character.[70] The question is whether there are three characters or simply one. To assert three different characters would bring with it a danger of increasing the number of sacraments beyond seven. To state simply that there is only one character would do insufficient justice to the teaching that each Order has its own specificity. One solution is to propose three characters which are incompletely distinct, rather like interlocking stacking rings which together look like one unit and when separated resemble three rings linked together. In this way, the character of the diaconate forms the basis on which the presbyteral character is added and thereafter sometimes the episcopal character. Nowadays, it is held generally that minor orders and ministries, though permanent, do not impart a sacramental character.

The sacramental character imparted in ordination also highlights the Christian tradition that even an unworthy minister validly performs his functions. A priest or bishop who, through grave sin, is no longer in a state of grace, still retains his sacramental character and thus the configuration to Christ the Priest still remains. Therefore, he can still validly celebrate Mass, hear confessions and perform the other sacred rites of the Church, even though he is doing so unworthily. This intrinsic efficacy of the sacraments is an expression of God's mercy, for in this way Christ's faithful are not abandoned to the uncertainty of whether a minister is worthy to perform a sacrament.

The grace of the Holy Spirit specific to the sacrament of ordination is configuration to Christ as Priest, Prophet, and King. This divine gift is also particular to each Order. For the bishop, it is primarily a grace of strength, "the grace to guide and defend his Church with strength and prudence as a father and pastor, with gratuitous love for all and a preferential love for the poor, the sick, and the needy. This grace impels him to proclaim the Gospel to all, to be the model for his flock, to go before it on the way of sanctification by identifying himself in the Eucharist with Christ the Priest and Victim, not fearing to give his life for his sheep."[71] The specific grace for the order of priests is especially connected with the worthy celebration of the Eucharist and other sacred rites. The grace proper to the diaconate is the service of the liturgy, of the Gospel and of works of charity, in union with the bishop and priests.[72]

7.6.2   Action of the recipient

The priestly function is essentially sacramental in the widest sense, for the cleric administers the sacraments and also propagates the sacramental reality of the Church. Certain recent approaches to the priestly function do inadequate justice to this perennial vision. These include the idea of the priest as a political liberator, as a social worker and also as a psychologist. The notion of the priest or bishop as a "manager" in the false and capitalist-inspired business model of the Church is likewise to be rejected.

Sacred orders involve the task of teaching, governing, and sanctifying within ecclesial communion, and in relation to the whole people of God. Within this context, the bishop, priest and deacon need to exercise prudence concerning any involvement in secular activities and politics. At one time, when the Church and State were more closely knit, socio-political involvement of the clergy was easier as the State more or less breathed a Christian ethos. However, even in those times, there was always the danger that a cleric, by becoming over-involved in the affairs of the political world, could lose contact with the saving mission with which he was entrusted. Nevertheless, the wondrous and unchanging doctrine of the Church concerning the true nature and mission of her sacred ministers, has been made visible across the centuries in the lives of so many clerics both famous and obscure, who have had their influence on the faithful of every race and nation. Ronald Knox expressed it thus: "There is one contact of our daily Christian life in which the priest becomes something more than the father who leads us and feeds us and fends for us. I mean the actual celebration of the Holy Mass, in which the priest becomes our representative before God, and even in some sense God's representative to us."[73]

Notes

1   *Roman Pontifical*, Ordination of Deacons 21.
2   *Roman Pontifical*, Ordination of Bishops 26.
3   *Roman Pontifical*, Ordination of Priests 22.
4   Eucharistic Prayer IV.
5   St. Thomas Aquinas, *Pange, lingua, gloriosi*, 5. See also idem, *Lauda Sion Salvatorem*, 8: "The old is by the new replaced; The substance hath the shadow chased; and rising day dispels the night."
6   *CCC* 1540. Cf. Heb 5:3; 7:27; 10:1–4.
7   Pope Leo I, *Sermon 22 on the Nativity*, cap. 2 in *PL* 54, 192.
8   Sequence of Easter Sunday, *Victimae Paschali*.
9   *CCC* 1545. See also I Tim 2:5–6 and Vatican II, *Lumen Gentium* 62.2.
10 See A. Piolanti, *I sacramenti* (Città del Vaticano: Libreria Editrice Vaticana, 1990), pp. 480–481.
11 See M. Schmaus, *I sacramenti* (Casale: Marietti, 1966), p.665.
12 See St. Irenaeus, *Against the heresies* Lib. 3, cap. 12, 10; Lib. 4, cap. 15, 1 in *PG* 7, 904–905, 1013.
13 See St. John Chrysostom, *Homilia 14 in Acta Apostolorum*, 3 in *PG* 60, 116.
14 See J. Galot, *Theology of the Priesthood* (San Francisco: Ignatius Press, 1985), pp.160–164.
15 St. Ignatius of Antioch, *Letter to the Trallians*, 3 in *PG* 5, 677–678.
16 St. Ignatius of Antioch, *Letter to the Ephesians*, 4 in *PG* 5, 735–736.
17 St. Irenaeus, *Against the heresies* Lib. 3, cap. 3, 1–4 in *PG* 7, 848–855.
18 St. Gregory of Nyssa, *In baptismum Christi* in *PG* 46, 581.
19 St. John Chrysostom, *On the Priesthood* 3, 5 in *PG* 48, 643.
20 St. Hippolytus, *Apostolic Tradition* 9: 1–5, 9–12 in G. Dix and H. Chadwick (eds.) *The Treatise on the Apostolic Tradition of St. Hippolytus* (London: The Alban Press, 1992), pp.15–18.
21 St. Ignatius of Antioch, *Letter to the Trallians* 2 in *PG* 5, 675–676.
22 See Eusebius, *Church History*, Lib. 6, cap. 43 in *PG* 20, 622.
23 See Blessed Rabanus Maurus, *De clericorum institutione* Lib. 1, 5 in *PL* 107, 300–301.
24 See St. Thomas Aquinas, *On the perfection of Spiritual Life*, 28.
25 See William of Auxerre, *Summa aurea* Lib IV, tr.8, q.1.
26 Bd. John Duns Scotus, *Reportata Parisiensia* IV, 9.
27 Council of Trent, Twenty-Third Session, *Doctrine on the Sacrament of Order* in ND 1707.
28 Council of Trent, Twenty-Third Session, *Doctrine on the Sacrament of Order* in ND 1710, 1720.

29   See Holy Office, Decree *Lamentabili* in ND [1729/49–50].
30   See Pope Pius XII, Apostolic Constitution *Sacramentum Ordinis*, 4 in ND 1737.
31   Vatican II, *Lumen gentium*, 21.2
32   *CCC* 1554.
33   Council of Trent, Twenty-Third Session, *Doctrine on the Sacrament of Order* in ND 1719.
34   Vatican II, *Lumen gentium*, 29.1.
35   *CCC* 1570.
36   Vatican II, *Lumen gentium*, 10.2.
37   See Congregation for the Doctrine of the Faith, Declaration *Mysterium ecclesiae* (1973), 6. See Idem, *Letter to the bishops of the Catholic Church on certain questions concerning the minister of the Eucharist*, III, 4.
38   See St. Augustine, *De Trinitate*, Lib. 15, cap. 26 in *PL* 42, 1093.
39   St. John Chrysostom, *Homilia 14 in Acta Apostolorum*, 3 in *PG* 60, 116.
40   Council of Florence, *Decree for the Armenians* in ND 1705.
41   Pope Pius XII, Apostolic Constitution *Sacramentum Ordinis* (1947), 4 in ND 1737.
42   The texts of these central portions have been taken from *Notitiae* 13 (1977) p.541.
43   See Pope Leo XIII, Bull *Apostolicae curae* in ND 1722–1728. See also Congregation for the Doctrine of the Faith, *Illustrative doctrinal note on the concluding formula for the Profession of Faith* (29 June 1998), 11.7, which indicates the definitive nature of the declaration *Apostolicae curae* on the invalidity of Anglican orders.
44   See St. Hippolytus, *Apostolic Tradition* 9, 7–8 as found in Dix and Chadwick *The Treatise on the Apostolic Tradition*, p.17 where it is stated: "For the presbyter has authority only for this one thing, to receive. But he has no authority to give holy orders."
45   *Didascalia Siriaca* III, 20.
46   See St. Epiphanius, *Haeresis* 75, 4 in *PG* 42, 507–508.
47   St. Thomas Aquinas, *Summa Theologiae* Supplement, q.38, a.1.
48   See Pope Boniface IX, Bull *Sacrae religionis* in ND 1704; see Idem, Bull *Apostolicae Sedis* in DS 1146.
49   See Pope Martin V, Bull *Gerentes ad vos* in DS 1290.
50   See Pope Innocent VIII, *Exposcit tuae devotionis* in DS 1435.
51   Council of Trent, Twenty-Third Session, *Doctrine on the Sacrament of Order* in ND 1711.
52   Vatican II, *Lumen gentium*, 28.1.
53   See CIC 1015–1023.
54   See CIC 1013–1014.
55   See *CIC* 1031.

56 See *CIC* 378 §3.

57 See *Didascalia apostolica*, 16.

58 St. Epiphanius, *Haeresis 79*, 2–3 in *PG* 42, 741–744.

59 See Sacred Congregation for the Doctrine of the Faith, Declaration, *Inter Insigniores* (1976).

60 Pope John Paul II, Apostolic Letter *Ordinatio sacerdotalis*, 4.

61 Congregation for the Doctrine of the Faith, *Reply to the "Dubium" concerning the doctrine contained in the Apostolic Letter "Ordinatio sacerdotalis"* as found in Congregation for the Doctrine of the Faith, *From "Inter Insigniores" to "Ordinatio sacerdotalis". Documents and commentaries* (Washington: US Bishops Conference, 1998), pp.196–197.

62 Vatican II, *Lumen gentium*, 62.2.

63 *CCC* 1580.

64 See C. Cochini, *Apostolic Origins of Priestly Celibacy* (San Francisco: Ignatius Press, 1990); S.L. Jaki, *Theology of Priestly Celibacy* (Front Royal: Christendom Press, 1997); R. M. T. Cholij, *Clerical Celibacy in East and West* (Leominster: Fowler Wright, 1989).

65 See Pope Paul VI, *Sacerdotalis coelibatus* (1967), 19–34.

66 St. Thomas Aquinas, *Summa Theologiae* III, q.63, aa.2 and 3.

67 St. Thomas Aquinas, *Summa Theologiae* III, q.63, a.5.

68 Council of Trent, Twenty-Third Session, *Doctrine on the Sacrament of Order* in ND 1710, 1717.

69 See Pope Pius XII, Encyclical Letter *Mediator Dei* (1947) in ND 1733; Sacred Congregation for the Doctrine of the Faith, Declaration *Mysterium ecclesiae* (1973) in ND 1750.

70 As regards the episcopate, see Vatican II, *Lumen gentium*, 21.2 and *CCC* 1558 ; for priests see Vatican II, *Presbyterorum ordinis*, 2 and *CCC* 1563 ; and for deacons see *CCC* 1570.

71 *CCC* 1586.

72 *CCC* 1588.

73 R.A. Knox, *The Hidden Stream* (London: Burns and Oates, 1952), p.191.

8

Holy Matrimony

The sacrament of Matrimony can be regarded in two ways: first, in the making, and then in its permanent state. For it is a sacrament like to that of the Eucharist, which not only when it is being conferred, but also whilst it remains, is a sacrament; for as long as the married parties are alive, so long is their union a sacrament of Christ and the Church.

St. Robert Bellarmine,
De controversiis: De matrimonio

8.1 Institution of marriage

Marriage as a human institution existed in some shape or form in most ancient cultures. The natural complementarity between man and woman expressed in various ways formed the basis of this union. In some ancient cultures, like that of ancient Rome, this noble institution was civilly enshrined. The old Roman law had proclaimed "Marriage is a union between a man and a woman, an association for the whole of life, in which both are under the same law, divine and human."[1]

8.1.1 Old Testament

From the book of Genesis, a picture can be built up of marriage in the order of creation (Gn 1:27–28 ; 2:18–24). Man and woman were entrusted by God with this office of nature deriving from the mutual attraction and union of the sexes (Gn 2:24). The union of man and woman was characterized by unity and indissolubility (Gn 2:24), and orientated towards procreation (Gn 1:28). Although it was given to human beings from their very nature, it still implied something sacred, since God blessed Adam and Eve (Gn 1:28). The holiness of Marriage is also apparent from other Old Testament texts such as the prayer of Tobias on the occasion of his marriage to Sarah:

> You are blessed, O God of our fathers;
> blessed, too, is Your name
> for ever and ever.
> Let the heavens bless You
> and all things You have made
> for evermore.
>
> It was You who created Adam,
> You who created Eve His wife
> to be his help and support;
> and from these two the human race was born.
> It was You who said,
> 'It is not good that the man should be alone;
> let Us make him a helpmate like himself.'
> And so I do not take my sister
> for any lustful motive;
> I do it in singleness of heart.
> Be kind enough to have pity on her and on me
> and bring us to old age together. (Tb 8:5–7)

Marriage reflected the covenant which God had made with His chosen people, when the Lord had said: "I will betroth Myself to you for ever, betroth you with integrity and justice, with tenderness and love; I will betroth you to Myself with faithfulness, and you will come to know the Lord" (Ho 2:21–22). The infidelity of the chosen people to the Lord was expressed in terms of the image of unfaithfulness within marriage as well as that of prostitution: "Only acknowledge your guilt: how you have apostatised from the Lord your God, how you have flirted with strangers" (Jr 3:13).

The institution of Marriage continued under the regime of sin; however, as a result of the Fall, during the period between the Old Adam and the New Adam, it was not always easy to observe monogamy, and even some great Old Testament figures such as Solomon exemplified this weakness. This infidelity and lack of single-heartedness in relation to women was related to an infidelity in Solomon's relationship with God: "King Solomon loved many foreign women: not only Pharoah's daughter but Moabites, Edomites, Sidonians and Hittites, from those peoples of whom the Lord had said to the Israelites, 'You are not to go to them nor they to you, or they will surely sway you hearts to their own gods....When Solomon grew old his wives swayed his heart to other gods; and his heart was not wholly with the Lord his God" (I K 11: 1-2, 4; cf. Si 47:19). The Law and Prophets attempted to correct man's waywardness in marriage as in other aspects of human life. The law given to Moses favoured the wife as well as the husband (Dt 24:5) but allowed divorce, because of the hardness of man's heart (Dt 24:1-4). Despite the fact that divorce was permitted in the Old Testament, it was not part of God's original plan: "For I hate divorce says the Lord the God of Israel, and I hate people to parade their sins on their cloaks, says the Lord of Hosts" (Ml 1:16).

The marriage contract was regarded as sacred in the Old Testament, as taught in the Decalogue (Ex 20:14, 17). Marriage was portrayed as a symbol of the covenant in the prophets who deepened the idea of the unity and indissolubility of marriage (Ho 1-3). Matrimony itself was also considered to be a covenant: "The Lord stands as witness between you and the wife of your youth, the wife with whom you have broken faith, even though she was your partner and your wife by covenant" (Ml 1:14). The books of Ruth and Judith offer a high vision of fidelity within marriage. The poetic presentation of the Song of Songs stresses the permanence of Matrimony: "Set me like a seal upon your heart" (Sg 8:6); and "Love is strong as death" (Sg 8:7). This text has been interpreted by many Fathers, like Origen and Gregory of Nyssa, as well as by later spiritual writers, such as St. Bernard of Clairvaux and St.

John of the Cross, as an image for the love bond existing eternally between Christ and His Church.

8.1.2   New Testament

Jesus performed His first sign at a wedding feast (Jn 2:1–11), henceforth Marriage was to be "an efficacious sign of Christ's presence."[2] It was thus raised to the dignity of a sacrament, for Christ has come to perfect the order of creation, and grace builds on nature. Therefore, Christ restored Marriage to its original purity, and bestowed the grace required to carry out the demands which this involves: "Have you not read that the Creator from the beginning made them male and female, and that He said: This is why a man must leave father and mother, and cling to his wife, and the two become one body? They are no longer two, therefore, but one body. So then, what God has united, man must not divide" (Mt 19:4–6; cf. Mk 10:6–8; Lk 16:18). Christ was emphatic in teaching that the man who divorces his wife and marries another "is guilty of adultery" (Mt 19:9; cf. Lk 16:18). The demanding standard which Jesus proposed concerning marriage, requires His grace in order to carry it out: "It is not everyone who can accept what I have said, but only those to whom it is granted." (Mt 19:11). These words also imply a special grace associated with Marriage, the grace imparted by the sacrament. Jesus employed wedding imagery in His parables (Mt 22:1–14), indicating once more the high esteem in which He held marriage.

St. Paul clearly indicated that Marriage was elevated to a sacrament (Ep 5:21–33). The marriage covenant is clearly intertwined with the image of the relation between Christ the Bridegroom and His Bride the Church: "Husbands should love their wives just as Christ loved the Church and sacrificed Himself for her to make her holy. He made her clean by washing her in water with a form of words, so that when He took her to Himself she would be glorious, with no speck or wrinkle or anything like that, but holy and faultless" (Ep 5:25–27). St. Paul wrote that Marriage is "a great mystery" which has many implications but which "applies to

Christ and the Church" (Ep 5:32). The Greek word *mysterion* is rendered by "mystery" in some modern translations, but in this context the word "sacrament" would be a more appropriate reading. In this sense we can say that Matrimony is the only sacrament which is called by that name in the Bible.[3] Moreover, in this perspective, if it is affirmed that the Church is the sacrament of Christ,[4] and if Marriage reflects the relation between Christ and His Church, then Marriage is also a sacrament. The Pauline letters contain many instructions about family life which indicate the Apostle's concern that the sacredness of this sacrament be upheld (I Co 7; Col 3:18–21; Tt 2:4–5). St. Peter made an important statement stressing that "husbands must always treat their wives with consideration in their life together" and that "the wife is equally an heir to the life of grace" (I Pt 3:7). In this way the Christian vision of the dignity of woman stands in sharp contrast to the oppression she suffered in pre-Christian and non-Christian circles.

8.2   Theological development

At the very beginning there was no specifically Christian form of Marriage, but Christians celebrated it like other people, in a ceremony presided over by the father of the family, employing simple rites and gestures like linking the hands of the man and woman. A Christian rite gradually developed. St. Ignatius of Antioch remarked that the faithful should obtain the bishop's permission before contracting Marriage.[5] The aim of this injunction was to dissuade Christians from marrying non-Christians. Tertullian also bore witness to the fact that Marriage was contracted before the Church: "How shall I be able to describe the happiness of a Marriage which the Church performs, the offering of the sacrifice ratifies, and the blessing seals, to which the angels assent, and which the heavenly Father recognizes."[6] By the fourth century, there is evidence of a priestly prayer and blessing for the rite of Matrimony. In the Roman Church, the first examples of a nuptial Mass for the celebration of weddings date from the fourth and fifth centuries. The rite of veiling (*velatio*) received a liturgical significance early on: "Like the virgin who is betrothed to Christ, her only Spouse, a Christian woman who is being joined to a Christian man in Marriage received a veil from the hands of the Church as a sign of her new state."[7]

In the West, the Christian vision of Matrimony was bound up with ideas derived from Roman law. Within this perspective arose a problem as regards deciding what was the essential element from the juridical viewpoint. It became established that the consent of the couple was the determining factor. For this reason, until the time of the Council of Trent, so-called *clandestine* marriages were considered valid in the West. In Eastern Christendom, on the other hand, right from ancient times, priests and bishops actively participated in the celebration of Marriage, along with the parents of the couple or even replacing them. This procedure took place at the request of the families and with the approval of the state authorities. Gradually, some of the rites which were originally used in the family sphere were absorbed into the liturgical rites. Thus, in the East, it became accepted that the ministers of the mystery of Holy Matrimony were not only the couple, but also the priest or bishop.

The Tradition of the Church concerning Matrimony gradually but surely unfolded. From the third to the fifth centuries, three concepts were often repeated by the Fathers. One of these was that Christian marriage is a symbol of Christ and His Church, and this idea is found, for instance in the writings of St. John Chrysostom and St. Ambrose. A second notable theme is that marriage confers grace, as Tertullian and Origen did not hesitate to point out. Third, the elevation of Marriage to the order of grace occurred at the Marriage Feast at Cana, according to St. Cyril of Alexandria and St. Maximus of Turin.

Furthermore, St. John Chrysostom stressed the complementary nature of marriage and virginity: "Whoever denigrates marriage also diminishes the glory of virginity. Whoever praises it makes virginity more admirable and resplendent. What appears good only in comparison with evil would not be truly good. The most excellent good is something even better than what is admitted to be good."[8] St. Augustine stressed the goodness of marriage against the Manichaeans, who taught that matter in general and Marriage in particular were evil; he firmly stated that the three goods of Marriage were fidelity, children and a sacrament.[9] According to Augustine, the essential content (*res*) of Marriage is indissolubility, which reflects the indissoluble mystical union between Christ and His Church: "The essence of this Sacrament is that the man and the woman, united in marriage as long as they live, remain unseparated."[10] He also stressed the concept of Marriage as a remedy for concupiscence, in continuity with the Pauline idea that "if they cannot control the sexual urges, they should get married, since it is better to be married than to be tortured" (I Co 7:9).

The Augustinian formulation was refined and broadened into a synthesis by St. Isidore of Seville[11] and this body of doctrine concerning Matrimony from a sacramental perspective was passed on to the medieval theologians. The Scholastics developed sacramental theology and applied it to Marriage, which was then seen as a sign and cause of grace. Among medieval thinkers, there were those such as Abelard, who maintained that Matrimony was a sacrament just for convenience and contained no merit for salvation.[12] However, St. Bonaventure and St. Thomas Aquinas followed the mainstream theological tradition concerning the sacramentality of Matrimony. In particular, the synthesis of St. Thomas went beyond the thought of St. Augustine and was more positive. The Angelic Doctor asserted with clarity that Marriage is a sacrament and confers grace.[13] This teaching was assumed by the Council of Florence in 1439: "The seventh is the sacrament of Matrimony which is the sign of the union of Christ and the Church."[14]

Right from the earliest days, the Church has had to proscribe the heresy that marriage is evil. St. Paul condemned the gnostic error that "marriage is forbidden" (I Tm 4:3). The Manichaean system maintained that matter was evil and therefore so was marriage. Several Manichaean and

Priscillianist errors were condemned by the First Council of Toledo in 400 and also by the Council of Braga in 561.[15] The goodness of Marriage was once more affirmed in 1208 against the Waldensians who, with a Manichaean touch, forbade Marriage to the perfect.[16] The Fraticelli, a heterodox offshoot of the Franciscans, were also negative towards marriage, and for this error as well as others they were roundly condemned in the year 1318 by Pope John XXII, who affirmed that the sacrament of Marriage was venerable.[17]

While the Reformers maintained that Marriage was sacred in the order of nature, they denied that Marriage was a means of grace. Therefore, if Matrimony was not a sacrament it became a civil affair in the eyes of the Reformers: it was drawn into Luther's separation of Church and State. Hence the Protestants handed over the solemnization of Marriage to the secular authorities.[18] Thus the reformed ecclesial communities permitted divorce in the case of adultery and other causes; the bedrock of indissolubility was thereby gradually eroded in the Protestant tradition. The Council of Trent refuted the Protestant errors and reaffirmed Catholic teaching on this sacrament. Trent defined that Matrimony was a sacrament instituted by Jesus Christ.[19] Moreover, it taught that the Church has power over the sacrament, including the authority to establish diriment impediments for Marriage.[20] The Council also taught solemnly that the state of virginity or celibacy is a higher calling than that of Matrimony.[21] It reiterated earlier Church teaching that a marriage which has been celebrated but not consummated can be dissolved by the solemn profession of one of the partners.[22]

In the period following Trent, marriage continued to be viewed as a contract until the teaching of the Second Vatican Council employed the use of the idea of covenant. St. Robert Bellarmine asserted against Melchior Cano that the contract and the sacrament are inseparable. The danger was that once a wedge was driven between the sacrament and the contract, the State could be given power over the contractual part of this institution. In the year 1880, Pope Leo XIII opposed various secularist tendencies which denied that the Church has authority over the sacraments. He also reaffirmed that the marriage contract and the sacrament are inseparable. "Hence it is clear that every valid Marriage between Christians is, in and of itself, the sacrament; and nothing is further from the truth than to say that the sacrament is a sort of ornament superadded, or an extrinsic property that can be dissociated and separated from the contract by human will."[23] A further step forward in the theology of Matrimony was provided by Pope Pius XI in his monumental encyclical, *Casti Connubii*. The Pope reaffirmed that each Marriage arises solely out of the free consent of the partners. The goods of Marriage are offspring, conjugal fidelity, and the sacrament, which is the "complement and crown of all." The mystical significance of the relation between Christ and Church was once more proposed by Pius XI, who also pointed out that although Marriage does not confer a character, nevertheless its efficacy remains permanently.[24]

The Second Vatican Council expressed Matrimony in terms of covenant rather than contract: "The intimate partnership of married life and love has been established by the Creator and qualified by His laws, and is rooted in the conjugal covenant of irrevocable personal consent."[25] The Latin Code of Canon Law further developed this concept of covenant and related it to the sacrament: "The matrimonial covenant, by which a man and a woman establish between themselves a partnership of the whole of life, is by its nature ordered toward the good of the spouses and the procreation and education of offspring; this covenant between baptized persons has been raised by Christ the Lord to the dignity of a sacrament."[26] Pope John Paul II has re-expressed Christian teaching that sexual self-giving only finds its true place in Marriage "the covenant of conjugal love freely and consciously chosen, whereby man and woman accept the intimate community of life and love willed by God Himself."[27] Christian Marriage is an echo or an extension of the Incarnation and furthermore, the Holy Spirit is the seal of the covenant of the marriage partners.[28]

8.3   The sacramental sign

8.3.1   Consent

The efficient cause of Matrimony is the mutual consent of the partners.[29] Consent affects the partners both as ministers (in the Western concept of Matrimony) and also as recipients of the sacrament. The exchange of consent is the essential component of Marriage, without which the sacrament does not take place.[30] Therefore, "a matrimonial contract cannot validly exist between baptized persons unless it is also a sacrament by that fact."[31] Matrimonial consent may be defined as an act of will by which a man and a woman, by an irrevocable covenant mutually give and accept one another for the purpose of establishing a marriage. In order to effect this consent in a valid manner, it is necessary that the contracting parties be present together either personally or by proxy, in order to give and exchange consent in one ceremony. Ecclesiastical law requires that the parties concerned must fulfil certain basic conditions for celebrating a valid marriage, which constitute a *capacity* in giving consent. These requirements include a sufficient use of reason, a sufficient discretionary judgment concerning the essential rights and obligations to be mutually given and accepted in the marriage covenant and also a psychological capability. A further necessity with regard to consent is sufficient *knowledge*. The partners must at least not be ignorant of the fact that Marriage is a permanent partnership between a man and a woman, ordered to the procreation of children. *Error* about a person renders a marriage invalid. If either of the parties by a positive act of the will should exclude Marriage itself, or all right to the conjugal act, or any essential property of Marriage, he or she contracts invalidly. A person who enters into a marriage deceived through fraud, contracts invalidly. Matrimony conditioned on a future event cannot be validly contracted. Marriage conditioned on a past or present event is valid or not as the event covered by the condition exists or not. A marriage is invalid which is entered into out of grave force or fear inflicted externally, even if not intentionally imposed, from which the person has no escape other than by choosing Marriage. The interior consent of the mind is presumed to correspond to the words or signs employed in the celebration of Marriage.[32]

8.3.2   The matter and form

Although the question has not been settled definitively by the Church, it is commonly held that the matter and the form are those same realities which constitute the contract. The matter is the mutual self-giving (*traditio*) of the spouses. The form is the mutual acceptance (*acceptatio*) of this self-giving. This mutual acceptance must be expressed in words or signs. "Hence by that human act whereby spouses mutually bestow and accept each other, a relationship arises which by divine will and in the eyes of society too is a lasting one."[33] The act of mutual self-giving involves two aspects, namely transmission of life and mutual love. Thus any decision made against transmission of life at the time that Matrimony is contracted, constitutes a defect of matter in the sacrament, so invalidating it.

In the Latin Church, the mutual consent expressed in words constitutes the form, as exemplified in one formula in use in Britain:

> I John Smith do take thee Jennifer Jones,
> to be my lawful wedded wife,
> to have and to hold from this day forward,
> for better for worse,
> for richer for poorer,
> in sickness and in health,
> till death do us part.

> I Jennifer Jones do take thee John Smith,
> to be my lawful wedded husband,
> to have and to hold from this day forward,
> for better for worse,
> for richer for poorer,
> in sickness and in health,
> till death do us part.

Other prayers used now or employed in the past, such as the prayer used by the groom to give the ring to his bride do not constitute the essence of the sacrament.[34]

In many Catholic Eastern Churches and among the Orthodox and Ancient Churches of the East, the priest's blessing at the crowning of the spouses constitutes the form. However, the mutual consent of the partners makes up the necessary basis, before the priest can give the blessing. Concerning this coronation, St. John Chrysostom commented: "Crowns are placed on the heads of the spouses as a symbol of their victory, for they have reached the port of marriage unconquered by pleasure."[35] For the groom, the priest says:

> The servant of God, Demetrios, receives as a crown the servant of God, Anastasia, in the name of the Father and of the Son and of the Holy Spirit.

For the bride, the priest says:

> The servant of God, Anastasia, receives as a crown the servant of God, Demetrios, in the name of the Father and of the Son and of the Holy Spirit.

In both East and West, the essential rite of Matrimony conveys the doctrine concerning Marriage as a gift of God, Marriage as a mutual giving and receiving between the spouses, and also the equality of the partners. The sacramental form of the sacrament leads to the idea of the canonical form of the sacrament, conducted by the partners in the presence of the Church's minister and two witnesses, which the Church has power to determine. Hence the canonical and liturgical form are related.

8.4   The ministers

8.4.1   Latin rite

In the centuries before the Council of Trent, clandestine marriages were allowed. These were marriages conducted by the couple concerned by themselves, without a presence of the Church community, and so without the assistance of the priest. The Council of Trent in its Decree *Tametsi* ended that state of affairs. Past clandestine marriages were said to be valid and true, though deplored and prohibited by the Church. Thereafter, those who married without a priest and two witness, would contact marriage invalidly.[36] However, Trent never defined the matter and form of Marriage, nor did it define who the minister was. In some parts of Europe, the decree *Tametsi* was not promulgated and therefore in those parts, the expression of matrimonial consent was governed only by the natural law. Often the act of living together as man and wife after engagement was regarded as sufficient to convey matrimonial consent. Finally, in 1907, under Pope St. Pius X the "obligation to marry according to the canonical form was extended to the whole Church."[37]

Most theologians of the Latin rite held that the spouses were the ministers of the sacrament of holy Matrimony. On the other hand, in the sixteenth century, the Dominican theologian Melchior Cano thought that the marriage contract was the matter of the sacrament and the form was the blessing given by the priest. His approach was unsatisfactory since it separated the contract from the sacrament of Marriage. In the seventeenth century, some Gallican and Josephinist theologians, who desired to stress the role of the State with regard to Marriage, proposed that the external sign of Matrimony was to be found in the priestly blessing. For these theologians, the contract of Marriage was merely a precondition for the sacrament and could thus be relegated to the authority of the State.[38]

The celebration of Marriage is possible, under certain circumstances such as the danger of death, in the presence only of witnesses, who are not clerics. The present Western canonical discipline stipulates the following conditions in this regard:

If the presence of or access to a person who is competent to assist at Marriage in accord with the norm of law is impossible without serious inconvenience, persons intending to enter a true marriage can validly and licitly contract it before witnesses alone: (1) in danger of death; (2) outside the danger of

death, as long as it is prudently foreseen that such circumstances will continue for a month.[39]

The Roman ritual, published in 1614 and used up until the
renewal of the liturgy after the Second Vatican Council, highlighted the role of the priest in the celebration of Marriage.
After the couple expressed their consent, the celebrant then
pronounced the words: "I join you in holy Matrimony in the
name of the Father and of the Son and of the Holy Ghost."[40]
Nevertheless, as Pope Pius XII formulated, the Western concept was that the contracting parties in Marriage minister
grace to one another.[41] This idea was reiterated and developed more recently in the Catechism: "In the Latin Church,
it is ordinarily understood that the spouses, as ministers of
Christ's grace, mutually confer upon each other the sacrament of Matrimony by expressing their consent before the
Church."[42]

8.4.2   Eastern rites

St. Ignatius of Antioch declared that Marriage should only be
contracted with the consent of the bishop and should only
take place in his presence.[43] St. Ambrose taught that Marriage should be sanctified by the priestly veil and blessing.[44]
These and other theological reflections led to the situation
whereby "in the Eastern liturgies the minister of this sacrament (which is called 'Crowning') is the priest or bishop
who, after receiving the mutual consent of the spouses, suc-
cessively crowns the bridegroom and the bride as a sign of the
marriage covenant."[45] For the Oriental Christians, who have
not experienced the separation of the Church and the world
that has marked Latin theology from the twelfth century, the
priest is regarded as the one who bestows the sacrament of
marriage.[46] Among the Eastern Catholic churches, the central minister of the sacrament of Matrimony is the bishop or
priest and never a deacon or lay-person.[47] The priest is the
minister of Marriage as he is also minister of the Eucharist so
that Marriage is assumed into "the eternal Mystery, where
the boundaries between heaven and earth are broken and
where human decision and action acquire an eternal

dimension."[48] While Oriental canonical discipline stresses the importance of the priest's blessing, nevertheless in the cases of danger of death or lack of a priest for at least a month, a couple can marry before lay witnesses like in the Latin discipline. However the priest's blessing has to be sought at a later stage, as soon as this becomes possible.[49]

8.4.3 The intention

According to the Western formulation, the ministers are the bride and groom, and these must have at least the intention of doing what the Church does. In current situations where many engaged couples are baptized but seem to have little faith, it has been asked if that impinges on the validity of the sacrament. First, of course, because a couple do not practise their religion does not necessarily indicate the absence of personal faith. Pope John Paul II has rooted the sacrament in the economy of creation, so that the commitment to marry "really involves, even if not in a fully conscious way, an attitude of profound obedience to the will of God, an attitude which cannot exist without God's grace."[50] By virtue of being baptized, an engaged couple already shares in Christ's marriage covenant with the Church, and if they have the right intention "they have accepted God's plan regarding marriage and therefore at least implicitly consent to what the Church intends to do when she celebrates Marriage."[51] It has been stated earlier, that even a minister without faith, provided he or she has the right intention can perform a sacrament validly,[52] and by this token, a marriage between the baptized must be assumed to have been celebrated sacramentally unless the contrary can be proven.

8.5   The recipient

8.5.1 Impediments

It is part of the doctrine of sacramental theology that sacraments are validly received where no obstacle is put in the way.[53] As with the other sacraments so also as regards Marriage, the Church has determined what is necessary for validity. In particular, the Church has indicated which circumstances according to divine law, ecclesiastical law or natural law render a person incapable of contracting marriage validly. There are several such diriment impediments. One of these is age, so that a man cannot marry validly before he has completed his sixteenth year of age, and similarly a woman cannot validly contract Matrimony before she has completed her fourteenth year of age.[54] Another impediment is impotence which is the inability to perform the marital act. "Antecedent and perpetual impotence to have intercourse, whether on the part of the man or of the woman, which is either absolute or relative, of its very nature invalidates marriage."[55] On the other hand, it is now accepted that persons who have undergone a vasectomy are free to marry. A further impediment is that of an existing marriage bond. A person who is held to the bond of a prior marriage, even if it has not been consummated, invalidly attempts marriage.[56] Disparity of cult is another impediment, which means that a "Marriage between two persons, one of whom is baptized in the Catholic Church or has been received into it and has not left it by means of a formal act, and the other of whom is non-baptized, is invalid."[57]

Those persons who are in major holy orders or who are bound by a public perpetual vow of chastity in a religious institute, invalidly attempt marriage.[58] Similarly invalid is an attempted marriage between a man and a woman "abducted or at least detained for the purpose of contracting marriage with her, unless the woman of her own accord chooses marriage after she has been separated from her abductor and established in a place where she is safe and free."[59] Crime is another impediment and covers three situations. The first is that of a person who murders his or her spouse in order to marry another person. Such a murder is the cause of the impediment, even if was carried out by someone acting under orders from the guilty spouse. The second situation concerns a spouse who kills another person's married partner in order to marry that person. The third case involves two people who conspire to murder the married partner of either, even if the desire to marry may not be the driving motive.[60] Consanguinity is also an impediment to marriage. "In the direct line of consanguinity, marriage is invalid between all ancestors and descendants, whether they be related legitimately or naturally. In the collateral line of consanguinity, marriage is invalid up to and including the fourth degree."[61] The relationship of affinity in the direct line in any degree whatsoever invalidates Matrimony. By affinity is meant the relationship arising between a man and the blood relations of his wife and vice-versa.[62] Another impediment is that of public propriety which arises from an invalid marriage after common life has been established or from notorious and public concubinage. Public propriety "invalidates marriage in the first degree of the direct line between the man and the blood relatives of the woman, and vice-versa."[63] Finally, adoption can also give rise to an impediment in the sense that a marriage is invalid between persons who are related in the direct line or in the second degree of the collateral line, through a legal relationship arising from adoption.[64] These impediments can be dispensed under different situations by different ecclesiastical authorities, apart from the impediment of consanguinity in the direct line or in the second degree of the collateral line.[65]

8.5.2   Special cases

a)   mixed religion

This concerns the marriage between a Catholic and a baptized non-Catholic. Permission is needed from the local Ordinary to celebrate this kind of marriage. In some territories, the parish-priest is empowered to dispense this impediment for his subjects. The Catholic party declares that they are to remove all dangers of falling away from the faith and makes a sincere promise to have all the children baptized and brought up in the Catholic Church. The non-Catholic party is to be informed in good time about these promises. The ordinary canonical form is necessary only for lawfulness when a Catholic marries an Orthodox or other Oriental Christian, though here the marriage must take place before a sacred minister for validity, because the Eastern Churches require this. In the cases of marriages between Catholic and members of other Churches and ecclesial communities, canonical form is required for validity. The Orthodox Churches would generally regard as invalid through defect of form a marriage between an Orthodox Christian and a member of the Reformed churches if such a marriage is carried out in a Reformed ceremony. If there are grave difficulties in observing the form, the local Ordinary has the power to dispense from it.[66] One may not celebrate two religious celebrations, nor is it allowed to have a service in which a Catholic cleric and a non-Catholic minister, each performing his own rite, ask for the consent of the parties.[67]

The Catholic Church considers marriages conducted among members of other Churches or ecclesial communities to be valid and sacramental. Therefore, a marriage between two Methodists or a Methodist and an Anglican would be valid and sacramental. Consequently, a member of one of these ecclesial communities who separates from his or her partner and subsequently wishes to marry a Catholic, is impeded by an existing bond. This holds irrespective of the form, including a civil ceremony, in which the marriage was held, since only baptised Catholics are bound by the canonical form, with the exception of cases provided for in law.[68] The basic reason is that, in the West, the baptized persons themselves are the ministers of marriage. On the other hand, the marriage of two unbaptized persons is governed only by the natural law and just civil laws.

b)   disparity of cult

This is a situation existing between a Catholic and a non-baptized person who desire to marry; the Church does not encourage this type of marriage. The impediment of disparity of cult can be dispensed by the local Ordinary when there is no danger of perversion to the spouse or offspring, and certain other conditions are satisfied. Namely, the Catholic party declares that they are to remove all dangers of falling away from the faith and makes a sincere promise to have all the children baptized and brought up in the Catholic Church. The non-Christian party is to be informed in good time about these promises.[69]

The question arises whether a marriage between a baptised and a non-baptised person be sacramental or otherwise. Pope Paul VI remarked that "Undoubtedly there exists in a marriage between baptized persons, since such a marriage is a sacrament, a certain communion of spiritual benefits which is lacking in a marriage entered into by a baptized person and one who is not baptized."[70] However some theologians say such a marriage cannot be hastily dismissed as non-sacramental, because according to St. Paul, the unbaptized partner is consecrated through his or her Christian spouse.[71] Some claim that Marriage between a baptized person and an unbaptized person is sacramental for the baptized person, since the baptized person is capable of receiving the sacrament, and the unbaptized person is capable of administering it.[72] Nevertheless, it is now accepted that Marriage between a baptized person and a non-baptized person results in a natural bond only, which nevertheless is to be respected since it has something of a sacred nature. Nevertheless it is not absolutely indissoluble, as consummated marriages between a Christian and a non-baptized person can be dissolved according to the Petrine privilege.

8.6   The effects

8.6.1   The bond

The sacramental bond is a God-given gift which is a source of grace and blessing to the couple for the whole of their married existence. "For the good of the spouses and their offspring as well as of society, the existence of the sacred bond no longer depends on human decisions alone. For, God Himself is the author of Matrimony, endowed as it is with various benefits and purposes."[73] The bond is technically the intermediate sign-effect (*res et sacramentum*) and is thus a sign and a cause; it is caused by the consent, and itself causes grace.[74]

A historical development took place concerning the relation between consent and consummation in the formation of the bond. In the early Church, the Roman view was accepted that consent and not sexual intercourse made a Marriage. An early statement on this question, made by Pope Nicholas I in the year 866, stated that consent was sufficient for Marriage.[75] Under the influence of Germanic law, on the other hand, consummation was seen as a determining factor in creating the Marriage. In the medieval canonical syntheses, Marriage was considered to consist of two stages, an exchange of consent and a consummation. Consummation was then regarded as conferring intrinsic and extrinsic indissolubility. This development leads to a consideration of various types of marital union. The first is ratified only: a valid marriage between baptized persons is called ratified only if it has not been consummated. The second type is ratified and consummated, and requires that the parties have performed between themselves, in a human manner, the conjugal act which is open to the generation of offspring. This act must take place after the celebration of a valid marriage. Once a ratified marriage between Christians has been consummated, the resulting bond cannot be dissolved by any human authority.

8.6.2   Sacramental grace

The sacrament of Marriage confers a special grace of state, which is the ultimate effect, or *res tantum*. It consists of a specific participation in Christ's life.[76] "By reason of their state in life and of their order, Christian spouses have their own special gifts in the People of God. This grace proper to the sacrament of Matrimony is intended to perfect the couple's love and to strengthen their indissoluble unity. By this grace, they help one another to attain holiness in their married life and in welcoming and educating their children."[77] Christ is the source and origin of this grace, and in the joys of their love and family life He bestows on the couple here on earth a foretaste of the wedding feast of the Lamb.[78]

8.7   The goods and requirements

8.7.1   Unity

The unity and unicity of Marriage are a consequence of the bond which reflects Christ's unique and only bond with His Mystical Bride the Church. The unity of Matrimony excludes all forms of polygamy, whether this be polygyny in which one man is linked to several wives or the rarer from, polyandry, in which one woman has several men. Similarly excluded are neo-pagan group marriages in which several men and several women live in common with respect to bed and board. Such relationships be they successive or simultaneous, are excluded by considerations of justice as well as sexuality. The unity of marriage is seen to be compromised in pre-Christian, non-Christian and post-Christian cultures.

8.7.2   Indissolubility

A natural bond is considered already worthy of respect, but the sacramental bond is even more worthy of veneration. It is the Church's conviction that although every contractually concluded marriage between Christians is indeed a sacrament, it only becomes absolutely indissoluble through its consummation; thus there is a close link between sacramentality, consummation and indissolubility. Divorce offends against this property of indissolubility. Many scholars hold that the supposed exceptions to Jesus' injunctions concerning divorce (Mt 5:32; Mt 19:9), can be interpreted in terms of "except on the grounds of unchastity", namely marriages which were already invalid because they lay within forbidden degrees of kindred. Some of the Greek Fathers like Origen and St. John Chrysostom and some Latin Fathers like St. Augustine regarded adultery as motives for separation, but not for re-marriage. During the Middle Ages, separation and re-marriage were allowed on grounds which later came to be known as impediments like consanguinity, affinity and impotence or grounds for nullity, like force or fear. The Council of Trent upheld the Church's teaching on the illicit nature of divorce.[79] The Orthodox Churches allow divorce and a simple second re-marriage in church under certain conditions. The ecclesial communities of the West deriving from the Reformation have, in general, fallen victim to permitting divorce.

The dissolution of a marriage bond can be granted by divine law, either by direct action owing to the death of one of the partners or by granting the power to dissolve the bond to the spouses themselves in the case of the Pauline privilege. A Marriage entered into by two unbaptised persons is dissolved in virtue of the Pauline privilege in favour of the faith of the party who received Baptism, by the very fact that a new Marriage is contracted by that same party, provided the unbaptised party departs.[80] The Pauline privilege does not apply to a valid Marriage between a baptised person and a non-baptised person, celebrated with a dispensation for disparity of cult. Another case is the Petrine privilege in which the Roman Pontiff has the power to dissolve a non-consummated Marriage between baptised persons or between a baptised person and a non-baptised person, for a just reason.[81] The Petrine privilege also extends to situations where the supreme authority of the Church dissolves a consummated natural (non-sacramental) bond, in favour of the faith. One such case would involve the dissolution of a consummated Marriage between a baptised non-Catholic person and a non-baptised person, upon the desire of the non-baptised person to marry a Catholic. Dissolution of the natural bond is also permitted between a baptised non-Catholic and an unbaptised partner, where the non-Catholic Christian wishes to marry a Catholic. Furthermore, a marriage solemnized with a dispensation from disparity of cult between a Catholic and a non-baptised partner, may be dissolved to allow the Catholic partner (or the unbaptised party after embracing the Catholic faith) to marry again this time with a Catholic spouse.

8.7.3   *Fidelity and openness to offspring*

Fidelity within marriage is based once more on the reflection of and participation in Christ's covenant love for His Bride

the Church. It excludes the sin of adultery, already condemned in the Old Testament (Ml 1:15), and rejected by
Christ and the whole of ecclesial Tradition. In particular, St.
John Chrysostom proposed that husbands should say to their
wives: "I have taken you in my arms, and I love you, and I prefer you to my life itself. For the present life is nothing, and
my most ardent dream is to spend it with you in such a way
that we may be assured of not being separated in the life
reserved for us.... I place your love above all things, and nothing would be more bitter or painful to me than to be of a different mind than you."[82]

The openness to procreation of a Marriage, or fecundity
"is a gift, an end of Marriage, for conjugal love naturally tends
to be fruitful. A child does not come from outside as something added on to the mutual love of the spouses, but springs
from the very heart of that mutual giving, as its fruit and fulfilment. So the Church, which is on the side of life teaches
that each and every marriage act must remain open to the
transmission of life."[83] Artificial contraception erodes this
basic good, and the contraceptive mentality attacks all
aspects of Marriage, reducing the self-giving and mutual love
to selfishness, jeopardizing fidelity, and unity, and impeding
the procreation of children.

Concluding thought

The theology of Marriage marks a fitting close to the study of
the sacramental mystery, because it does not only symbolize
the union of Christ and his Church on earth, but also prefig-
ures her definitive triumph in heaven. When the Marriage of
the Lamb has come (Rv 21:2) the Church will have no further need of sacraments, since her members will see God
face to face; the veil will have been removed from the face of
the Bride. The eternal union of the Mystical Bride with the
Most Holy Trinity is ever being prepared and prefigured in
the saving sacramental signs which God bestowed upon His
Church, through Christ in the Love of the Holy Spirit, while
she makes her earthly pilgrimage towards the final consummation of her love.

Before the dawn comes round
Here is the night, dead hushed with all its glamours,
The music without sound,
The solitude that clamours,
The supper that revives us and enamours.

Now flowers the marriage bed
With dens of lions fortified around it,
With tent of purple spread,
In peace securely founded,
And by a thousand shields of gold surmounted.[84]

Notes

1   "Nuptiae sunt conjunctio maris et feminae et consortium omnis vitae, divini et humani juris communicatio." See Modestinus, *Libro I Regularum*, in *Digest*, Book 23, title 2, *De ritu nuptiarum* frag. 1.

2   *CCC* 1613.

3   See R.A. Knox, *The Hidden Stream* (London: Burns and Oates, 1952), p.194.

4   See chapter 1, section 1.2.

5   See St. Ignatius of Antioch, *Letter to Polycarp*, 5 in *PG* 5, 723–724.

6   Tertullian, *Ad uxorem*, Lib. 2, 8, 6 in *CCL* 1, 393.

7   J. McAreavey, *The Canon Law of Marriage and the Family* (Dublin: Four Courts Press, 1997), p.148.

8   St. John Chrysostom, *De virginate*, 10 in *PG* 48, 540.

9   See St. Augustine, *De nuptiis et concupiscentiis*, Lib. 1, cap. 11, 13 in *PL* 44, 421; Idem, *De bono coniugali*, 24, 32 in *PL* 40, 394.

10   St. Augustine, *De nuptiis et concupiscentiis*, Lib. 1, cap. 11, 10 in *PL* 44, 420.

11   See St. Isidore of Seville, *De ecclesiasticis officiis*, Lib. 2, cap. 20 in *PL* 83, 809–814.

12   Peter Abelard, *Epitome theologiae*, 31 in *PL* 178, 1745–1746.

13   See St. Thomas Aquinas, *Summa Theologiae* Supplement, q.42, aa.1,3.

14   Council of Florence, *Decree for the Armenians* in ND 1803.

15   See First Council of Toledo in DS 206 and Council of Braga in ND 402/11–12.

16   See Pope Innocent III, *Profession of Faith prescribed to the Waldensians* in ND 1802.

17   See Pope John XXII, Constitution *Gloriosam Ecclesiam* in DS 916.

18 See W. Kasper, *Theology of Christian Marriage* (London: Burns and Oates, 1980), p.40.
19 Council of Trent, Twenty-Fourth Session, *Doctrine on the Sacrament of Matrimony* in ND 1806, 1808.
20 *Ibid.*, in ND 1811.
21 *Ibid.*, in ND 1817.
22 *Ibid.*, in ND 1813. See Alexander III, Letter *Verum post* to the Archbishop of Salerno in DS 755.
23 Pope Leo XIII, Encyclical *Arcanum Divinae Sapientiae* in ND 1823.
24 See Pope Pius XI, Encyclical *Casti connubii*, in ND 1824–1833.
25 Vatican II, *Gaudium et spes* 48.1.
26 *CIC* 1055 §1.
27 Pope John Paul II, *Familiaris consortio*, 11.7.
28 See *CCC* 1624, and also Knox, *The Hidden Stream*, p.197.
29 See Council of Florence, *Decree for the Armenians* in ND 1803:
30 See *CCC* 1626; *CIC* 1057 §1.
31 *CIC* 1055 §2.
32 As regards consent see *CIC* 1095–1107.
33 Vatican II, *Gaudium et spes* 48.1.
34 The old prayer used by the groom ran "With this ring I thee wed; this silver and gold I thee give; with my body I thee worship; and with all my worldly goods I thee endow." It sounded like a formal expression of what Marriage is all about, but did not constitute the from of the sacrament.
35 St. John Chrysostom, *Homily 9 on I Timothy 9*, 2 in *PG* 62, 546.
36 See Council of Trent, Decree *Tametsi* in DS 1813–1816.
37 McAreavey, *The Canon Law of Marriage and of the Family*, p.136. See Sacred Congregation of the Council, Decree *Ne temere* in DS 3468–3469.
38 These errors were condemned in the Letter *Deessemus nobis* in the year 1788 as found in DS 2598 and in the condemnation of certain errors of the pseudo-synod of Pistoia in the Constitution *Auctorem fidei* in the year 1794 as found in DS 2658–2659.
39 *CIC* 1116. See Decree *Ne temere* in DS 3471.
40 Ego conjungo vos in matrimonium, in nomine Patris, et Filii, et Spiritus Sancti.
41 See Pope Pius XII, Encyclical *Mystici Corporis*, 20.
42 *CCC* 1623.
43 See St. Ignatius of Antioch, *Letter to Polycarp*, 5 in *PG* 5, 723–724.
44 See St. Ambrose, *Letter 19*, 7 in *PL* 16, 984.
45 *CCC* 1623.
46 See Kasper, *Theology of Christian Marriage*, p.40.

47   See D. Salachas, *Il sacramento del matrimonio nel nuovo diritto canonico delle chiese orientali* (Bologna: EDB, 1994), pp.29–34.
48   J. Meyendorff, *Marriage: an Orthodox Perspective* (New York: St. Vladimir's Seminary Press, 1970), p.27.
49   See CCEO 828, 832.
50   Pope John Paul II, Apostolic Exhortation *Familiaris consortio*, 68.3.
51   *Ibid.*, 68.5.
52   See chapter one, section 1.8.
53   See chapter one, section 1.9.
54   See *CIC* 1083.
55   *CIC* 1084.
56   See *CIC* 1085.
57   *CIC* 1086 §1.
58   See *CIC* 1087–1088.
59   *CIC* 1089.
60   See *CIC* 1090.
61   *CIC* 1091 §§1–2.
62   See *CIC* 1092.
63   *CIC* 1093.
64   See *CIC* 1094.
65   See *CIC* 1078 §3.
66   See *CIC* 1127 §1–2. See also *ED* 153.
67   See *CIC* 1127 §3. *ED* 156–157.
68   See Decree *Ne temere* in DS 3474: "Acatholici sive baptizati sive non baptizati, si inter se contrahunt, nullibi ligantur ad catholicam sponsalium vel matrimonii formam servandam." See also *CIC* 1117.
69   See *1086* §2.
70   Pope Paul VI, Apostolic Letter *Matrimonia Mixta* in *AAS* 62(1970) p.258.
71   See P.J. Elliott, *What God has joined* (Homebush: St. Paul, 1990), pp.199–200, who cites I Corinthians 7:12–14.
72   See L. Ott, *Fundamentals of Catholic Dogma* (Rockford, Ilinois: Tan Books, 1974), p.468.
73   Vatican II, *Gaudium et spes* 48.1.
74   See Pope John Paul II, *Familiaris consortio*, 13 in ND 1843.
75   Pope Nicholas I, response *Ad consulta vestra* in DS 643.
76   See Pope John Paul II, *Familiaris consortio*, 13 in ND 1843.
77   *CCC* 1641.
78   See *CCC* 1642.
79   Council of Trent, Twenty-Fourth Session, *Doctrine on the Sacrament of Matrimony* in ND 1814.
80   See I Co 7:10–16; see also *CIC* 1143–1149.

81   See *CIC* 1142.
82   St. John Chrysostom, *Homily 20 on Ephesians*, 8 in *PG* 62, 147.
83   *CCC* 2366.
84   St. John of the Cross, *Songs between the soul and the bridegroom* as found in Elliott, *What God has joined*, p.221.

Select Bibliography

Auer, J., *Dogmatic Theology Volume 6: Mystery of the Eucharist* (Washington, D.C.: Catholic University of America Press, 1995).

Beasley-Murray, G.R., *Baptism today and tomorrow* (London: Macmillan, 1966).

Behrens, J., *Confirmation, Sacrament of Grace. The theology, practice and law of the Roman Catholic Church and the Church of England* (Leominster: Gracewing, 1995).

Bligh, J., *Ordination to the Priesthood* (New York: Sheed and Ward, 1956).

Bradshaw, P.F., *Ordination Rites of the Ancient Churches of East and West* (New York: Pueblo Publishing Co., 1990).

Catholic Bishops' Conferences of England & Wales, Ireland and Scotland, *One Bread One Body* (London/Dublin: CTS/Veritas, 1998).

Cholij, R.M.T., *Clerical Celibacy in East and West* (Leominster: Fowler Wright, 1989).

Connolly, H., *The Irish Penitentials : and their significance for the sacrament of penance today.* (Portland, OR: Four Courts Press, 1995).

Elliott, P.J., *What God Has Joined. The Sacramentality of Marriage* (New York: Alba House, 1990).

Emminghaus, J. H., *The Eucharist* (Collegeville: The Liturgical Press, 1997).

Everett, L.P., *The Nature of Sacramental Grace* (Washington: Catholic University of America, 1948).

Finn, T.M., *Early Christian baptism and the catechumenate* (Collegeville: The Liturgical Press, 1992).

Galot, J., *Theology of the Priesthood* (San Francisco: Ignatius Press, 1985).

Gihr, N., *The Holy Sacrifice of the Mass* (St. Louis: Herder, 1951).

Halligan, N., *The Sacraments and their Celebration* (New York: Alba House, 1986).

Howell, C., *Of Sacraments and Sacrifice* (Collegeville, Minn.: Liturgical Press, 1952).

Jaki, S.L., *Theology of Priestly Celibacy* (Front Royal, VA: Christendom Press, 1997).

Kasper, W., *Theology of Christian Marriage* (London: Burns and Oates, 1980).

Kavanagh, A., *Confirmation. Origins and Reform* (New York: Pueblo, 1988).

Kolbe, F.C., *The Sacrament of Confirmation* (London: Burns & Oates, 1930).

Laurentin, R., *The Eucharist and Mary* (Dayton: Marian Library Studies-University of Dayton, 1964).

Lawler, M.G., *Symbol and sacrament : a contemporary sacramental theology* (Omaha, Neb.: Creighton University Press, 1995).

Leeming, B., *Principles of Sacramental Theology* (London: Longmans, 1963).

Lynch, K.F., *The Sacrament of Confirmation in the early-middle scholastic period* (St. Bonaventure:1957).

Macquarrie, J., *A Guide to the Sacraments* (London: SCM, 1997).

McPartlan, P., *Sacrament of Salvation. An Introduction to Eucharistic Ecclesiology* (Edinburgh: T & T Clark, 1995).

Meyendorff, J., *Marriage: An Orthodox Perspective* (Crestwood: St. Vladimir's Seminary Press, 1975).

O'Dwyer, M., *Confirmation. A study in the development of sacramental theology* (Dublin: Gill, 1915).

Osborne, K.B., *Sacramental Theology* (New York: 1988).

Palmer, P.F., *Sacraments and Worship. Liturgy and Doctrinal Development of Baptism, Confirmation and the Eucharist* (Westminster, MD: The Newman Press, 1955).

Palmer., P.F., *Sacraments and Forgiveness. History and Doctrinal Development of Penance, Extreme Unction and Indulgences* (Westminster, MD: The Newman Press, 1961).

Pham, J.-P., *The Sacrament of Penance. In the Teachings of the Last Five Popes* (Chicago: Midwest Theological Forum, 1996).

Poschmann, B., *Penance and the Anointing of the Sick* (New York: Herder, 1964).

Tierney, C., *The sacrament of repentance and reconciliation* (Dublin: Dominican Publications, 1983).

Scheeben, M.J., *The Mysteries of Christianity* (St.Louis, MO: B. Herder, 1961).

Schleck, C.A.,*The Sacrament of Matrimony* (Milwaukee: Bruce, 1964).

Schmaus, M., *Dogma 5: The Church as Sacrament* (London: Sheed and Ward, 1975).

Schnackenburg, R. *Baptism in the thought of St.Paul. A Study in Pauline Theology* (Oxford: Blackwell, 1964)

Searle, M., *Documents of the marriage liturgy* (Collegeville: The Liturgical Press, 1992).

Semmelroth, O., *Church and Sacrament* (Dublin : Gill, 1965).

Thornton, L.S., *Confirmation. Its place in the baptismal mystery* (Westminster: Dacre Press, 1954).

Van Roo, W.A., *The Christian Sacrament* (Roma: Editrice Pontificia Università Gregoriana, 1992).

Vorgrimler, H., *Sacramental Theology* (Collegeville, Minn.: Liturgical Press, 1992).

Walsh, L., *The Sacraments of Initiation* (London: Geoffrey Chapman, 1988).

Wengier, F.J., *The Eucharist-Sacrifice* (Milwaukee: Bruce, 1955).

Woolley, R.M., *Coronation rites* (Cambridge: University Press, 1915).

Index

Aaron, 114, 164–165
Abraham, 164, 166,
Adam, 41, 198–199
Aerius of Sabaste, 184
Albert the Great, St., 38, 152, 175
Alexander III, Pope (see also Bandinelli, R.), 10, 38, 55, 88, 221
Alexander VIII, Pope, 26, 38
Alexander of Hales, 131
Ambrose, St., 24, 30, 31, 36, 37, 54, 64, 68, 74, 87, 186, 202, 210, 221
Ambrosiaster, 175
Anglican communion, 11, 98–99, 128, 183–184
Anselm, St., 82
Aphraates the Syrian, 145
Apollinaris of Laodicaea, 81
Apostolic succession, 105–106, 160, 170–173, 183.
Aquinas, St. Thomas, 8, 22, 24, 25, 26, 30, 31, 35, 36, 38, 53–55, 57, 65, 69, 73–74, 89, 92, 97, 103, 109–112, 129, 131, 140, 141, 152, 161, 175, 184, 190, 193–195, 203, 220
Athanasius, St., 5, 30
attrition, 130–131, 160

Augustine, St., 7, 8, 10, 12, 22, 25, 26, 30, 33, 36, 52, 54, 57, 68, 87, 96, 100, 110–112, 123, 181, 194, 203, 217, 220

Bandinelli, R. (see also Alexander III, Pope), 10, 88
Barnabas, St., 171
Basil, St., 54, 83, 124, 141
Bede the Venerable, St., 30, 150, 161
Bellarmine, St. Robert, 197, 204
Benedict XIV, Pope, 67
Benedict XV, Pope, 154, 162
Berengar of Tours, 88
Bernard of Clairvaux, St., 5, 199
Bonaventure, St., 31, 38, 52, 131, 152, 161, 175, 203
Boniface IX, Pope, 184, 194
bridal imagery, 5–6, 23, 108, 166, 189–190, 197–201, 219–220

Cabasilas, N., 83, 109
Caesarius of Arles, St., 125, 141, 149, 161
Cain, 114
Cajetan, Cardinal, 52

229

Printed in the United Kingdom
by Lightning Source UK Ltd.
113571UKS00001B/241-423